Managing

(Alan Fyall) To Lise

(Brian Garrod) To Alison and Lydia

(Anna Leask) To Malcolm and Euan

Managing Visitor Attractions

New Directions

Edited by

Alan Fyall, Brian Garrod and Anna Leask

OXFORD AMSTERDAM BOSTON LONDON NEW YORK PARIS
SAN DIEGO SAN FRANCISCO SINGAPORE SYDNEY TOKYO

Butterworth-Heinemann
An imprint of Elsevier Science
Linacre House, Jordan Hill, Oxford OX2 8DP
200 Wheeler Road, Burlington MA 01803

First published 2003

British Library Cataloguing in Publication Data
A catalogue record for this book is available from the British Library

Library of Congress Cataloguing in Publication Data
A catalogue record for this book is available from the Library of Congress

ISBN 0 7506 5381 7

For information on all Butterworth-Heinemann publications visit our website at
www.bh.com

Composition by Genesis Typesetting, Rochester, Kent
Printed and bound in Great Britain

Contents

Contents

Figures

Tables

Editors and contributors

Editors

Alan Fyall is Senior Lecturer in Tourism Marketing in the International Centre for Tourism and Hospitality Research, Bournemouth University, UK. E-mail: afyall-@bournemouth.ac.uk. He lectures in marketing and strategy on postgraduate programmes in tourism, and has a particular interest in collaborative forms of marketing and strategy in the tourism and hospitality industries. Alan has conducted contract research and consultancy for a variety of large and small organizations, and has also taught and conducted research in a number of countries around the world, including the USA, India, Malaysia and Australia. Alan has published widely in the academic press, with articles featured in the likes of *Annals of Tourism Research*, *Tourism Management* and *Services Industries Journal*, and is consulting editor for the *International Journal of Tourism Research*.

Brian Garrod is Senior Lecturer in Environmental Economics in the Faculty of Economics and Social Science, University of the West of England, Bristol, UK. E-mail: Brian.Garrod@uwe.ac.uk. He lectures in environmental economics and specializes in sustainable tourism, with a particular emphasis on the interface between environmental economics and tourism analysis. Brian has had articles published in a wide range of academic journals, both tourism related and non-tourism related. He has twice been retained by the World Tourism Organization as an expert adviser on the subject of sustainable tourism. Recent projects include updating and revising 'Agenda 21 for the Travel and Tourism Industry: Toward Environmentally Sustainable Development', an agenda for sustainable tourism published by the World Tourism Organization in collaboration with the World Travel and Tourism Council and the Earth Council.

Anna Leask is Senior Lecturer in Tourism Management in the School of Marketing and Tourism, Napier University, UK. E-mail: a.leask@napier.ac.uk. She lectures in tourism management on both undergraduate and postgraduate programmes in tourism, with particular specialisms in heritage, visitor attraction and conference management. Anna has presented and published a wide variety of articles in the UK and in the international academic arena. Anna was lead editor of the textbook *Heritage Visitor Attractions: An Operations Management Perspective* published by Cassell.

Contributors

Stephen W. Boyd is Senior Lecturer in the Department of Tourism, University of Otago, New Zealand.

Bradley M. Braun is Associate Professor of Economics in the Department of Economics, University of Central Florida, USA.

Philip Feifan Xie is Assistant Professor in the School of Human Movement, Sport and Leisure Studies, Bowling Green State University, USA.

Philip Goulding is Visiting Lecturer in Tourism in the School of Marketing and Tourism, Napier University, UK.

C. Michael Hall is Professor and Head of the Department of Tourism, University of Otago, New Zealand, and Honorary Professor, Department of Marketing, Stirling University, UK.

Joan Henderson is Assistant Professor in the Nanyang Business School, Nanyang Technological University, Singapore.

Martin McCracken is Lecturer in Human Resource Management in the School of Management, Napier University, UK.

Victor T. C. Middleton is an Independent Management Consultant and Visiting Professor at the University of Central Lancashire and Oxford Brookes University, UK.

Rachel Piggin is a former graduate student at the Department of Tourism, University of Otago, New Zealand.

Bruce Prideaux is Senior Lecturer in the School of Tourism and Leisure Management, University of Queensland, Australia.

Derek Robbins is Senior Lecturer in Transport in the School of Service Industries, Bournemouth University, UK.

Myra Shackley is Professor of Cultural Resource Management, Nottingham Trent University, UK.

Mark Soskin is Associate Professor of Economics in the Department of Economics, University of Central Florida, USA.

Terry Stevens is Managing Director of Stevens & Associates, Swansea, UK, and Visiting Professor at Bournemouth University, UK.

Richard Voase is Senior Lecturer at the Lincoln campus of the University of Lincoln, UK.

Geoffrey Wall is Associate Dean, Graduate Studies and Research, at the University of Waterloo, Ontario, Canada.

Stephen Wanhill is Professor of Tourism in the International Centre for Tourism and Hospitality Research, Bournemouth University, UK, and Head of the Tourism Research Centre, Bornholm, Denmark.

Sandra Watson is Head of Human Resource Management in the School of Management, Napier University, UK.

Foreword

Tim Smit

When first asked to contribute a foreword to this book I was naturally pleased to accept, despite the fact that I loathe the words 'visitor attraction'. Although this may sound contradictory, I believe that the world has moved on from the time when the term held meaning. It is now an umbrella term, covering such a wide range of activities, interests and ambitions that new descriptive phrases will have to evolve.

That being said, one thing they all share is visitors; what has changed is the motivation behind many of the visits. My experience may perhaps be informative to others. I began in this arena by undertaking a garden restoration which was to open to the public under the name, 'The Lost Gardens of Heligan'. We opened while the restoration was in its early stages and we found that people took real ownership over what we were doing and returned time and again and told their friends about us, to the point that Heligan is now the most visited private garden in Britain. I then became involved with the creation of the Eden Project, the largest conservatories in the world, home to a new scientific foundation and an educational and entertaining visitor destination which attracts around 2 million people a year.

What makes them successful? They are both physically beautiful and of a status that has guaranteed them miles of newsprint and television coverage; but the secret of their continuing success comes from two things. First is a recognition that most people are to a lesser or greater degree lonely (how many couples or families do you entertain who seem to have lost the art of conversation?). They want to have their attention engaged, but they actually desire something deeper – a connectedness that links to their lives either actually or wishfully. This may sound pretentious but it is not. The great visitor attractions understand this and are selling what they do in terms of lifestyle choices, not passive entertainment and a great day out. The eye for detail, the curious, the talking point are the seducers of conversation and they are often fired up by the second factor, staff. We employ massively more people than an MBA manual would advise (over 600 by March 2002). We do this because visitors like nothing more than to talk to someone who is enthusiastic about what they are doing. People love people who love people, and they return time after time to enjoy the experience. This is only a truth that everyone reading this book knows in their heart, but most do not translate it into their businesses. If you would love to go to the place you work at you are probably not doing much wrong: if you would not pay to go there, fire yourself. The best form of marketing is word of mouth and the best ambassadors are your visitors.

Tim Smit
The Eden Project

Foreword

Sir Neil Cossons

Visitor attractions are surprisingly complicated to run. The apparently simple task of opening an attraction to the public involves potentially a great many skills and disciplines and often raises conflicts which have to be reconciled. Conservation, entertainment, education, visitor orientation and interpretation all feature to a greater or lesser extent in most, resulting in complex and sophisticated products which have to hold their own in a diverse market. This market is immature, fickle and widely misunderstood but it lies at the heart of what is one of the world's largest industries – tourism.

One of the great breakthroughs of recent times, particularly in the heritage sector, has been the realization that it is not a business based on buildings or monuments or even shops and cafés. It is about people, their inspiration and professionalism. The attractions business is universally characterized by the need to deliver excellence in visitor service. But this excellence can only be delivered if supported by exemplary management standards and practices.

In recent years the sector has come to appreciate this. Much greater emphasis is now placed upon good management, recruitment, training, appraisal procedures and the development of career structures. This has produced numerous benefits. The principal one though is the change in perception of careers in a sector often characterized as low paid and seasonal to ones which offer real opportunities for long-term development.

Now this perception has been overturned and visitor attractions are able to recruit, develop and keep real talent. This improvement has translated to the bottom line, to better quality for visitors and the beginnings of sound, professional management and operation. This book establishes the complex of parameters that define this increasingly sophisticated sector. Its expert contributors bring a wealth of experience, from all over the world, to point the way ahead for attractions and the people who work in them.

Sir Neil Cossons OBE FSA
Chairman English Heritage

Preface

As is so often the case with collaborative projects, the genesis of this book arose out of an informal discussion over coffee between the three editors, on this occasion in Edinburgh, toward the end of November 1999. The catalyst for discussion was the vast number of visitor attraction projects due to open in the early months of the new millennium, both in the UK and in other countries around the world. This fact alone was not that much of a revelation. Rather, what raised an inquisitive eyebrow were the huge sums of capital investment injected into many of the developments at a time when the rate of growth in attendance at 'traditional attractions' was beginning to experience a distinct slowdown. Two trains of thought presented themselves. On the one hand, the willingness of investors to put their money into these developments perhaps demonstrated a confidence that there was a pool of latent demand waiting to be drawn to their attractions. On the other hand, the evident eagerness to invest in such projects perhaps demonstrated a naive understanding of the visitor attraction marketplace and reflected a misplaced confidence in the wildly optimistic visitor projections advanced by those putting themselves forward as 'experts' in the field. It is easy to be critical with the benefit of hindsight, but the aftermath of the 'millennium exuberance' phase in visitor attraction development merely demonstrates the need for a much greater understanding of the visitor attraction domain. For example, we need to understand more fully what visitor attractions actually are, what forces drive their development, who visits them and why, how they are funded, and what the numerous day-to-day challenges are in respect of their management, marketing and, perhaps most importantly, their long-term viability.

The paucity of reliable research data, particularly of a comparable nature, and the general lack of published work available in the field of visitor attractions, makes answering many of the above questions difficult. Unlike other sectors of the tourism industry where there is a continual supply of new academic and practitioner-focused sources of information and analysis becoming available, it remains a mystery that so little has been published on visitor attractions. After all, they represent the very aspect of tourism that acts as the principal tourist draw to so many destinations around the world. There are some books that focus specifically on cultural and heritage attractions, national parks, historic cities, event management and the management of museums. However, publications with a sector-wide focus on visitor attractions have been conspicuous by their absence. One of the possible explanations for such a vacuum lies in the fact that visitor attraction sectors around the world are often typified by a very large number of small, geographically fragmented and resource-poor members trying to meet a multitude of objectives for a diverse set of owners. This can be demonstrated by the fact that historic monuments, castles and battlefields, zoos, theme parks, industrial attractions, museums and galleries, visitor centres, churches and cathedrals and, increasingly, retail sites and sporting arenas, to name but a few, can all to varying degrees be legitimately classified as visitor attractions. Addressing the sector in its entirety is therefore a challenging proposition and raises the question as to how worthwhile such an endeavour is in the first place.

In 1972, in his seminal work *Vacationscape*, Gunn refers to visitor attractions as 'the first power, lodestones for pleasure and the real energizer of tourism in a region . . . without attractions there would be no need for other tourism services' (Gunn, 1972). This viewpoint has our unequivocal support. Visitor attractions as a sector may lack the glamour of international airlines, the diversity and appeal of destinations, or the political and critical challenge of tourism policy. Individually and collectively, however, they represent the catalytic focus for the development of tourism infrastructure and services. For this reason alone they warrant academic attention and deserve a research base equivalent to, or even better than, other much more talked about and researched sectors of the wider tourism industry. Visitor attractions represent a complex sector of the tourism industry and are generally not very well understood. It is thus the principal aim of this book to generate greater interest and discussion of visitor attractions, to stimulate critical debate and to provide a foundation for a much greater research contribution from both the academic and practitioner communities.

One factor that has clearly ignited debate, as evidenced by the development of many millennium attractions, is the burgeoning supply of visitor attractions in recent years and the corresponding slowdown in visitor demand. Understandably, the oversupply of visitor attractions in many developed destinations has started to cause real concern. Considerable capital outlays have been invested in a vacuum of policy – be it at the local, regional or national level – and a complete void of strategic direction and guiding management principles. It therefore comes as no real surprise to find many attractions, both old and new, struggling to achieve viable visitor numbers. This said, there have been some considerable successes, most recently in the UK with the innovative Eden Project.

The issues discussed in this book were selected carefully to address the areas considered to be of the utmost importance to the future direction of the management of visitor attractions. With the book divided into five parts, focusing on the *nature and scope* of visitor attractions, and their *development, management, marketing* and *future directions*, an attempt has been made to identify and address thematic issues that connect a variety of seemingly disparate elements in the visitor attraction sector. Issues explored in the book include the nature and purpose of visitor attractions, economic aspects of their development, issues pertaining to the development of visitor attractions on the geographic periphery and in urban locations, and the integral part played by transport in the success or otherwise of visitor attractions. Management issues covered include discussion on attraction authenticity, the management of visitor impacts and seasonality, the challenge for religion-based attractions and the importance of recruiting and managing an effective human resource base. The book also examines a number of marketing issues relating to heritage attractions, the branding of World Heritage sites, competitive strategies of theme parks, and the emergence of a more collaborative approach to the marketing of visitor attractions. The book concludes with a review of the visitor and visitor motivation to visit attractions, an argument in support of a national strategy for attractions, and a crystal-ball gazing exercise as to what the future holds in terms of scope, form, number and likely popularity of visitor attractions. No doubt this list omits many other issues considered to be of great significance. What the list does represent, however, is a genuine attempt to bring together issues that are important to both academics and practitioners, and are likely to be of real value to students of this dynamic sector of tourism.

Of great significance to all of the above is the role and experience of the visitor at attractions. Without visitor attractions, one could argue there is no basis for tourism; yet without visitors there is clearly no market for visitor attractions. Tim Smit stressed the importance of the visitor in his foreword to the book and there is no doubt that this principle cannot be emphasized enough. Despite the slowdown in visitor demand in many markets, visitors are still frequenting attractions in very large numbers indeed. However, the nature of their visits, their motivations and expectations, their experiences and perceived 'value for money', their willingness and readiness to act as ambassadors for attractions and their readiness to return, are likely to change over time and be influenced by the vast array of alternative 'things to do' in their leisure time. Visitor attractions are not only competing for visitors with other attractions, they are in the market for 'people's time'. Time is continually at a premium for many people around the world. Visitor attractions need to understand their visitors, understand what draws them to attractions in the first instance and understand what satisfies their thirst for fun, education or whatever it is that the visitor of the future is searching for.

In putting this book together, the editors are in considerable debt to the efforts of all the contributors for their acceptance of initial interest and readiness to participate in the project, and for their hard work and valued contribution with regard to subject matter and ideas. All contributors are either recognized academic experts in their field or well-respected and highly experienced practitioners in the visitor attraction sector. In view of the busy schedules of everyone concerned, the prompt response to invitations for contributions, the speed with which ideas were forthcoming and the efficiency with which deadlines were met, all contributors are worthy of praise. In particular, we are delighted with the geographic coverage of both our contributors and their chosen themes and case material. Contributions span England, Scotland and Wales in the UK, and Australia, Singapore, Canada, New Zealand and the USA worldwide. The authors make no apology for the English-speaking bias of the contributors and their examples. This has more to do with their shortcomings and limited abilities in speaking foreign languages than any attempt deliberately to exclude many other worthy examples and notable authors from other countries around the world.

In closing this preface, the editors wish to place particular emphasis on the chosen title of the book. Rather than merely to report the status quo, it has been the aim throughout the project to advance 'new directions' in the management of visitor attractions. We hope this has been achieved. What perhaps is still lacking, however, is the necessary research base upon which to compare and contrast international best practice, to provide a national or international benchmark of visitor attraction quality or to provide a foundation for the advancement of some of the issues discussed in this book beyond national boundaries. It is hoped that *Managing Visitor Attractions: New Directions* will serve as a catalyst for change and help raise the study of visitor attractions to a higher level.

Alan Fyall
Bournemouth University, UK

Brian Garrod
University of the West of England, UK

Anna Leask
Napier University, UK

April 2002

Reference

Gunn, C. (1972). *Vacationscape: Designing Tourist Regions*. Bureau of Business Research, University of Texas.

Abbreviations

AIM	Association of Independent Museums
ALVA	Association of Leading Visitor Attractions
ASVA	Association of Scottish Visitor Attractions
CPI	consumer price index
DCMS	Department of Culture, Media and Sport
ERDF	European Regional Development Fund
ETAG	Edinburgh Tourism Action Group
ETB	English Tourist Board
ETC	English Tourism Council
EU	European Union
HKTB	Hong Kong Tourism Board
HKTC	Hong Kong Tourism Commission
HRM	human resource management
IAAPA	International Association of Amusement Parks and Attractions
ICCROM	International Center for Conservation in Rome
ICOMOS	International Council for Monuments and Sites
IiP	Investors in People
IT	information technology
ITP	International Theme Parks Pte Ltd
IUCN	International Union for Conservation of Nature and Natural Resources
LPG	liquid petroleum gas
MBO	management by objectives
MD	management development
MGC	Museums and Galleries Commission
MS	margin of safety
NGO	non-government organization
NTS	National Travel Survey

OD	organizational development
OECD	Organization for Economic Co-operation and Development
RTB	regional tourist board
SAR	Special Administrative Region
SEZ	special economic zone
STB	Singapore Tourism Board
SWHC	Scotch Whisky Heritage Centre
SWNZ	Southwest New Zealand
TNP	Tongariro National Park
UKDVS	United Kingdom Day Visitor Survey
UNESCO	United Nations Educational, Scientific, and Cultural Organization
VOC	volatile organic compounds
WDW	Walt Disney World
WHC	World Heritage Convention
WTO	World Tourism Organization

Part One

Introduction: the role and nature of visitor attractions

Part One of this book explores the broad context within which visitor attractions operate and provides a historical overview of how the visitor attraction product has developed over time. While the overall focus of the book is on the role of visitor attractions as a major component of the tourism system, it is important to recognize that visitor attractions operate within a number of interrelated internal and external environments. For example, many visitor attractions play a vital role in conserving and protecting the natural and built historic heritage. Others have an explicit educational function or are important in helping to maintain specific cultural identities and practices. As a result, the management of visitor attractions is influenced by a range of complex issues in addition to those arising out of their role as tourism resources. The key themes identified in the first part of this book therefore cover a broad range of issues relating to the context in which visitor attractions are managed.

After providing an introduction to the variety and scope of visitor attractions, Chapter 1, by Anna Leask, considers how visitor attractions may best be defined and categorized. Definitions of visitor attractions vary significantly around the world, as does the basis for the categorization of different types of visitor attraction within a certain definition. This gives rise to a major dilemma for the conduct of research into the management of visitor attractions. On the one hand, the lack of a common definition of what constitutes a visitor attraction can frustrate efforts to compare management concepts and identify best practice across different categories of visitor attraction, as well as across the visitor attraction sectors of different countries. On the other hand, the existence of a wide diversity of visitor attractions may call into question the necessity and desirability of a common definition. Indeed, visitor attraction sectors around the world are often characterized by a very large number of small attractions that have poor access to resources and are diffuse in spatial terms, yet are trying to meet a wide range of objectives set by a multitude of stakeholders. It might be argued that in the presence of such diversity, any attempt to analyse the sector as a whole constitutes a fundamentally worthless exercise.

Chapter 1 then goes on to explore how visitor attractions fit into the overall tourism product. Visitor attractions are clearly only one part of a complex network of tourism service providers. Leask considers the main interrelationships and interdependencies between visitor attractions and the wider tourism industry. Visitor attractions are then discussed in relation to the wider political and sociocultural environment. The degree to which the focus of analysis should be at the level of the individual attraction, at the destination level or at the national level is also explored. This, in turn, raises the question of whether the focus of analysis should be on the management of the attraction as a whole or on particular management functions, such as marketing or human resource management. This book has adopted an inclusive and flexible approach to the questions of definition, categorization and analytical focus in a deliberate attempt to stimulate debate and discussion. The collective thoughts of the editors can be found in the concluding section of this book. From the beginning of the writing process, contributors were encouraged to sow the seeds of thought and question the existing status quo within the visitor attraction sector. The contributors responded enthusiastically, particularly so in the case of the contribution of Stephen Wanhill, who in Chapter 2 introduces the concept of the market–imagescape mix. He then goes on to use a framework based on the market–imagescape concept to suggest a revised classification of attractions which, he argues, will contribute to the better understanding and management of both individual visitor attraction products and the wider visitor attraction sector.

The third major issue explored in Part One relates to the multiplicity of objectives arising from the wide range of stakeholder interests that is typically evident among visitor attractions. Despite the diversity of objectives in evidence around the world, increasingly competitive market conditions are serving as a catalyst for the adoption of more common approaches to attraction management. However, the current lack of commonality in objective setting continues to generate conflicting management pressures. It also continues to provide a diversity of challenges and impediments to the effective management of visitor attractions. The opening two chapters offer some valuable insights into how such challenges and impediments may best be addressed and ultimately overcome.

Finally, Part One considers the perceived economic benefits of visitor attractions and, in particular, the extent to which the development of visitor attractions represents a viable means of economic development and/or regeneration. In so doing, Chapter 2 offers some insights into the criteria that are likely to determine the success, or otherwise, of visitor attractions.

The nature and purpose of visitor attractions

Anna Leask

Aims

The aims of this chapter are to:

- introduce the variety and scope of visitor attractions
- discuss the various definitions and categories of visitor attractions
- identify the range of purposes that visitor attractions have in international, national, regional and local environments.

Introduction

There can be no doubting the crucial role that visitor attractions have in the development and success of tourism destinations. At their most basic level they work to attract visitors to an area, while they may also operate on much broader levels as agents of change, social enablers and major income generators. Indeed, Boniface and Cooper (2001: 30) state that 'attractions are the *raison d'être* for tourism; they generate the visit, give rise to excursion circuits and create an industry of their own'.

The purpose of this chapter is to introduce the variety of visitor attractions, their definitions and purposes in differing destinations. This allows authors of subsequent chapters to concentrate on the specific management issues as they relate to visitor attractions, without each needing to discuss the broad context within which they operate. While no set definition of visitor attractions is to be used for this book, the following discussion will allow for the whole gamut of the sector to be explored, thus setting the international context of this sector. The chapter starts with an explanation of the huge variety of visitor attractions that exists around the world, followed by a brief discussion of the key working definitions currently in use. The chapter finishes with an assessment of the purposes that visitor attractions may have within a range of tourism destinations.

The variety and scope of visitor attractions

Visitor attraction categorization

There have been many attempts to explain the multitude of forms in which visitor attractions may manifest themselves (Holloway, 1995; 1998; Smith, 1998) with classification generally being on the basis of the natural or built nature of the resource. However, this appears to be a rather narrow, single-dimensional view of a sector which often has multiple stakeholder involvement in individual properties and, consequently, an extensive range of management objectives. Figure 1.1 attempts to describe the various approaches that could be considered in classification of this dynamic sector of the tourism industry.

At the centre of Figure 1.1 is the core product offered by the visitor attraction, which focuses mainly on the resource that attracts the visitors to visit in the first instance. The increasing need to generate alternative revenue streams has led to an expansion of the core activities in many new and existing attractions, with very few now opening without some element of retail or catering, and many others also investing in conference rooms for hire or various off-site activities to boost income. As Bland (2001: 14) states, '[f]unding visitor attractions in the 21st Century is not an

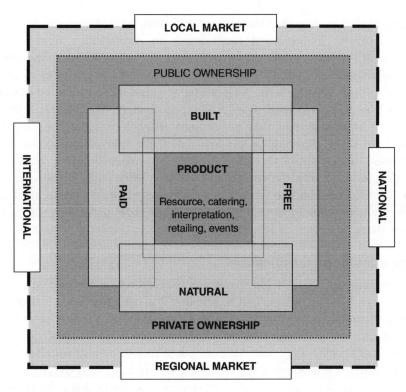

Figure 1.1 Classification of visitor attractions

insoluble problem, but most will involve packaging with other less risky cash flows or with the generation of indirect benefits for investors'. The interpretation of the resource should, however, remain the key feature of the attraction visit, with increasing focus on catering for broader markets or more specific niche markets. The use of technology to enhance the presentation of the resource is currently a popular approach, with the development of hands-on interactive exhibits, such as those seen at Glasgow's new Science Centre, and virtual reality shows, such as those at Hellenic Cosmos in Athens. While these developments may well cater for specific markets, usually children, they are costly both to install and to maintain, and they may serve to exclude other markets that are not impressed with or predisposed to use this style of presentation.

The next stage in classification usually focuses on the nature of the resource itself, be it natural or built (Millar, 1999). The main reasons for this categorization result from the different approaches required for their management, with natural sites usually requiring fewer staff, incurring lower fixed costs and having a more open attitude towards access than in the case of built properties. This is not to say that natural sites such as the Grand Canyon require no management, but that the objectives of site management often focus on conservation issues and the management of visitors, rather than increasing visitor spend and entertainment. Built sites may also be subdivided into those built for the purposes of tourism, such as the Alton Towers theme park in England, and those converted from other uses, such as Robben Island, the former prison of Nelson Mandela in South Africa. The significance of this is apparent when looking at the design and operation of these differing properties, where the conversions often have to compromise on operational issues in order to meet building conservation legislation. Additionally, the converted buildings often carry higher fixed costs and a need to consider the wishes of existing users, for example, in religious buildings where worshippers stand next to vast hordes of tourists (discussed in Chapter 10).

Visitor attraction classification

The other main approach to classification often centres on the pricing policy for access to the visitor attraction, that is, whether it is paid admission or free access. While government policy on this varies internationally, there is usually some provision for key national sites to offer free access to visitors on either a permanent or specific-day basis. An example of this is the year-round free access for all to national museums in the UK and free Sunday access to Greek national sites in the off-peak season. This often overcomes the perception of local residents that the attractions are purely there for use by tourists, and meets the broader educational and social inclusion aims of many institutions. The management objectives of the managing body usually determine the admission-charging policy for the visitor attraction. One example of this is Historic Scotland, the executive agency responsible for many of Scotland's historic monuments, who charge admission at approximately sixty of their 330 sites in order that money raised at the revenue-generating sites can be used to support conservation work at less-visited sites. Additionally they offer free education visits in the shoulder months to help meet their broader educational objectives.

The differing objectives of public and private bodies will naturally affect the operation and management of their visitor attractions. Quite different approaches to management issues such as pricing, visitor access, interpretation and marketing, can be seen across the world (Deloitte & Touche, 1997; Fyall and Leask, 2002), though an increasingly competitive market is encouraging more common approaches to be adopted.

The final point shown in Figure 1.1 is that the operating environment for visitor attractions will vary depending on the market in which it exists. Some may cater mainly for the local market and require facilities that allow this, for example, flexible use of space to allow community use, while others may cater more significantly for the international market, acting as key flagship attractions within a destination. The target market for an attraction may well determine the nature and management of the product offering, particularly in terms of pricing, visitor spend and interpretation. One evident implication of the market in which an attraction operates is the potential pool of visitors that might be attracted. Very few visitor attractions attract large numbers of visitors on a regular basis, while most, particularly in rural areas, rely on a much smaller visitor throughput. This can be clearly seen in the UK, where only 7 per cent of visitor attractions record visitor numbers above 200 000, while 57 per cent attract less than 20 000 per annum (ETC, 2000a). Attempts to broaden an attraction's visitor appeal may entail increased collaboration and training, as will be discussed in Chapter 15.

The classification methods suggested in Figure 1.1 are not exhaustive but serve to indicate the main features of classification used in various settings. Each national tourist board or attraction governing body has its own classification mechanisms appropriate to its own context. What it does do, though, is demonstrate the diverse range of attractions around the world and offers some explanation as to how this variety has evolved over time. The variety of visitor attractions on offer around the world has developed significantly in the past twenty years (Stevens, 2000), no doubt influenced by the increased ability and propensity to travel. While more traditional museums and galleries have long attracted local markets, they can now also look to international audiences both in attracting actual visitors to their properties and in providing remote access via the use of advanced technology. Changes in funding structures often influence the available stock of facilities within a country, seen significantly since the introduction of National Lottery funding in the UK in the 1990s and the availability of European Union structural funding in the 1980s and 1990s. Similarly, changes in access to public finance for ongoing revenue support or to capital funding priorities by enterprise companies, can make vast differences in the development and reinvestment in the visitor attraction product. Current trends indicate an increasing need for attractions to appeal to broader audiences and to generate ever greater levels of external income, resulting in an increased mix of product offering and choice for the visitor (STB, 2001). Changing patterns of leisure time and discretionary income are influencing the form of attractions wanted by consumers, calling for products that meet their needs and quality expectations (CBI, 1998; Cooper et al., 1996), rather than a decision taken by the attraction operators on the basis of what they feel the visitor wants. According to Stevens (2000: 64) 'attraction designers will innovate to create a new generation of all-inclusive, multi-faceted destination attractions capable of year-round operation, appealing to different markets and providing sound returns on large-scale investments'.

Defining visitor attractions

There is a temptation to aim to define visitor attractions for research and management purposes, although views on how they should best be defined and categorized vary around the world. This variety frustrates efforts to compare management concepts and management practices, but is acceptance of a common definition necessary or even desirable?

Visitor attraction sectors around the world are often typified by a very large number of small, geographically fragmented, resource-poor members, trying to meet a multitude of objectives for a diverse range of owners. Although agreement of definitions can sometimes cause unnecessary delay in a research study, a universal definition of attractions is required in order to 'record, map and monitor attractions for information and statistical purposes' (ETC, 2000b: 24). This having been said, once a definition is set and used for certain purposes, for example, annual visitor surveys, it is considered inadvisable to change the basis because this will alter the comparability of results (Chapter 17 discusses this point in the context of developing a national strategy for visitor attractions). This has resulted in the continued, though slightly amended and out-of-date, use of the following definition for visitor attractions in the UK.

> A permanently established excursion destination, a primary purpose of which is to allow public access for entertainment, interest or education; rather than being principally a retail outlet or venue for sporting, theatrical or film performances. It must be open to the public without prior booking, for published periods each year, and should be capable of attracting tourists or day visitors as well as local residents. In addition, the attraction must be a single business, under a single management . . . and must be receiving revenue directly from visitors. (ETC, 2000b: 24)

Changing leisure patterns and product development have meant that the above definition, currently espoused by the UK national tourism boards, has begun to be questioned. Although ostensibly inclusive, there are a number of weaknesses, both domestically and internationally, of using the English Tourism Council (ETC) definition for research purposes. The main reason for developing a definition is to allow international comparison. For example, a new generation of 'destination' attractions is emerging wherein consumers are offered a comprehensive range of services and facilities for entertainment, shopping, eating and drinking, and other aspects of leisure (Stevens, 2000). Although not a permanent attraction, the much-derided Millennium Dome in London is typical of such developments, which in turn make a succinct definition both elusive and increasingly irrelevant. This issue of definition is highly pertinent, as numerous retail and sporting attractions that are included in studies conducted in other countries, such as Canada, would be excluded if one were to adopt the ETC definition. Likewise, the condition that to be considered an attraction for sightseeing purposes it should be possible (but not compulsory) to charge an admission fee for access would exclude many monuments and historic battlefields in Scotland. One part of the definition that the ETC proposes changing is the element of the definition which relates to 'without prior booking'. As so many visitor attractions now have pre-booking facilities, this item no longer appears valid (ETC, 2000b).

Related to the question of definition are the issues of comparability and equivalence. In particular, such issues relate to the means by which visitor attractions are categorized. As with any changes to the definition of an attraction, category data must be manageable, meaningful and usable. Duplication of any categories should be avoided (ETC, 2000b). The incorporation of all attractions across all countries into standard visitor attraction categories would prove highly complex and not necessarily advantageous. For example, the National Historic Site category used in Canada does not correspond with any category used in other countries. From a marketing standpoint, the newly introduced Wilderness, Thrill Zone, Heartland, Kiwi Spirit and Chill Out categorizations of attractions used in New Zealand are highly pertinent and facilitate consumer choice. However, they serve as obstacles to the researcher trying to achieve comparability and equivalence in international studies. Although the broad classification of attractions as either natural or built, whether for tourism-specific reasons such as a museum or for other reasons such as a castle, does alleviate the problem, it does so somewhat artificially. Perhaps even more challenging is the means by which the researcher classifies visitor attractions by ownership and whether or not a charge is levied on entry. In previous studies conducted on Scottish visitor attractions (Garrod, Fyall and Leask, 2002; Leask, Fyall and Goulding, 2000), ownership category proved to be a key dependent variable with regard to determining the entire approach to attraction management. This is particularly the case for managing revenue and overall yield, visitor management strategies and the management of environmental impacts at attractions. Although there are similarities across many of the ownership categories used, misrepresentation of the terms 'public', 'charity', 'trust' and 'society' on occasion make for spurious accuracy of comparison. Equally challenging is the means by which the researcher defines an attraction which charges, or does not charge, for visitor entry. Although there are a large number who clearly charge for admission, there are a significant proportion of visitor attractions which rely on voluntary donations and alternative 'pricing' mechanisms. For example, many churches, historic properties and gardens in Scotland rely heavily on visitor donations, while in New Zealand the enormous number of wineries do not charge for visitor admission but set token prices for wine tasting. In this instance, the New Zealand winery is similar to the Scottish whisky distillery in that it serves both tourism and non-tourism objectives such as brand building.

Thus, it is difficult to determine an internationally recognized definition for visitor attractions, mainly due to the variety of product offerings and scope as discussed above. For the purposes of this book, authors were invited to determine their own definitions, within the generally accepted categories as discussed.

The purpose and role of visitor attractions

As stated by Swarbrooke (2000: 267), 'Visitor attractions are at the heart of the tourism industry, they are motivators that make people want to take a trip in the first place'. Richards (2001: 4) points out that while it can be argued that attractions do not always literally 'attract' visitors, they 'certainly do provide a focus for much tourist activity, and are an essential weapon in the arsenal of tourism destinations engaged in a competitive struggle for tourist business'.

Their role within a destination forms only one part of a complex network of tourism service providers within the broader tourism product; however, they are often used as key products in marketing activities. Examples of this are the use of images of the Taj Mahal when marketing India or those of the British Airways London Eye in publications promoting England. The main interrelationships and interdependencies between visitor attractions and the wider tourism industry appear to focus on standard areas of mutual benefit, with an increasing move to develop more formal partnerships and collaboration being seen in recent years (Fyall, Leask and Garrod, 2001). Declining visitor numbers to attractions, in an environment of decreasing public capital and revenue funding, have encouraged visitor attractions to expand their revenue streams into areas such as conference venues, events and off-site activities. These all require attractions to work effectively with other tourism operators within a destination, such as accommodation providers, food and beverage suppliers, destination management companies and transport operators.

The value of specific visitor attractions within a destination can also be a key motivator in attracting business to the destination, for example, the wealth of heritage attractions in Edinburgh or access to mountain ranges for team-building courses. Therefore the quality and success of these interrelationships depend not only on the visitor attraction itself, but its contribution to the development of the critical mass of the destination product offering itself. Within the business tourism context, visitor attractions may also be an important part in the decision to return to a destination for a leisure visit, thus attracting those elusive repeat visitors.

Visitor attractions may also play a crucial role in the revitalization of an area or destination, one example of this being the Guggenheim in Bilbao. The creativity shown in the nature of the architecture of a building to house a key development may in itself elevate the purpose of the attraction to flagship proportions. Another classic example of this would be the success of the National Museum of New Zealand and its contribution to the development of Wellington as a destination. Flagship attractions can be used to pull in visitors, meet needs of local residents and develop stronger tourism activities within the destination. While a destination rarely survives long term on the basis of one attraction, it can be the key 'pump-primer' in more sustainable development of a destination, for example, the opportunities now available within Bilbao to develop further their existing stock of internationally significant cultural offerings. The purpose of visitor attractions in this manner should form part of a general strategic tourism plan that may identify such opportunities to 'use' the attraction as a management tool within the destination, rather than in isolation. Examples of this might include the location of some of Scotland's newest visitor attractions: the Royal Yacht *Britannia* in the new Ocean Terminal complex in Leith, Edinburgh, Our Dynamic Earth as part of the Holyrood North project at the base of the Royal Mile in Edinburgh, or the new Science Centre on Glasgow's abandoned waterfront. These ventures all offer opportunities to tackle management issues such as seasonality, economic benefit and the development of civic pride.

In considering the purpose of visitor attractions within a destination it is important not only to consider the views of visitors and how they might be attracted and catered for. The needs of the local population must also be met and may indeed play a more significant role in the success of an attraction, particularly in rural settings, where their support for repeat visits, staffing, recommendation and participation may be vital. There is also the issue of social inclusion to be considered, to encourage cultural awareness within the local population and meet educational objectives. The maintenance of specific cultural identities and practices can often only be achieved via the involvement of those from the local population.

The multiplicity of stakeholders involved in the operation and use of visitor attractions can create difficulties in identifying the future practices of a development. Objectives may include revenue generation, enterprise, conservation, cultural issues or simply entertainment. The market might be local, national or international, resulting in differing needs and product offerings. It is unlikely that any one attraction can be directly compared with another in terms of its role and purpose within a setting, as these will vary considerably between destinations. However, certain policies can be set in place to encourage successful management of the variety of visitor attractions that exist. While individual attractions may achieve certain levels of success according to their own set of objective criteria, it usually falls to national bodies and organizations to determine the parameters and structure for long-term success. It is important that these structures, be they strategic policies, funding principles or quality standards, take account of the variety of purposes that visitor attractions may have within their particular contexts. What might be considered appropriate in one area or country may not be in another. International benchmarking initiatives may well offer opportunities in this area, though there is limited evidence of their use in this sector to date. Much of this can be attributed to the fact that the focus of existing schemes can often reflect the organizer's particular interest or background, or meet institutional administrative requirements. As with all issues pertaining to the definition of visitor attractions, there is also the need for a cross-sectoral benchmarking scheme that concentrates on visitor, marketing, commercial and quality aspects, and perhaps most importantly is in a format suitable to both large and small attractions (ETC, 2000b).

Conclusion

There is no doubt that the international visitor attractions sector is facing a challenging time ahead. Uncertainties over the continued growth of tourist movements in light of the 11 September 2001 attacks on America, changing patterns of leisure time and use, the current oversupply of visitor attractions in some regions and the potential product developments in the field of technology in particular, all pose the need for new directions to be taken in the management approach at visitor attractions. The multiple objectives of which visitor attractions need to be aware in determining their nature, role and resultant success, also invite change. Meanwhile the wide range of stakeholder interests relating to an attraction, whether such interests are related to education, revenue generation or conservation, will inevitably lead to conflicting management pressures. The purpose of this book is to identify what the main challenges might be in the future and how they can be overcome to the benefit of all concerned.

References

Bland, N. (2001). *Leisure Review: A Digest of Corporate Financial Activity.* 2nd quarter. Deloitte & Touche.

Boniface, P. and Cooper, C. (2001). *Worldwide Destinations: The Geography of Travel and Tourism.* 3rd edn. Butterworth-Heinemann.

CBI (1998). *Attracting Attention: Visitor Attractions in the New Millennium.* Confederation of British Industry.

Cooper, C., Fletcher, J., Gilbert, D., Shepherd, R. and Wanhill, S. (1996). *Tourism: Principles and Practice.* 2nd edn. Longman.

Deloitte & Touche (1997). *Survey of Continental European Visitor Attractions*. Deloitte & Touche Consulting.

ETC (2000a). *Sightseeing in the UK 1999*. English Tourism Council.

ETC (2000b). *Action for Attractions*. English Tourism Council.

Fyall, A. and Leask, A. (2002). Managing visitor attractions: an international comparison of management practice. *Journal of Hospitality and Tourism Management* (in press).

Fyall, A., Leask, A. and Garrod, B. (2001). Scottish visitor attractions: a collaborative future? *International Journal of Tourism Research*, **3**, 211–228.

Garrod, B., Fyall, A. and Leask, A. (2002). Scottish visitor attractions: managing visitor impacts. *Tourism Management*, **23**, 265–279.

Holloway, J. C. (1995). *The Business of Tourism*. 4th edn. Longman.

Holloway, J. C. (1998). *The Business of Tourism*. 5th edn. Longman.

Leask, A., Fyall, A. and Goulding, P. (2000). Scottish visitor attractions: revenue, capacity and sustainability. In *Yield Management Strategies for the Service Industries* (A. Ingold, U. McMahon-Beattie and I. Yeoman, eds), 2nd edn, pp. 211–232, Continuum.

Millar, S. (1999). An overview of the sector. In *Heritage Visitor Attractions: An Operations Management Perspective* (A. Leask and I. Yeoman, eds) pp. 1–21, Cassell.

Richards, G. (2001). *Cultural Attractions and European Tourism*. CABI.

Smith, R. (1998). Visitor attractions in Scotland. In *Tourism in Scotland* (R. McLellan and R. Smith, eds) pp. 187–208, International Thompson Business Press.

STB (2001). *The Scottish Visitor Attraction Monitor*. Scottish Tourist Board.

Stevens, T. (2000). The future of visitor attractions. *Travel and Tourism Analyst*, **1**, 61–85.

Swarbrooke, J. (2000). *Sustainable Tourism Management*. CABI.

2

Interpreting the development of the visitor attraction product

Stephen Wanhill

Aims

The aims of this chapter are to:

- show how the nature of the visitor attraction product has changed over time
- explain the nature of visitor attraction development
- explore the concept of the market–imagescape mix and present a revised classification of attractions based on this dimension
- discuss the criteria which can determine the success or otherwise of visitor attractions.

Introduction

A visitor attraction is a focus for recreational and, increasingly, educational activity, undertaken by both day and stay visitors, and frequently shared with the domestic resident population. Every region and every town boasts at least one attraction, adding to its appeal as a destination. Thus, the range of visitor attractions is extensive and there are numerous variations in respect of the product concept or creativity of the design and its appeal. This will be termed the 'imagescape' to match the use of the word 'imagineers' by the Disney Corporation when describing its designers (Kirsner, 1988). The concept is based on the fact that all attractions, in some part, measure their performance by the number of visitors, for which the output is the visitor experience. To enhance the latter, the modern approach is to place tangible objects, say, a thrill ride or a collection of artefacts, within the context of a specific theme or image in a particular setting or environment; hence the word 'imagescape'.

It is possible to classify attractions along a number of different dimensions: ownership, capacity, market or catchment area, permanency and type. The simplest classification by type is to group attractions into those that are gifts of nature and those that are human-made. The former include the landscape, climate, vegetation, forests and wildlife, embodied in, say, country parks in Britain, lakes in Canada, mountains in Switzerland, the coast in Spain or game reserves in Africa. The latter are principally the products of the historical development of countries and civilizations, but also include artificially created entertainment complexes, that is, attractions designed almost exclusively for amusement and enjoyment such as theme parks. Among the most well known of these are the Walt Disney parks, the imagescape originating in California (in 1955) but since reproduced in Florida, Tokyo and near Paris.

Going further, it will be appreciated that this basic classification may be subdivided again into attractions which are site-specific because of the physical location of facilities and therefore act as a destination, and attractions which are temporary because they are events. International events that are regarded as world class normally stand alone as 'hallmark' activities, while others may be used to complement site-specific attractions. What is happening at the time is usually more important for events than their location, so mega-events such as the Olympics, and exhibitions, for example, world trade fairs, may move around the globe. However some mega-events do evolve in and become specific to their location, so that they become branded by it. Thus several of the most spectacular events in the form of parades or carnivals have become associated with major cities, for example, the Lord Mayor's Show in London or the Calgary Stampede in Alberta. This is because cities provide access to a large market and have the economic base to support them. Similarly, important religious festivals are often connected with locations that are considered the foundations of the faith, such as Mecca and Jerusalem.

Complementarity may be achieved, for example, by staging a festival of the countryside to enhance the appeal of a country park, or markets and fairs in towns and villages of historic interest. Similarly, complementarity may be achieved by staging a performance of a Shakespeare tragedy in the courtyard of a historic castle. Janiskee (1996) examines three event models as suitable attractions for historic houses – community festivals, stand-alone tours and living history portrayals – and deduces that the latter, which include holiday celebrations, ceremonies, rituals and parties, historic re-enactment and the learning of vernacular skills, crafts and household 'chores', are best suited to such venues.

The attraction product

In the post-industrial society that Pine and Gilmore (1999) label the 'Experience Economy', it is argued that the production system should be re-engineered to add value through marketing experiences. This implies producing services with attached goods, rather than the traditional mass production process in which commodities are uniformly produced and sold on price. In this way, customers are able to receive a package that can be tailored to their needs. In fact, Pine and Gilmore draw many of the examples in their work from the leisure industry. Following this line of reasoning, Figure 2.1 presents an abstract construction of an

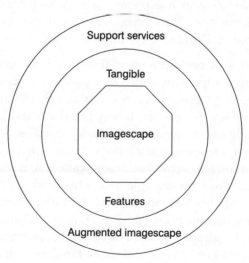

Figure 2.1 The attraction product

attraction product where the core is the imagescape, the purpose of which is to convey the essence of the visitor experience to the potential market. Thus the intangible output of a constructed imagescape is central to the visitor experience. The core is surrounded by commodities and services, which are combined to add value or support the imagescape. The right imagescape portrays, through the functional aspect of theming, all four realms of the visitor experience, namely, entertainment, education, aesthetics and escapism. These four aspects are embodied in all truly successful visitor attractions, be they theme parks in the private domain or heritage attractions in the non-commercial sector. As commercial operators know well, failure to distinguish between the core and peripherals designed to augment the imagescape, or lack of content control, as in the case of exhibitions that are made up of a variety of sponsors, or failure to communicate the imagescape to the market, will lead to underperformance and possible project failure.

When presenting the core, the diversity of imagescape themes for visitor attractions is beyond doubt extensive, as indicated in Table 2.1. But in essence, there is very little new in what draws visitors. The main attractions are still the wonders of the natural and physical world and the endeavours of human society, including, albeit to a much smaller extent, dark subjects that deal with what are considered to be behaviour inversions, such as the grim consequences of war, crime and punishment, and the unusual, for example, catastrophes and the erotic.

While the broad themes indicated in Table 2.1 may be globally enduring, their presentation within the context of an imagescape may not be. The acceptance of

Table 2.1 Imagescapes

Armed forces	Industry
Art and media	Miscellaneous
Built environment	Myths and fantasy
Childhood	Natural world
Civilizations	Physical world
Dark subjects	Politics
Entertainment	Religion
Famous and notorious	Retailing
Food and drink	Science and discovery
Future	Society and culture
History and heritage	Sport
Hobbies and pastimes	Transport
Human body	War and conflict

the content and style of production of the imagescape is determined by fashion, which has its own dynamic that is born out of the spirit of enquiry and competition within society to alter its patterns of consumption and value systems. Thus, animals in captivity in zoos or safari parks are no longer acceptable to many people and there is a marked decline of interest in static attractions and object-oriented museums, unless they are national collections (Swarbrooke, 1999) or they are best presented in this way, as for example jewellery. Despite the intrinsic value of historic buildings and collections, presentation, interpretation and good support facilities have become increasingly important. On the other hand, historical tableaux (which have developed from static wax museums to animatronic figures and even fantasy presentations), the performing arts, sporting events and thrill rides seem to have universal appeal. To complete the attraction product, the core imagescape in Figure 2.1 is supported by facilities such as retailing, catering, cloakrooms, first aid, special needs access, internal transport and car parking, as well as an augmented imagescape designed to ensure that all customers' experiential requirements are met, for example, visitor orientation, queue entertainment, complaints handling, puppet characters, shows, presentations, and so on.

A significant aspect of the core of the attraction product, which is sadly lacking in many visitor attractions, is the encouragement of repeat visits. This is a necessary requirement for long-term success, unless the market for the experience is global, which therefore provides a catchment population that is to all intents and purposes infinite in size, since it is continually being replenished. This, of course, may not be an issue with public attractions that are free, depending on whether or not visitor numbers are used as a performance indicator. Entertainment attractions, such as cinemas and theatres are able to survive on one-time-only purchases of the experience, because they continually change the core attraction (the film or show). Meanwhile, theme parks embody thrill rides for which there is a repetitive demand that they reinforce with a rolling programme of replacement and re-theming to persuade their customers to return. Leisure shopping facilities continually replace their merchandise in line with fashion but, for the majority of visitor attractions that were not built for such purposes, their ability to maintain attendances is functionally related to the size and dynamics of their market, as well as to their capacity to alter the core imagescape and supplement it by special events (giving animation to object-oriented attractions such as museums) and other supporting features. To this extent, national museums are at a considerable advantage because the size of their collections enables them to change the imagescape. For example, the Victoria and Albert Museum in London has only about 3 per cent of more than 4 million objects on public display, although more are accessible in its reading, study and print rooms.

However, small attractions that are exhibiting collections, whether they are in the public or private domain, need to change their displays by, say, borrowing objects and works from elsewhere, or to stage events in order to tempt visitors to return. Looking at the revenue side, a local residents' privilege card, season tickets and promotions such as allowing the local community free access if they bring a guest, are all ways of encouraging attendance.

Attraction development

Within different subject disciplines, the development of new commodities and services in the marketplace are termed 'innovation' in economics, 'new product development' in marketing and management, and 'design' in engineering. In order to give a historic context, the term 'innovation' will be used here to encompass all these notions, but it is acknowledged as a very wide term that has been used to describe a concept, a process or the product of the process. This leads to the seminal work of Schumpeter (1934), wherein the key concept is the linking of long-wave business cycles to innovative change. This arises because, as Schumpeter observed, major innovations (whether they are new products, markets, sources of supply, or organizational changes leading to increased market power) are not spread evenly over time but tend to come in swarms and are therefore discontinuous in their occurrence. Invention may take place any time, but innovation, that is, putting a new product to the market, comes about in the upswing of the cycle when the economic climate looks favourable. The essence of Schumpeter's theory is that the vehicle of economic growth is 'creative destruction' through innovation that disrupts existing technologies and creates new markets, collapsing old ones.

The above is, however, a rather special case, for transcribing what has been said so far across the landscape of natural and human-made attractions serves to show that commerciality and consumer choice are rather modern concepts, in the sense that the majority of today's attractions have not been brought into existence for visitor purposes. The innovation process in terms of imagescape creation is therefore a gradation from a situation of no adaptation (but, rather, controlled management), to visitor attractions that are fashioned for the purpose, which is very different from the stereotypical image of monumental change as understood by Schumpeter's theory. More recent literature recognizes a much greater variety in the nature and classification of innovations (Booz, Allen and Hamilton, 1982; Hjalager, 1994), although these are not necessarily relevant to many attraction developments because of the degree of adaptation permitted. This is because alterations in the cultural capital stock (by which is meant tangible or intangible assets that hold cultural value, irrespective of any economic value they may

Table 2.2   Agencies owning attractions

Public
- Central government
- Government agencies
- Local authorities
- State industries

Voluntary organizations
- Charitable trusts (incorporated)
- Private clubs and associations

Private
- Individuals and partnerships
- Private companies
- Corporations

possess) are, in the main, irreversible. The actuality of having a spectrum of innovations with regard to visitor attractions is reflected also in the pattern of ownership, as shown in Table 2.2. Here the public sector is more likely to take on a stewardship role of what are considered to be national assets, where innovation is constrained, while private sector firms may be much more innovative because of the need to maintain contact with consumers and their position in the marketplace. Observed ownership models indicate that most attractions are non-corporate, which absolves them of public shareholding constraints, while many are in the non-profit sector (public or voluntary) and so have a myriad of objectives (often conflicting), and mixed funding and operating methods arising from different ideals. This makes performance measures, particularly financial ones, hard to achieve and assess.

Development process

From a commercial standpoint, to paraphrase the famous dictum about hotels that has been attributed to Conrad Hilton: 'There are only three things you need to know about attractions: visitors, visitors and visitors!' No better example of this principle can be found than the Millennium Dome at Greenwich, in London. It was designed as a celebration for the year 2000, but was judged by the press as a commercial attraction, so that the out-turn of 6.5 million visitors for the year as against a forecast of 12 million was declared a financial 'disaster' in the media and the political arena, and an embarrassment to the government.

Once paying visitors are introduced to attractions in the public and voluntary sectors, the pressure builds up for the visitor experience, in support of admissions, to become the marketed output, as in the commercial sector. This has its own dynamic in terms of fashion and tastes, and so creates a momentum for change in the nature of the imagescape and, perhaps, the presentation of the overall product. This is something that is often resisted by the curatorial side of these attractions, who are rightly concerned about the authenticity of the visitor experience. For example, in the 1980s the Victoria and Albert Museum was heavily criticized for using the marketing strap-line 'Ace café with a rather nice museum attached!' to stimulate a reappraisal of the museum by the public, a marketing strategy that would be considered quite acceptable today. But although these changes bring the public and voluntary sectors closer to the market, their mixture of ideological objectives such as conservation, authenticity and education, along with their charitable status and sunk capital costs, imply that they cannot be matched completely with commercially established visitor attractions. This is because the latter are seeking a return on capital invested and attempting to maintain a strong, if not dominant, position in their marketplace.

Key features

The key aspects to consider in developing an attraction from a demand perspective are indicated in Figure 2.2. Ideally the system is sequential, which begs the question of the running order. Commercial logic dictates that the optimum path is Market → Imagescape → Location, but given the fact that most attraction developments are limited by their type, conditions of ownership and location, this only applies to what are termed 'footloose' attractions that have flexibility across all three aspects in order to ensure economic success. A good example are sea-life centres, which are modern aquariums (a subject that has an enduring interest). These are not too sophisticated and require relatively small visitor numbers to succeed. They may therefore be found in many coastal locations. The instances of theme and ride parks, which are also seeking to maximize their visitor potential, are discussed in Chapter 3. In comparison, there are limited adjustments that can be made to the imagescape of a country park because the location is fixed and it has fairly unalterable intrinsic elements. This means that change is restricted to adding support facilities to augment the imagescape, such as a visitor centre. Similarly, a mining museum, that has a mine visit as part of the attraction, is tied by its location (Wanhill, 2000). What is important here is to recognize that location, market assessment and imagescape are bound up with one another. Thus, if site selection becomes at most a second-best choice, this throws greater weight on to the market–imagescape mix in order to achieve visitor numbers commensurate with notions of the economic viability of the attraction. But precisely how these factors are balanced depends on the objectives of the attraction. Thus a botanical garden has other aims than simply

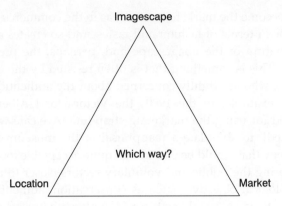

Figure 2.2 The development process

maximizing visitor numbers. Similarly, wildlife sanctuaries and other natural attractions do not want to be swamped by visitors. This brings the debate back to ownership patterns and the organization's objectives, because once the commercial pathway to development is abandoned, financial viability may be difficult to attain.

Regeneration

The regeneration and property development model typically follows a reverse pathway, Location → Imagescape → Market. In such cases, where old industrial buildings, disused market halls, railway stations and docks are located close to urban centres, it is fairly widespread to find public sector intervention, both at national and international levels to convert them into tourist zones which serve both visitors and residents alike. Since leisure shopping is an increasingly important visitor and resident activity, there has been a focus on speciality shopping – as in Covent Garden, London – intermingled with hotels, leisure attractions and also business facilities. Such facilities can include a convention centre, an exhibition hall or trade centre, and offices in order to attract commercial developers. In this way, tourism has replaced manufacturing and distribution industries, which have left the inner core for more spacious and cheaper locations on the outskirts of the city. Thus tourism has been recognized as a feasible economic option and catalyst for community regeneration. The development of Baltimore's Inner Harbor from the 1960s, for example, became an inspiration for revitalization of decaying industrial waterfronts in other parts of the world (such as the Albert Dock in Liverpool, Darling Harbour in Sydney and the Victoria and Alfred Wharf in Cape Town). In this way, tourism can become the 'glue' that holds the area together, particularly where there is little else the local authority can do with such assets. Ownership of regeneration development is mixed, frequently resulting from a private–public sector partnership in which the revenue earning activities are commonly in the hands of the private sector and the rationale for public participation is vested in the wider economic, social and environmental benefits that are bestowed. Even for commercially desirable urban sites, there is usually a proportion, of around 15 to 20 per cent, devoted to leisure in order to obtain planning permission. However, the leisure development may be drawn from the local authority's 'wish list' of amenities for local residents and could be unsuitable for tourism purposes. On the other hand, the trend in modern retail malls is to provide an entertainment experience for the whole family through adding themed areas, health clubs, cinemas, performance venues, restaurants and bars to traditional shopping facilities in an enclosed space that can be open all year round. Such developments, which have become increasingly commonplace in North America and Europe (for example, West Edmonton Mall in Canada and the Mall of America in Minneapolis), have become noted visitor attractions in their own right, with high levels of repeat visitation giving attendance levels in tens of millions that match those of destinations.

From a pure attraction (as opposed to a mixed development) standpoint, the reverse pathway of regeneration strategies may carry a high degree of risk, in that they can result in an 'outside-in' project and/or project inflation. The former is used to describe an investment that goes from the physical structure to the imagescape, as opposed to an 'inside-out' project that takes as its starting point the imagescape and then creates the structure around it. The latter is the case for most visitor attractions that appear to be flourishing. For example, the structure of the Millennium Dome in London was finalized long before the content was known, so it had to be designed to give maximum exhibition space. The creativity of the imagescapes, and how they linked together, were not effectively communicated to the general public and allowed the media to satirize the project as ersatz and of no substance, even though the satisfaction rating amongst those who had visited the Dome was well over 80 per cent (NAO, 2000).

Where public authorities are involved, there is always the danger of project inflation in response to civic pride and the vainglory of local politicians. This results in an exaggeration of employment creation to obtain development grants, increased complexity, which boosts consultants' fees, and substantial capital structures to the benefit of the architects. Several millennium projects sponsored by the Heritage Lottery Fund in the UK have gone this way. Some have had to be closed, for example, the National Centre for Popular Music in Sheffield, the Centre for the Visual Arts in Cardiff and the Earth Centre near Doncaster, although there are plans to re-launch the latter. The lesson for the UK Millennium Commission from these examples is straightforward. Major capital projects

25

should not be undertaken unless their market function is clear, visitor displacement from other attractions has been considered and a 'proper' feasibility study has been carried out so that the nature of the risks involved is thoroughly understood and accepted.

Industrial developments

Industrial visitor attractions tend to pursue a path, Location → Market → Imagescape. In the first instance, natural association with the place of production dictates the location, as for example, Cadbury World, Bourneville, near Birmingham, UK (opened in 1990), Tetley's Brewery Wharf, Leeds, UK (opened in 1994), Universal Studios, Hollywood (opened in 1964), Ford at Dearborn, USA (opened in 1999), and Glenturret Whisky, Crieff in Perthshire, Scotland (opened in 1980). Almost all of these attractions have developed by capitalizing on the demands of consumers to visit the factory, brewery, studio or distillery. Not all are successful. Tetley's Brewery Wharf was closed in 2000 due to visitor numbers falling away. The imagescape of the attraction is built on consumer interest in the product and its history, and may be regarded as brand stretching or brand extension, so as to associate the attraction with the merchandise of the organization and distinguish it from its competitors (Grant, 1999). Legally registering a brand, be it a name, logo or design, protects the organization's right to use it exclusively and enables the business to harvest the benefits of customer loyalty, reduced sensitivity to price, and added value. Many industrial businesses go further than brand extension, as has, for example, the LEGO Corporation (for which there is a case study in Chapter 3). LEGO sees the primary role of its parks as one of brand support. Similarly, the Anheuser Busch brewing corporation entered the leisure entertainment arena to provide a showcase for its beer interests, Budweiser being the best known of its brands.

The market–imagescape mix

The great array of imagescapes has already been noted, but it is significant that they are inextricably bound up with assessment of the market, as indicated by the classifications given in Figure 2.3, and vice versa. Thus, while there is a clear demand for entertainment attractions, success is related to the creativity of the design and its appeal. Both axes are defined from the stance of a developer of a new attraction project, whether in the commercial or not-for-profit sector or in some private–public partnership. The development is taken to be the establishment of a new business, a new activity in a current attraction, or a reformulation of an existing attraction. In the last two instances, it should be appreciated that there are likely to be more limitations on the development of the imagescape, either because it has to be in keeping with the overall branding of the attraction product or it is constrained by the nature of available resources. For example, heritage attractions yield both cultural as well as economic values, but there is no *a priori* reason for these values to move in the same direction, and changes in the stock of cultural assets will usually lead to the loss of that which is authentic through irreversibility. This limits the scope of what is possible in the creativity of the imagescape. What is also important is scale. Thus, small attractions may offer only a single imagescape, often proscribed by the resource base, while created attractions like theme parks promote multiple imagescapes structured around different rides and features in order to achieve the required market penetration rates.

'Me too' attractions

The common attraction experience is linked to the first quadrant of Figure 2.3, since this involves least risk, which in turn has implications for finance and operational viability. It involves the least risk because it is possible to look at parallel projects (tried and tested imagescapes) to see whether or not they are

Image　Market	Current	New
Current	Q I 'Me too' attraction	Q II 'Grand inspiration' attraction
New	Q III 'New version' attraction	Q IV 'Wonder' attraction

Figure 2.3　The attraction market–imagescape mix

successful. It should also be possible to obtain reliable data to be combined with overall market trends to see what the market absorption capacity is likely to be. Where there is public sector involvement, the danger to guard against is 'me tooism' on the part of local politicians who see a political opportunity arising from the location of the project in their area. An example of this can be seen in the development of coal-mining museums/heritage centres in the valleys of South Wales, during the late 1980s, following the closure of the collieries (Wanhill, 2000). A number of developments went ahead in spite of survey evidence which suggested that only about 7 per cent of visitors were likely to visit more than one mining attraction in the area. Politically, 'me too' projects can always be justified on the basis of need, but whether it is possible to turn need into demand at a price which will make the project financially or economically viable is another question. From the perspective of the economy in general, such projects should not go ahead until questions over displacement of visitors from other attractions have been considered, since oversupply can result in a series of non-viable attractions that end up wasting resources. Commercial feasibility studies often do not take sufficient account of this aspect when looking at the competition for market share, or the irreversibility of most attraction investments. The innovation process at this stage is usually minor since it is based on followership, but it can have a cumulative impact over time from a series of adaptive improvements that raise visitor throughput and enhance the experience. There is no disruption to existing imagescape delivery and markets. Innovative changes simply strengthen the dominant design and its appeal, in clear contrast to Schumpeter's position stated earlier.

'Grand inspiration' attractions

One of the difficulties of evaluating attraction investments in this quadrant is weighing up whether the 'grand inspiration', in terms of the imagescape, will work in relation to the market or whether it is simply the sole brainwave approach to project development. The latter could be an indulgence that is unnecessarily or unrealistically costly in the context of what the market can afford. To counter this, major players now have whole sections devoted to creativity, with the opportunity to bring in design consultants. This is not to undermine the importance of the single genius such as Walt Disney, whose personal inspiration was the creation of Disneyland in 1955. On the public sector side, the North of England Open Air Museum at Beamish was the personal inspiration of Frank Atkinson, a local museum curator, who had to 'drive' the project for fourteen years before it finally opened in 1972 (Johnson and Thomas, 1992).

In terms of assessment, a common strategy in this area is to try to reverse the project evaluation sequence by estimating the volume of visitors needed to make the project both feasible and viable at a price the market is prepared to pay. Even if this hurdle is passed, however, delivering projects in this quadrant is very much dependent on the track record of its proposers, so that it is possible to raise the necessary finance and to obtain various planning consents. The latter is a 'minefield' of issues in the developed world, as most important sites are under local authority control and local government culture is not noted for being receptive to new ideas or being able to think in ten- to fifteen-year trends. The innovation process in this quadrant should make the existing imagescape delivery style obsolete and is therefore radical in approach (corresponding to Schumpeter's view of innovation as carrying out new combinations or ways of doing things), yet it deals with existing market structures. While it may build competitive advantage and take market share from others, it does not destroy the competition, which may, in any case, have the opportunity to copy the new ideas.

'New version' attractions

The innovation process here may be the opening up of new market opportunities while preserving the existing imagescape in content and format, having the effect of rejuvenating the existing attraction because the current public has become too familiar with the product or the market has moved on, or a combination of the two. Spatial division of markets can be important, thus old concepts can work in new destinations, while new concepts are needed to move forward in established destinations. An example of the former is the gradual movement of Disney overseas, beginning with the establishment of Tokyo Disneyland (in 1983). Similarly, Universal Studios has sought to increase their global presence through park development. This innovation route is analogous to yield management procedures, and heritage associations may partake of this by acquiring new properties and adapting them to visitors in areas where there is an undersupply of castles, palaces and stately homes open to the public. National museums and galleries have a public duty to display their collections and may open branches in different parts of their home country. Such developments are supply led, as they are generating demand in spatial terms where it has not been previously. This means that in order to attain visitor targets there is a need for substantial market research and forecasting to take account of both the short-term conditions (economy, financial climate and the political situation) and the longer-term ones (demographics, social values and lifestyle, technology, climate and environment).

Clearly, product rejuvenation is a defensive strategy to retain existing attendances, requiring careful monitoring of key market trends affecting attractions. These currently include:

- continued growth in multiple, shorter vacations, so that main attractions are likely to receive the lion's share of any new growth, with the exception of visits that are repeats
- the rise in the allocation of the household budget to 'quality' leisure time
- increasing influence of children on the use of leisure time in families with both partners working

- growth in concern for environmental issues and the recognition of the need for sustainable environmental management practices
- other leisure activity spending, namely in-home leisure, retailing and computer systems.

It is readily apparent that current markets in themselves are not static, so the key question for 'new version' attractions is whether, for example, by their use of new technology for better visual interpretation, experiences and sales, they are leading the market or simply catching up in terms of product formulation, the communications proposition and the channels of communication. Meeting the needs of new and future markets may require a much greater leap forward in terms of imagescape development for the new version to be successful. This is something that was achieved by the opening in 2000 of the Tate Modern Gallery in the old South Bank Power Station on the River Thames in London.

'Wonder' attractions

The term 'wonder' attraction is used here to describe those very large projects that have major economic impacts on their location and are eagerly sought after as flagship enterprise. Maximum uncertainty holds in this quadrant in Figure 2.3 because of the number of unknowns and often the scale of the project, which on the one hand deters competition but on the other increases financial exposure. However, this quadrant only applies to relatively few projects (examples being Disneyland in California, EPCOT (opened in 1982), the Sydney Opera House (opened in 1973), Baltimore's Inner Harbor and London's Millennium Dome). This is because well over 90 per cent of all attractions are geared to fewer than 200 000 visitors, which minimizes the risk of scale in developed destinations. Governments, very large attraction operators or major corporations with a leisure interest are the ones who fund projects of this kind.

Commercial operators are careful to limit their financial exposure, so 'wonder' projects usually proceed with public sector support, both in terms of kind (usually land) and cash, so as to spread the risks and help draw in external finance. Their downfall on the financial side has commonly come from:

- too large a capital cost, making the project unfundable from the standpoint of raising equity to match debt. Examples include the proposed theme parks in the UK of Wonderworld near Corby in Northamptonshire and the Battersea Project in London, that approached the City of London for finance during the 1980s

- delays in building or underestimation of construction costs which lead to serious cost overruns and the need for refinancing, as in the case of the Sydney Opera House, which was completed ten years late and at fourteen times more than its original budget
- ignoring funders' demands by bringing them in at the end of all the feasibility work, when it would have been more appropriate to have them in at the beginning.

Alternatively, money may come solely from public or quasi-public funds. The spate of 'millennium vision' attractions sponsored by the Heritage Lottery Fund in the UK fell into this category, though not necessarily, as noted earlier, to good effect. In Europe, many large projects have been initiated through the European Regional Development Fund and most members of the European Union offer some form of investment support to new tourism projects. Such funding is in addition to the many other ways where the public sector has tried to set the 'right climate' for tourism development.

For 'wonder' attractions, the innovation process can be one that departs from established imagescape delivery systems and sets down a new marketing agenda and communication strategy, which then becomes an inspiration for subsequent development. Projects of this kind lay down a new structure for the industry (Abernathy and Clark, 1985) and the new framework in which competition will occur and develop, setting future standards for some time to come. Market assessment for such unique attractions is notoriously difficult. For example the estimates of visitor numbers for the Millennium Dome ranged from 9 million to 17 million. Twelve million was the figure that the government was prepared to accept and budget for, on the basis that it was meant to be a public festival, so that everyone who might want to come should be able to do so. In these circumstances, there is a need to build up a large database of market trends in different leisure activities, make future change assumptions (predictions) and consider the project in a 'with and without' situation. Developing project scenarios so as to give a thorough understanding of what is being proposed and the risks involved is more important than the actual projections, though the latter are required to give dimensions to the project and to assess its impact on the economy.

Successful attractions

With visitor attractions covering such a wide setting and mixture of ownership, it is a moot point as to whether anything can be concluded as to what constitutes successful innovation and development. But on the supposition that attendances (and in certain circumstances membership) are a performance target, then critical to the prospects of new attraction investments, whether they are low-risk 'me too' developments or high-risk 'wonder' projects, is how the creativity of the imagescape connects to the market. The imagescape does not have to be revolutionary as in the Schumpeterian concept of innovation. In fact few are, but the imagescape needs to be flexible if the attraction has to rely on repeat visits to meet its performance targets.

The creation of imagescapes suggests that in those sectors of the economy where the marketed output is experiences, the transformation of invention to innovation cannot be compared with the processes seen in manufacturing. It appears that some of the winning attractions are those that have followed a reverse product development cycle to that normally understood in the production of commodities (Barras, 1986). For commodities, development starts with the invention and introduction of the product, then qualitative process innovation, which is the setting up of the manufacturing systems (capital widening), and finally quantitative process innovation that takes the form of improvements and rationalization of the production system for mass supply (capital deepening).

In the case of the majority of attractions, the reverse appears to be true. Products either exist in the natural world or in the physical environment, or they are at the end of the supply chain where they have been developed for other purposes and in other economic sectors. They are then adapted to provide a visitor experience with the aid of new communication techniques. In the latter case, public monuments, buildings and infrastructure are obvious examples. Even in the commercial sector, however, it may be observed that the Disney characters were well known in the entertainment industry and as toys before the development of Disneyland at Anaheim. Similarly, Asterix the Gaul was widely read in several languages as a cartoon character before the opening of Parc Asterix in 1989. Many companies are now going down this 'post-Fordist' road of building on their customers' association with their products to stretch their brands into industrial tourism. Similarly, museums and galleries also follow this formula by presenting objects and works, many of which may already have a high intrinsic value and association in the public's mind, in ever more stimulating ways.

In essence, the reverse product development cycle, when applied to visitor attractions, is trying to minimize the risks of failure through building imagescapes around already well-received environments, artefacts, commodities or services so as to call to mind positive images or happenings. These may be termed 'reproductive' imagescapes. For many cultural resources, monuments and works of art, which are now venerated by certain segments of the visitor market, this was not always so. Thus one of the best-loved of Verdi's operas, *La Traviata*, was not that well-received when it was first performed, there was fierce opposition to the Eiffel Tower and Van Gogh only ever sold one painting in his lifetime. This was because the audience had no prior perceptual experience of the creativity put before them and acknowledgement, which can come from experts in the field, as to its acceptability. This supports the view that an 'avant-garde' or 'anticipatory' imagescape is difficult to evaluate in the marketplace, thus separating cultural value from economic value because there is no recognition at large of its worth. Such imagescapes run the risk, as in the case of the Millennium Dome, of being lampooned as the 'emperor's new clothes', or causing public outrage when they run counter to what is currently accepted as 'good' taste.

By way of contrast to the Millennium Dome, another millennium project in the UK that has been generally regarded as very successful is the London Eye, a giant Ferris wheel on the southern bank of the Thames, near to the Houses of Parliament. It is selling a tried and tested product (reproductive imagescape) in a setting of superb quality. The media are also capable of taking unknown attractions and developing them as reproductive imagescapes through their use as backdrops for films and television programmes. It seems, therefore, that creating a reproductive imagescape is a sufficient condition for attraction success with the public, but not a necessary condition for all attractions. So, for example, the Sydney Opera House became an immediately popular symbol once the financial embarrassment was put aside.

While imagescape association can be seen as a significant ingredient in the popularity of an attraction, there is also the question of fashion and taste. Fashion exists and is encouraged in the branding of everything that is purchased, resulting in the obsolescence of commodities and service provision long before their use value is exhausted. Thus, as noted earlier, object-oriented museums are, by and large, no longer considered fashionable. Taste balances the desire to conform to the established fashion against the desire to be different. Therefore, while all attractions aim to achieve an element of surprise, it is important for public acceptance that the content of imagescapes conforms to styles that are characteristic of the time so as not to exceed the bounds of taste. There are some commercial attractions, such as the London Dungeon (a macabre exposition of medieval crime and punishment), which are designed to shock and appeal to the voyeur and the bizarre. They have a particular target market and their style of presentation would not on the whole be acceptable in the public and voluntary sectors.

Conclusion

When dealing with visitor attractions it will be readily appreciated that the number of permutations to do with the variety of imagescapes (Table 2.1), organizations (Table 2.2) and ways of classifying attractions are immense. From an innovation perspective, a useful classification is to place attractions on a scale that has at one end those that have been built or designed for visitor purposes, which are in the minority, and at the other, resources and facilities that are neither for visitors nor can be adapted for them. The bulk of attractions would then be spread out between these two poles. This, in turn, is linked to the pattern of ownership and the multiple objectives that beset different ownership structures. Once attractions have been adapted for visitors, pressure builds up to interpret success in terms of the quality of the experience, visitor numbers (to capture the spill-over benefits of visitor expenditure) and, where admission is charged, some level of financial viability. The latter brings the non-profit sector closer to the workings of commercial operators.

On the presumption that visitor numbers are a performance target, key attraction demand concepts – the market, imagescape and location – and their linkages have been identified, noting that for the majority of attractions their location is already proscribed by circumstances. This in itself has inherent dangers to do with being able to reach out to the market, which in turn throws greater weight on the market–imagescape mix (Figure 2.3), the degree of uncertainty associated with the level of innovation and the need to develop an imagescape, at whatever level of the attraction, for which demand is more or less continuous through the universality of its popularity. While this is readily accepted in the case of entertainment attractions, in the museum world the commitment to populariz-ing the product has raised concerns about overstaging the experience, in the sense of being too technologically driven, overemphasizing the media rather than the message embodied in the resource base.

Within the commercial sector, attractions that are flourishing are, as a rule, those that have followed the reverse product development sequence, namely, the creation of reproductive imagescapes from products designed for other purposes and in other industries. Similarly, in the not-for-profit sector, the reverse product development model supports the observation that award-winning museums are those that have good collections and use technology to add value to the experience. To take the technology route alone is to embark on a fashion cycle that may be unsustainable in the longer term, though this route is not to be confused with major museums that sequentially update or renew their various depart-ments as a matter of course. A sufficient condition for successful innovation in attraction development concerns the creation of imagescapes that have strong associations, are different (but not too different) and are flexible enough to encourage visitors to return. Avant-garde or anticipatory imagescapes have a high probability of economic failure, although they may be judged to have significant cultural values. This implies that non-market models of resource allocation are needed for many such attraction developments to occur.

Acknowledgements

The author is grateful to the Danish SSF, which helped fund his work through the Danish Centre for Tourism Research, and discussions with many industry colleagues, especially Chris Evans, Andy Grant, Alan James, Henning Nørbygaard, Ken Robinson, Mads Ryder, Brian Terry and Derek Walker. The views expressed here are the responsibility of the author.

References

Abernathy, W. and Clark, K. (1985). Innovation: mapping the winds of creative destruction. *Research Policy*, **14**, 3–22.

Barras, R. (1986). Towards a theory of innovation in services. *Research Policy*, **15**, 161–173.

Booz, Allen and Hamilton (1982). *New Product Management for the 1980s*. Booz, Allen and Hamilton.

Grant, A. (1999). *Marketing Opportunities: The Growing Phenomenon of Brand Extension and Industrial Tourism*. Grant Leisure Group.

Hjalager, A.-M. (1994). Dynamic innovation in the tourist industry. In *Progress in Tourism, Recreation and Hospitality Management* (C. Cooper and A. Lockwood, eds) pp. 197–224, Wiley.

Janiskee, R. (1996). Historic houses and special events. *Annals of Tourism Research*, **23**, 398–414.

Johnson, P. and Thomas, B. (1992). *Tourism, Museums and the Local Economy*. Edward Elgar.

Kirsner, S. (1988). Hack the magic: the exclusive underground tour of Disney World. *Wired*, March, 162–168, 186–189.

NAO (2000). *The Millennium Dome*. National Audit Office and The Stationery Office.

Pine II, B. and Gilmore, J. (1999). *The Experience Economy*. Harvard Business School Press.

Schumpeter, J. (1934). *The Theory of Economic Development*. Harvard University Press.

Swarbrooke, J. (1999). *The Development and Management of Visitor Attractions*. 2nd edn. Butterworth-Heinemann.

Wanhill, S. (2000). Mines: a tourist attraction: coal mining in industrial South Wales. *Journal of Travel Research*, **39**, 60–69.

Part Two

Developing visitor attraction provision

The wide variety of different types of visitor attraction arguably explains, at least in part, why no unified theoretical framework currently exists to explain and guide the development of either individual attractions or the visitor attraction sector as a whole. Part Two takes four different approaches to examining the development of visitor attractions: a resource-based approach, a geographical approach, a geopolitical approach and a broadly strategy-based approach.

In Chapter 3, Stephen Wanhill begins to address resource-based issues, particularly those of an economic and financial nature. Obtaining funding is problematic for most visitor attractions, not only in terms of the initial capital investment required to develop the visitor attraction, but also in relation to the day-to-day financing of the attraction once it has come into operation. After outlining the historical development of theme parks, Wanhill identifies the major economic and financial challenges, and considers some important aspects of their planning and development. He then goes on to suggest why such challenges arise, and explores how they manifest themselves. Examples are provided throughout Chapter 3 to demonstrate the economic and financial aspects of visitor attraction development, as well as to serve as a vehicle to answer what individual attractions, and the sector as a whole, can do to attract the funding they require. A detailed, 'true-to-life' case study of the LEGO Company is also provided. The historical context of the development of the company is presented in order to help enhance understanding of contemporary funding issues. As with some of the examples used elsewhere in the chapter, the LEGO case study emphasizes the importance of scale, ownership and location on funding decisions. Chapter 3 concludes by identifying the current trend followed by major operators of theme parks, both in the USA and the UK, toward growth strategies based on acquisition rather than organic growth.

While focusing on the same theme of visitor attraction development, Chapter 4 adopts a geographical rather than a resource-based approach to the development of visitor attractions. After defining the meaning of peripherality as it applies to visitor attractions and identifying a range of factors that affect the success of attractions in the periphery, Bruce Prideaux discusses the significance of these factors using a case study of the town of Burra in South Australia. This explores the vital contribution that the development of visitor attractions can make in meeting the challenges faced by peripheral locations.

By way of contrast, Chapter 5 selects two heavily urbanized locations, namely Hong Kong and Singapore, to explain and illustrate the tendency for visitor attractions to be used as instruments of local, regional, national and international political agendas. In this chapter, Joan Henderson explores the political drivers and implications for the development of visitor attractions in East Asia. Although sharing similar urban characteristics, the different political backgrounds of the two countries provide an interesting contrast of how notions of culture, nationhood and ethnicity can be incorporated into the development of modern visitor attractions and manifest themselves in traditional, predominantly heritage-based attractions. Case studies on the forthcoming Hong Kong Disneyland and Singapore's Haw Par Villa are then used to illustrate the social and political role of visitor attractions in expressing national and cultural identities.

The final chapter in Part Two adopts a broadly strategy-based approach to the development of visitor attractions by addressing a variety of transport-related issues and their impact on attraction development. In many countries, the majority of visitor attractions rely on the private car as the principal means of transport for their visitors. Derek Robbins examines the major implications of this by exploring the relationships between private and public transport in developing effective access strategies. Thereafter, the chapter analyses the impact of tourism transport on the environment and the case for sustainable transport policies. It then evaluates how and why the transport service, and in particular the vehicle itself, can become the visitor attraction in its own right. This is demonstrated in the case study on Guide Friday, the world's largest operator of specialist sightseeing bus tours. The chapter concludes with an investigation of the impact of seasonality on the profitable operation of the transport-based visitor attraction.

3

Economic aspects of developing theme parks

Stephen Wanhill

Aims

The aims of this chapter are to:

- analyse the historical development of theme parks
- discuss key economic and financial aspects in developing theme parks
- demonstrate these issues using a contemporary case example of the LEGO Company.

Introduction

The most frequently quoted definition of a theme park is that of the American Marriott Corporation: 'A family entertainment complex oriented towards a particular subject or historical area, combining the continuity of costuming and architecture with entertainment and merchandise to promote a fantasy provoking atmosphere'. But, as is well known, the Disney Corporation has moved beyond fantasy to encompass learning experiences, so that fun is also educational, for which the word 'edutainment' has been coined. Nevertheless, the underlying principle of the theme park product remains – to provide a pleasurable day out for the family. It is founded on resolving a long-established market research outcome – that families cannot stay together for more than two to three hours without bickering – through the provision of a variety of distractions (McClung, 1991).

For the purposes of this discussion, the meaning will be restricted to that commonly recognized by the general public, namely, modern leisure or amusement parks that have their lineage in the fairgrounds of former times. The working definition used here will be 'a family amusement complex oriented towards a range of subjects or historical periods, combining the continuity of costuming and architecture with entertainment through rides, attractions, catering and merchandising, to provoke an experience for the imagination'. Normally, such facilities have a single all-in admission charge, but may provide free entry with the opportunity to buy an all-inclusive ticket or book of tickets, alongside a 'pay-as-you-go' system.

Historical development

The earliest amusement park, which still exists today, is the 'Bakken', north of Copenhagen, that dates from 1583. Thereafter, pleasure gardens began to appear in Europe during the late seventeenth century. For example, in 1661 Vauxhall Gardens was established in London at the time of Charles II, featuring music, entertainment, fireworks, games and, even, primitive rides. In France, these gardens were created by full-time showmen. Thus the Ruggieri family opened the Ruggieri Gardens in Paris in 1766. The royal parks at Versailles and the Prater in Vienna introduced similar attractions and traditional rides such as the carousel. These activities, although hugely popular, were not without criticism, as they were thought to encourage lax moral behaviour.

The first Tivoli amusement park appeared in Paris in 1771 and was originally a rich man's 'folly' that was swept aside in the Revolution, as were the frivolous activities of the pleasure gardens. But the idea and name were copied elsewhere in Europe, the most notable being Copenhagen's Tivoli that was created in 1843 and survives to this day, drawing in around 4 million visitors per year. As a result, Tivolis became somewhat commonplace and the public's appetite moved on, so that many disappeared in the 1850s.

It was the growth of urbanization, together with the Industrial Revolution, that gave the next major impetus to amusement park development, through being able to harness power, at first steam and then electricity, to build and regulate more powerful rides, while the railways brought the visitors to their destination. The stereotype for the innovation process is the new product that disrupts existing competencies and creates new markets, which cause the collapse of old structures. In this instance, the developments were technically radical in the sense that they made existing park facilities obsolete, but as all were able to copy these improvements there was no great change in the traditional fairground style of marketing the attractions to the public. In Europe this took the form of developing attractions at the growing coastal resorts (Blackpool Pleasure Beach was established in 1896) and, particularly in Britain, at the ends of piers where seventy-eight were developed between 1860 and 1910. Very few piers were built on mainland Europe. At the same time, in the USA the increased urbanization following the Civil War gave rise to 'trolley parks'. They came about because the utility companies charged the new electric traction (trolley) companies a monthly flat fee for the use of their electricity. As a result, to stimulate weekend use they created amusement parks, typically at the end of the line. The success of these parks caused them to spread across the USA. The innovation process at this stage was minor since it was based on followership and did not disrupt existing reproduction systems and markets, but simply strengthened the dominant design and its appeal in the market. Nevertheless, in time, followership can have a cumulative impact through a series of adaptive improvements by new entrants that raise visitor throughput and enhance the experience.

But it was at the 1893 Chicago's Columbian Exposition that a major architectural innovation (conforming to the stereotype of new product development) took place with the introduction of George Ferris's Giant Wheel and the Midway Plaisance with its wide array of rides and concessions. The success of these dictated amusement park design and framework in which competition would occur and develop for the next sixty years, both at home and abroad. As a result, the industry in the USA experienced strong growth over the next three decades, its heart being Coney Island in New York (1895), but this was to end with the Wall Street Crash of 1929. Thereafter the industry struggled to survive and, apart from a short-lived post-Second World War boom, parks were now out of vogue as people in the television age were looking for more sophisticated entertainment than could be found in these old-fashioned and, in many instances, shabby parks.

To restore the fortunes of the US industry, a new architectural innovation was needed and this was created by Walt Disney in Anaheim, California, in 1955. Built at a cost of some US$17 million, Disneyland was the largest park investment that had ever been made. As often happens with new ideas, there were many sceptics who were unable to see how an amusement park without any of the traditional attractions could be successful. Instead of the fairground style of a Midway Plaisance, with numerous concessionaires, Disneyland offered five distinct themed areas (Main Street USA, Adventureland, Frontierland, Fantasyland and Tomorrowland) that provided 'guests' with the fantasy of travel to different lands and times, all designed and managed by one organization. In Europe, De Efteling in the Netherlands was created in 1951, with fairy tales as the central theme, and drew in 300 000 visitors in 1952, but it was Disneyland that set the agenda for the theme park developments that are so familiar around the world today. Confounding its critics, the park drew 3.8 million visitors in its first year; a figure that reached 13.9 million in 2000 as the number of attractions has grown from seventeen to sixty-one and the area has become a fully-fledged resort. The Disney Corporation uses the term 'imagineers' to describe its designers and what they create are 'imagescapes' through sophisticated 'audio-animatronics' tableaux that blend fantasy with reality around an activity in a spatial setting. Imagescapes compress history and culture, and thus time and space into marketable entertainment experiences that have been criticized as 'no place places' (Zukin, 1991). On the other hand, complex or scholarly themes have difficulty producing the emotional experiences necessary to attract family groups and have limited repeat visit potential. This market wants easy access, fun rides and attractions, little waiting in queues, good weather and scenery, and a 'clean' family atmosphere.

Economic issues

In a broad sense, the key economic aspects to consider in developing any attraction are the imagescape (or a number of imagescapes, thus giving a place within a place), the location and the market. Demand-oriented logic dictates that the optimum path is Market → Imagescape → Location. However, given the fact that the majority of today's attractions, whether natural or human-made, have not been brought into existence for visitor purposes and so are already proscribed by their nature and location (and are also non-commercial), this is a counsel of perfection that only has true force in terms of footloose attractions. These can present subjects that are the focus of attention in a broad range of ways, so that it is only a matter of choosing the appropriate imagescape and scale.

Location

Theme parks are the most obvious examples of attractions that can follow the Market → Imagescape → Location pathway, because they are seeking to maximize their level of attendance. Attendance is functionally related to the population catchment area within a specified drive time of up to two hours for cars and three to four hours for coach, bus or train. Opinions vary as to what is the appropriate catchment size. Thus Oliver (1989) argues, within a European context, for a location to be found within a population catchment of 15 million within ninety minutes drive by motorway or other rapid transit system. In the 1990s, the English Tourist Board proposed a standard of 12 million residents within two hours' drive or approximately half that number when the location is close to a major resort. But, whatever the particular norms that may apply, it is generally agreed that the two hours driving edge is critical, so that in North America, parks attracting up to 3 million visitors are located within this drive-time band from large cities.

In practice, the availability of large sites for land-extensive entertainment complexes is often limited. In America, the 1960s and 1970s saw the closure of large inner city parks to be replaced by corporate-backed theme parks outside cities. Parks in major cities are now more valued for their environmental benefits than being locations for amusement activities. Europe, too, can trace modern theme park development back to the 1970s, but at lower intensity than in the USA, given the much richer tradition of alternative visitor attractions. Initially, European parks were concentrated in the north, where the highest levels of disposable income and car ownership were to be found. France experienced a building boom in the 1980s, and in recent years the concept has spread to Italy, Portugal and Spain. Theme parks are also spreading into central and southern America and Australasia, where site provision is much easier. But, both in Europe and North America, desirable sites near major cities are somewhat rare, unless they become available under an urban renewal programme. By and large, these sites are usually under the control of local governments or public development agencies, with strong environmental and physical planning controls that permit them to dictate terms. For example, it took Thorpe Park in Britain six years and 150 planning applications before it could open in 1979, and permission is still needed for every new ride.

Therefore, site availability may limit commercial attraction developers to a second-best pathway that runs Imagescape → Location → Market, which incurs the risk of 'talking up the market' to justify the location. This happened in the case of Disneyland Paris where the site was offered at 1971 agricultural prices as part of the French government's regional policy, in spite of the fact that it had already been zoned for urban development. What is important here is to recognize that location, market assessment and imagescape are bound to each other, so that the sequential process may go through several iterations over the development period of the park. For example, once the site is selected then the development can come into place, but the further the location is away from the optimal market position, the more appealing and exciting the design content has to be in order to 'pull' visitors in. Alternatively, the market assessment may be changed, which in turn can affect the imagescape. Either way, the calculations for the feasibility study will need to be revised at this stage and most likely continuously during the time it takes to translate the imagescape from idea into practice, in order to keep abreast of market trends.

Development

Theme park planning is normally centered on the first and fifth years of operation, the latter being the design standard, when park operations should have settled and the future of the park is established. The market potential is made up of the resident population in the specified catchment area, visitors to the area and groups. The latter includes schools, company outings, clubs and associations. In the calculation of market penetration rates for the park to ascertain likely visitor numbers, account has to be taken of disposable income, accessibility, competing attractions, the appeal of the imagescape and the level of capitalization required to ensure that visitors have a variety of activities to enjoy during their stay and, so, want to return. The latter is termed the 'warranted' level of investment.

The evidence indicates that to minimize the risks of failure, 'reproductive' imagescapes that evoke known products or events in the mind of the public are most suitable. Thus the LEGO brick was well established as a toy, the Disney characters were well known in the entertainment industry and as toys, and Universal Studios was famed for its cinematography long before the creation of the parks. They are in fact 'branded' parks that have been established around the success of the core business. 'Anticipatory' or 'avant-garde' imagescapes, on the other hand, are difficult to evaluate in the marketplace, because there is generally no recognition of their value. Thus they run the risk of being lampooned as the 'emperor's new clothes', or causing public outrage when they are controversial and are not considered to be in good taste.

As theme parks are for the family, then the importance of the children's influence on the decision to visit, particularly when both partners are working, must not be overlooked in the images that are portrayed (McClung, 1991). To balance this, an evening theme with shows and good restaurants will attract adults to the park. Generally speaking, US parks have a greater level of warranted investment and, thus, higher market penetration rates than European parks. In part, this can also be explained by closer proximity of parks to each other in Europe, which means greater competition through overlapping catchment areas. In addition, parks in the USA have a larger percentage of admissions as groups than in Europe: established parks should generate 35 per cent to 50 per cent of their market as groups.

Planning

Planning may best be understood by taking a simple numerical example, say, a theme park designed for 1 million visitors, with a catchment area of about 9 million people as presented in Table 3.1. The overall penetration rate is estimated at 9 per cent in the first year, dropping down in the second year after the celebratory phase of the launch year, but with market growth to the design level in the fifth year of operation. The park is open all year and has some seasonality, the peak month being August with an anticipated 200 000 guests in the design year. There are eight weekend/holiday days in August and twenty-three weekdays, with attendance at weekend days being 2.5 times those of weekdays. From this it follows that the design day is $200\,000 \times 2.5/(2.5 \times 8 + 23) = 11\,628$ guests, which is typically 10 per cent to 20 per cent below peak numbers. As a rule, seasonal parks in the USA may expect to have a design day of 1 per cent to 1.2 per cent of annual attendances.

The design day is used to determine the time period in which the 'peak in ground' number would occur. The latter is arrived at by first recording likely

Table 3.1 Design characteristics for a 1 million visitor theme park

Item	Year 1	Design Year 5
Population catchment	9 000 000	9 000 000
Penetration rate	9%	11%
Visitor numbers	810 000	1 000 000
Peak month	162 000	200 000
Design day	9 419	11 628
Peak in ground	7 064	8 721
Average entertainment units/hr	1.5	1.5
Total entertainment units/hr	10 596	13 081
Average ride throughput/hr	550	550
Number of rides	19	24

hourly arrival numbers during opening hours and then deducting departure patterns, recorded on the same basis, from arrivals. Let this value be 75 per cent of the design day occurring late in the morning (though it can be as high as 85 per cent), giving a peak in-ground figure of 8721 upon which the infrastructure, facilities and attractions in the park will be based. The industry standard is that, given queuing time (about 25 per cent on average), 'walk-around' time and miscellaneous activities, the average guest should participate in 1.5 to 2.5 entertainment units per hour, the lower figure being typical in dry parks with a higher figure being more appropriate for water parks. Taking 1.5 as the standard, then, this park should have an hourly operating capacity of $1.5 \times 8721 = 13\,081$ entertainment units. Major roller coasters have ride throughputs that range from 1000 to 2000 entertainment units per hour, but the simple provision of thirteen coasters is not the planning answer. While some park operations, such as Six Flags and Wet 'N' Wild, specialize in 'white knuckle' rides (although health reasons do not allow them to go much above G-force 4), most provide a mix of rides and shows to entertain the whole family. This will reduce average hourly throughput because, while an average coaster ride may only last around two minutes (the larger ones lasting up to four minutes), a show can be up to half an hour in length. Applying an overall hourly throughput standard of 550 entertainment units indicates an 'adequate' provision of twenty-four attractions made up of key rides that can be the focus for promotion, several medium-sized round rides, capacity-filling flat rides that appeal to young children, and live shows, play areas and film-based activities to round out the mix. The latter are continually improving, thus Futurescope, which was established at Poitiers in 1987, is made up entirely of three-dimensional films, 360° cinema, simulators and other audio/visual attractions.

The figure of twenty-four attractions is stated only as 'adequate' because several judgemental factors need to be considered before placing the mix on an overall plan for the park, namely:

- Does this level of investment warrant the market penetration rates used at the proposed admission charges?
- Are there enough attractions to encourage sufficient repeat visits? In the best parks, repeat visit rates can run at 80 per cent and certainly should not be below 40 per cent for established parks.
- What will the queues be like for the principal rides?

The consequences of not achieving the right level of investment can be seen in these examples:

- Undercapitalization was one amongst a number of reasons for Britannia Park in England opening and closing in 1985.

- In 1987, Zygofolis in Nice had serious cost overruns, resulting in the 'skimping' of the theming.
- Also in 1987, Mirapolis in Paris had too small a number of attractions.

The outcome was that Zygofolis and Mirapolis failed to meet their design standard and went into liquidation in 1991. Parks encourage repeat visits through events, re-theming old attractions and spending 5 per cent to 10 per cent of their initial investment on launching new rides every few years. If such activities are not carried out, the catchment area simply becomes exhausted and attendances fall away.

It is becoming evident in the major parks that in spite of improvements in the design of queues as part of the fabric of the attraction, guests are becoming ever more irritated with paying high entrance fees, only to wait for hours for a two-minute ride. Traditional solutions have been to increase capacity and try to manage visitor flows around the park, but recent direction has been the introduction of timed ticketing, such as Disney's Fastpass, for the anchor rides. Given the variable movement of guests around the park, arrivals at the various attractions tend to exhibit a Poisson distribution, so the standard of 1.5 entertainment units would cover the activities of approximately 70 per cent of the guests. Increasing this design level by plus one standard deviation, to just over 2.7, would account for 90 per cent of guest activity and so reduce the length of queues. In terms of the example, this would raise the required number of attractions to forty-three, if overall throughput were not increased. It is likely that higher capacity rides will be added so that the park would settle at thirty to thirty-five attractions and some rides may be phased in as visitor numbers adjust to the park's design year. The benefits of reducing waiting times go beyond guest satisfaction, as more time is now available to spend in the restaurants and shops.

Once the number of rides has been agreed, they are evaluated for their place on the master layout, their suitability for the range of imagescapes proposed in the park and their contribution to the balance of the experience provided by each zone. A popular layout is the 'hub and spoke system', where the hub is a central facility offering restaurants, shopping arcades, entertainment, conference rooms and other amenities (benefiting from economies of scale in infrastructure provision), while the spokes are the themed areas connecting the visitor experience. Locating refreshment points, souvenir sales and amenities appropriate to the imagescape in each themed zone is also necessary in order to create additional spending opportunities and allow flexibility of provision in accordance with the daily and seasonal fluctuations of visitor numbers. It is likely that the master layout will go through several iterations in refining the details, so as to optimize the park's creative appeal, effectiveness and affordability, and to ensure that no particular cultural habits are overlooked (for example, the tendency of the family always to lunch together in a fixed one-hour period, as in France). Of course, it is possible to overdesign a park, so a normal tenet is that the 'soft' costs for professional services, pre-opening expenses and other incidental costs, should not exceed 30 per cent of the total investment.

Theming

Theming allows imagineers to give new meaning to attractions, park facilities and infrastructure, and can cost as much again or more than the attractions themselves. To be effective the message is continually repeated in the imagescape of each zone so as to have the highest visitor impact and to solidify the entertainment value through the illusion and sense of role-play created by the use of different story lines and settings. Beyond this there are a number of other advantages:

- Park operators are in continual touch with the main ride and attraction manufacturers, so that there is a broad element of similarity in terms of what is on offer. Theming allows parks to develop a sense of individuality and product differentiation.
- The imagescapes provide passive entertainment for seniors and family members with young children who may not wish to participate in the anchor rides, but enjoy watching others, particularly members of their group, having a good time.
- Themed entertainment and waiting spots make queuing a less frustrating experience.
- Well-themed areas, restaurants and shops can help in managing visitor flows by increasing walk-around time as well as raising secondary spend.

Finance

Table 3.2 draws up a hypothetical income statement for the design year of the theme park used earlier as a numerical example. The park is estimated to cost US$100 million and is positioned to charge an adult entrance of US$30, with the child price being close to this, so that the average rate of discount is no more than 20 per cent. The pay-one-price admission system is generally regarded as advantageous for marketing, family budgeting and enjoyment, is cost-efficient and also serves to deter those who may want to come to the park and create a disturbance through rowdy behaviour. Ideally, parks try to achieve a secondary

Table 3.2 Summary income statement for a 1 million visitor theme park

Item	Design Year 5 US$	Revenue percentages
Revenue		
Admissions[1]	24 000 000	55.6
Catering	9 600 000	22.2
Merchandising	7 200 000	16.7
Miscellaneous[2]	2 400 000	5.6
Total	43 200 000	100.0
Cost of sales		
Catering	3 072 000	7.1
Merchandise	3 168 000	7.3
Total	6 240 000	14.4
Gross profit	36 960 000	85.6
Other income[3]	3 888 000	9.0
Total income	40 848 000	94.6
Controllable expenses		
Payroll	11 923 200	27.6
Marketing	3 780 000	8.8
Admin and general	1 339 200	3.1
Maintenance	1 101 600	2.6
Operating supplies	885 600	2.1
Utilities	1 447 200	3.4
Insurance	1 123 200	2.5
Total	21 600 000	50.0
Cash flow	19 248 000	44.6
Capital expenses		
Occupation costs[4]	4 200 000	9.7
Attraction replacement and renewals	10 000 000	23.1
Total	14 200 000	32.9
Net income before taxation	5 048 000	11.7

Notes: 1 Adult admission is US$30, giving an average discount of 20 per cent.
2 Includes rentals, arcades and vending machines.
3 Sponsorship, corporate hospitality and rental of facilities.
4 Rental provision for site and premises.

spend in the grounds equivalent to the revenue gained from admissions, but the former normally settles at 80 per cent or less of the latter. Income from sponsorship, corporate hospitality and the rental of facilities is often difficult to predict, so it is included as a separate category, 'Other income'.

The largest item of controllable expenses is payroll, but only about 30 per cent of this is for salaried staff, the remainder being for seasonal employees, whose numbers are variable in line with attendances. Marketing expenses account for 5 per cent to 7 per cent of revenue in Europe but can rise to 10 per cent in US parks. Generally speaking, the operating expenses for theme parks are relatively low, yielding a high cash flow, which makes them attractive to multiproduct firms or conglomerates such as Anheuser-Busch, who own SeaWorld, where the ability of the facility to contribute to the cash flow of the overall business and promote the product line (Budweiser) may be given a higher priority than return on capital. Production industries frequently have long lead times between incurring costs and receiving revenues. In these circumstances, the ownership of subsidiaries capable of generating ready cash inflows into the organization on a daily and weekly basis can contribute greatly to total financial stability. However, it is the capital expenses relating to site occupation costs (20 to 30 per cent of the initial investment) and the provision for the replacement and renewal of attractions that make inroads into long-run profitability, thus rendering parks as somewhat risky investments.

To understand the nature of this risk, it is necessary to manipulate the data shown in Table 3.2. Let N stand for net income before taxes, R for revenue, I for other income, C^k and C^o for capital and operating expenses (cost of sales plus controllable expenses) respectively. Then the basic income model for this park is:

$$N = R + I - C^o - C^k \tag{3.1}$$

It may be seen from Table 3.2 that C^o constitutes 64.4 per cent of R, of which 40 per cent of R is estimated to be the variable component C^o_v and 24.4 per cent the fixed element C^o_f. From this it follows that the breakeven revenue, say, R^*, when only fixed and variable operating costs are accounted for, is:

$$R^* = (C^o_f - I)/(1 - C^o_v/R)$$

$$= (24.4 - 9.0)/(1 - 40.0/100) \tag{3.2}$$

$$= 25.7 \text{ per cent}$$

This result corresponds to US$11 120 000 of revenue and 257 407 visitors respectively, and gives a substantial margin of safety (MS), defined as the excess of actual (or planned) revenue over breakeven revenue, which in percentage terms is:

$$MS = [(R - R^*) \times 100]/R$$

$$= [(100 - 25.7) \times 100]/100 \tag{3.3}$$

$$= 74.3 \text{ per cent}$$

However, once C^k (the capital expenses total in Table 3.2) is introduced into equation (3.2), the situation changes quite radically, for now:

$$R^* = (C_f^o + C^k - I)/(1 - C_v^o/R)$$

$$= (24.4 + 32.9 - 9.0)/(1 - 40.0/100) \qquad (3.4)$$

$$= 80.5 \text{ per cent}$$

At this point, the park needs to earn US\$34 786 667 from 805 247 visitors to remain viable, and the margin of safety is reduced to 19.5 per cent.

The different situations are illustrated in Figure 3.1 in which C^oC^o is the operating cost line, giving rise to the first breakeven point at V_1, representing 257 407 visitors. Beyond this point the theme park is said to be economically feasible in that $R + I$ is in excess of operating costs, but it is not viable until V_2 admissions are reached at 805 247 visitors. At this point, the park covers all costs, including capital expenses. The triangle ABD indicates the area on the graph where long-run losses occur if attendances fall below V_2 and clearly the gap between C and $R + I$ grows alarmingly as $V_2 \rightarrow V_1$. Thus parks such as Zygofolis (design 900 000) and Mirapolis (design 2 million) mentioned above, quickly closed when attendances settled at 350 000 and 650 000 respectively. Thus the cost structure of theme parks makes them inherently risky projects, the financial term for this being a 'high operating leverage'. This means that parks generally have a high level of fixed costs in relation to variable costs, which makes them financially

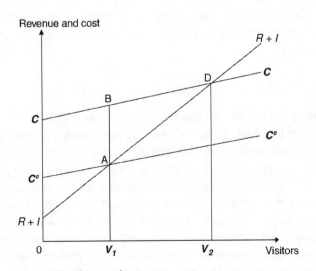

Figure 3.1 Theme park breakeven chart

vulnerable to downturns in the market. As a consequence, providing the capital funding package for theme parks is often difficult. Banks will not usually lend more than 40 per cent of the required sum and so the rest has to be found from equity investors who carry the risks. Sponsorship of attractions also helps, but another important component has been public money. Because parks can generate significant 'spill-over' benefits at the destination, many have been given government assistance, either through benefits in kind, such as site and infrastructure provision, or grant in aid. Support of this kind acts as substitute equity by reducing investment costs, but is likely to be no more than 25 per cent of the capital provision, with an absolute ceiling of 50 per cent for public funds made available from all sources.

Case study: the LEGO Company

The Legoland parks come under the Global Family Attractions division of the LEGO Company and as they are branded parks, their history and development has been, and still is, very much bound up with the core business of the company, which is toy manufacturing. Since the early 1960s, the company has become truly international: it has fifty-seven subsidiaries spread around thirty countries, with worldwide sales of its product in over 130 nations. It is wholly owned by a Danish family, the Kirk Christiansens, which is somewhat unusual for a company of its size, with some 7700 employees and a turnover of over US$1000 million. The basis of the company's growth has been the eight-stud plastic brick that offers creative play to children in the form of a new toy every day. This may be appreciated when it is realized that the mathematics of combinations dictates that six bricks can be combined in 102 981 500 ways.

History

Understanding some of the history of the company is significant for comprehending the development of the Legoland parks, as they are a cross between the usual themed ride park and the 'brand'. The story begins with Ole Kirk Christiansen establishing his joinery and carpentry business in Billund, Jutland, in 1916. But like most of Denmark, Billund was an agricultural area that suffered greatly during the interwar depression and in order to find alternative employment, since construction work had come to a halt, Ole started manufacturing wooden products in 1932, both household goods and toys. He saw particularly good prospects for the latter, since children will always need playthings. In 1934 he called both his toys and his company LEGO, which is an abbreviation for the Danish words *leg godt*, meaning 'play well'. He also inscribed his aim on a wooden sign in his workshop that read 'only the best is good enough', which has remained the motto of the company to this day.

The next major step took place in 1949 when, based on the ideas of an English inventor, Hillary Page, the company produced interlocking plastic bricks. In 1954 Ole's son, Godtfred, realized that the bricks could be worked into countless combinations and developed the 'LEGO System of Play', which was introduced into the Danish market in 1955, using a town plan as the basis for building houses, shops and other buildings with small plastic bricks. But the breakthrough came in 1958, when the company patented a way to improve the clutching strength of the bricks (and therefore structural stability) by placing inner tubes inside the hollow underneath part. In 1960 the wooden toy workshop burnt down and the company decided to concentrate on a single product idea – the LEGO building bricks. This 'one-brand company' phase was to last until 1979, when Kjeld Kirk Christiansen (Godtfred's son) took over as managing director and developed the product along the following lines:

- Duplo, for the one to three year-olds
- LEGO System for the three- to nine-year-olds
- LEGO Technic for the nine- to sixteen-year-olds
- LEGO Dacta for use in schools.

The parks

As shown in Table 3.3, there are currently four parks, one of which is still establishing itself. The accepted thesis in post-Fordist society is that to retain market position, suppliers should no longer sell goods with attached services but, rather, sell services with attached goods to create experiences (Pine and Gilmore, 1999), so that each customer receives a bespoke package. It might be thought that the park at Billund, which is the home of LEGO, is an early

Table 3.3 LEGO global family attractions

Legoland	Opening Year	Area (hectares)	Visitors 2000 (millions)	Design standard (millions)
Billund, Denmark	1968	10	1.55	Site restricted
Windsor, UK	1996	60	1.41	1.40
Carlsbad, CA, USA	1999	52	1.48	1.80
Günzburg, Germany	2002	140	–	1.50

development of this concept, but the reality was somewhat more indirect and personal as it was born out of Godtfred's frustrations with disruptions caused by visitors to the factory and the desire to be rid of them. Its development came about from three sources of inspiration:

- Godtfred had seen a miniature park in Holland, which gave the idea for the 1:20 scale Miniland to be found in every park today.
- Godtfred was impressed with the Louisiana movement in modern art and hired its chief of exhibitions, Arnold Boutrup, to mastermind the development of the park.
- The creative ability of his cousin, Dagny Holm, in using the brick to make outstanding models.

Nevertheless, it has turned out that the Billund park, unlike its replicates in Windsor and Carlsbad, which principally serve the domestic resident population, has become a flagship international tourist attraction that reaches sacred-like status amongst LEGO enthusiasts, who may perhaps even be regarded as 'pilgrim tourists'. Replication has only served to elevate the standing of Billund (MacCannell, 1989), which is now suffering from too many visitors on peak days. This is, however, difficult to control through 'de-marketing' methods because they are tourists, many being international, who are hard to reach through normal communication channels such as local radio announcements telling listeners that the park is likely to be full early on that particular day.

The gap in theme park development is also explained on personal lines, arising from the involvement of the company in a consortium to create the Hansa-Park in Germany during the late 1960s. This was not a success and LEGO withdrew from the venture, leaving Godtfred determined neither to co-operate with anyone in the park business nor undertake any park expansion outside Billund. At the beginning of the 1990s, under Kjeld's stewardship, the latter policy was changed and park development was seen as a way of growing the market for the core business. The planning for the Windsor project was started in 1990 and since opening it has been an undoubted accomplishment. The parks are planned along the following guidelines:

- The overall strategy is that their design and existence is to support the toy sales. Thus, for example, Castle Land/Hill is themed on the LEGO Castle Play System and the Dragon Ride contained within it tends to be the most popular activity.
- Prospective locations are in regions where sales are substantial and there is strong brand awareness.

- They are family parks for children aged two to thirteen years and the investment requires a resident catchment area of around 20 million, with about 50 per cent or more being target families.
- Locations are in an established tourist area yielding a steady flow of visitors.
- The parks are set in attractive rural surroundings, with planning permission for leisure development.
- The minimum site requirement is 40 hectares.
- There are locally available support services in terms of suppliers and general tourist infrastructure.

In current terms, the parks cost about US$150 million each to build and to date the company has financed them internally. The latter gives advantages in decision speed and ensuring minimal information leakage to competitors. For this money, taking Günzburg as an example, there will be more than forty rides and attractions covering 12 hectares of land, with a further 20 hectares allocated for parking and the remainder of the site used for administration, park expansion, woodlands and other 'green' areas. Günzburg will have a full-year staff of about 120 and a seasonal workforce of around 600 employees. As a rule, branding with LEGO lifestyle goods and services enables the company to take as much money inside the parks as it does at the turnstiles. Sponsorship of attractions is accepted but there is no franchising. The company mimics Disney in quality and it sees this as being achievable only through complete control, so that every day can be seen as 'fresh as springtime' by visitors.

Given that LEGO toys have a worldwide distribution, the aim is to develop each park optimally, but in a way that specifically supports the brand. It follows, therefore, that the parks have a high degree of commonality in their imagescapes, save where local cultural adjustments are clearly necessary. Thus Legorado in Billund, which has a Wild West imagescape, is not suitable in Carlsbad in the light of current American cultural attitudes towards this period of their history. As a counterpoint to the company's strategy, it should be noted that a new line of toys can fail or have a short lifetime, while investments in new rides in the parks are expensive and have to be depreciated over four to six years. The risk is therefore that the parks end up with rides that have no reference to the LEGO product portfolio. The hybrid nature of the parks also has consequences for performance measurement. For example, it is customary to measure capacity in theme parks by ride throughput, but the LEGO parks have a great deal of 'soft' capacity in the form of workshops where model-makers are on display and give advice to visitors.

Similarly, Miniland is a passive visual activity that can absorb a variable number of visitors. Calculating the return on capital employed is also problematic, as the role of the parks in uplifting toy sales creates a longer payback time.

Future strategy

Towards the end of the 1990s the company set itself a mission statement of being the strongest global brand among families with children by 2005. However, although acclaimed as the toy of the last century and widely admired by developmental psychologists for the scope it offers for children's inventiveness and experimentation, and by parents for creativity and the quiet absorption that results, the brick has been a casualty of the advance of high-technology gadgetry (with instant action and gratification). The tide has slowly been turning against the simpler toys of yesteryear, and for LEGO this has resulted in sales growth falling back, forcing the company to trim its costs and embark on new developments. The company has fought back with the introduction of robotics (LEGO Mindstorms), Bionicle (LEGO Technic) and licensing agreements with the Walt Disney Corporation, Lucas Licensing Ltd (Star Wars) and Warner Bros to obtain characters, in particular Harry Potter, which has turned out to be very successful for the company. It will be readily appreciated that from the perspective of the parks, the LEGO Company has no iconic children's characters as can be found in the theme parks of Disney or Universal Studios. Plans have been mooted for further parks in Japan (Tokyo) and the USA (Florida being an obvious choice), but these have been sidelined for the present due to the restructuring of the brand and the decision for the fifth park is to be made after the opening of Günzburg.

Conclusion

The architectural innovations created by Disney in 1955 spread outwards as they were adopted by the amusement park industry. By 1975, the top thirty parks drew in some 65 million visitors. Ten years later this number had risen to 95 million, reaching 160 million in 1995 and 185 million in 2000. Of the latter figure, 89.3 million attendances were attributable to Walt Disney attractions. To cope with this growth in numbers, the most recent change has been the introduction of timed-ticketing, but there are a number of other new directions that are emerging. In terms of the industry structure, there has been a move away from organic growth towards acquisitions (which simplifies planning issues) and joint ventures. Thus as the US market has matured, so the major operators, such as Disney, Six Flags,

Cedar Fair, Universal Studios, Paramount, Anheuser-Busch and Alfa SmartParks (Wet 'N' Wild) have used their economic 'muscle' and expertise to expand overseas by these means. Similar trends can be detected elsewhere. For example, the three parks of the Tussauds Group in the UK (Alton Towers, Chessington World of Adventures and Thorpe Park) were all obtained through acquisition. The LEGO Company, as noted above, is exceptional in this instance, for by establishing a park in California it has bucked this trend.

The next radical innovation coming from imagineers is the combination of the physical and virtual worlds, producing an enhanced fantasy imagescape, though at much greater cost. Thus Universal Studios, in their Islands of Adventure at Orlando, has established a Spider-Man ride at the cost of US$200 million. Costs of this kind can only be endured in parks that are resort destinations, which further increases the competitive advantage of chains over independents. The ride matches three-dimensional imagery with structured sets, as opposed to back-drops, and a motion simulator that culminates in a 400-foot drop. In like manner, the new DisneyQuest is an enclosed, interactive theme park covering five floors with virtual reality video games that can be located in the downtown areas of cities. Not to be outdone, production industries have also seen the benefits of creating experiences for their customers, notably the branded parks established by the motor car industry, for example, the Spirit of Ford at Dearborn, USA, and Volkswagen with Autostadt, and Opel with Opel Live in Germany.

Acknowledgements

The author is grateful to the Danish SSF, who helped fund his work through the Danish Centre for Tourism Research, and discussions with many industry colleagues, especially Ken Robinson, Henning Nørbygaard, Mads Ryder, Brian Terry and Derek Walker. The views expressed here are the responsibility of the author.

References

MacCannell, D. (1989). *The Tourist: A New Theory of the Leisure Class*. 2nd edn. Schocken Books.

McClung, G. (1991). Theme park selection: factors influencing selection. *Tourism Management*, **12**, 132–140.

Oliver, D. (1989). Leisure parks: present and future. *Tourism Management*, **10**, 233–234.

Pine II, B. and Gilmore, J. (1999). *The Experience Economy*. Harvard Business School Press.

Zukin, S. (1991). *Landscape and Power: From Detroit to Disneyworld*. University of California Press.

4

Creating visitor attractions in peripheral areas

Bruce Prideaux

Aims

The aims of this chapter are to:

- define the meaning of 'periphery' as it applies to visitor attractions
- identify factors that affect the success of attractions in the periphery
- discuss the significance of these factors in the development of the town of Burra, South Australia, as a visitor attraction located in a peripheral area.

Creating visitor attractions in peripheral areas

Attractions are an integral part of the tourism industry, provide an important focus for tourism activity (Richards, 1996), and influence travel decisions. Attractions range from iconic in nature to relatively minor and of only local significance. In all cases, a site, event or place can only become an attraction when some special and significant value is given to it, and that value is communicated to visitors through interpretation and promotion (MacCannell, 1976). The process of converting a potential site, place or event into an attraction is the essence of tourism's unique ability to turn a resource into a product to which visitors must travel, rather than a product that can be transported to customers for consumption. This process lies at the core of developing a tourism industry and is responsible for the flows of visitors from generating regions to destination regions. At another level, tourism exhibits a core–periphery relationship reflecting the flow of tourists from a developed core to a less-developed periphery in search of new icons and novel experiences not available in the core. The volume of the tourism flows that are generated is governed by the significance of the site, technology of travel, cost of the experience, degree of hardship endured during travel to the attraction and conditions encountered in the locality of the attraction. Peripheral areas seeking to build a tourism industry must first overcome impediments to tourism flows by offering a tempting visitor experience built on the pulling power of their visitor attractions and supported by associated tourism infrastructure.

In peripheral areas, the desire to build visitor attractions is often a response to the declining health of regional economies. The twentieth century witnessed a remarkable transformation of city and country landscapes, as rural dwellers migrated into urban enclaves in search of employment and services not available in the country. As a consequence, the countryside has suffered from a range of problems including depopulation, declining education, commercial and health services, deteriorating infrastructure, high living costs and high business costs. This rapid transformation of the rural landscape has generated significant social and economic problems for remaining rural residents creating a city–country dichotomy that can be described in terms of a core–periphery relationship. The search for new industries to revitalize the rural economy has often identified tourism as a potential candidate. Perhaps part of this interest in rural tourism may be more to do with city dwellers' attempts to harness postmodern nostalgic desires for returning to rural origins and values as a form of personal identity building than with creating viable industries for rural residents. Yet, possession of an interesting landscape, old building, unique event or historic site is no guarantee that tourism will flourish in peripheral areas. Success lies beyond preservation of the past and construction of the new to celebrate the old. Success has much more to do with the decidedly un-nostalgic issues of marketing, pulling power, viability and informed management.

Potential attractions in peripheral areas may include natural features such as wildlife, landscapes and unique ecosystems, built heritage, events and sites of historic interest. Attempting to exploit these resources for touristic purposes is not a simple matter, with complex problems including competition, community support and funding posing significant obstacles. As will be argued later in this chapter, the sense of periphery imposed by the time and length of travel from origin to destination and by access difficulties further complicates attraction development in the periphery.

Defining periphery areas: how far is peripheral?

Contextualizing peripheral areas is difficult because the concept of distance is very much governed by spatial factors, human perceptions and the technology of transport. Distance and location have traditionally defined the degree or scale of isolation of the periphery from the core. New technologies have altered traditional perspectives of isolation by reducing travel times and bridging communication gaps. The core–periphery argument has attracted the attention of tourism researchers and has been interpreted in a number of ways, including an international core–periphery dynamic, an internal core–internal periphery dynamic (Weaver, 1998), the 'plantation tourism model' (Weaver, 1988) and the distinction between formal and informal tourism space (Oppermann, 1993). Weaver (1998: 292) argues that the core–periphery model 'provides a valuable and fundamentally geographical framework for contextualizing and comprehending spatial disparities in power and levels of development'. Wall (2000) takes a slightly different approach defining the core–periphery, or alternatively the centre–periphery, relationship as the link between a powerful urban concentration of demand and distant less powerful areas where the supply of tourism opportunities is dispersed. This chapter adopts the view that the periphery is defined by a number of factors including distance, accessibility, visitor perceptions and scale, which can be measured from slightly peripheral to very peripheral, or exhibit location characteristics which describe the periphery as near or far. Degrees of peripherality affect investment decisions, management practices and marketing strategies leading to a co-dependent relationship involving the scale of an attraction and the degree of its remoteness. As remoteness increases, the scale of attractions must grow if they are to offer the inducement of uniqueness or 'differentness' needed to attract visitors who might otherwise confine their travel to less remote sites. Concurrently, attractions in the periphery need to attract investment in infrastructure and tourism products that collectively build an attractive tourism experience from the visitor's perspective.

In most circumstances, access to the periphery declines as distance and the difficulty of travel increases. Peripheral areas are generally regarded as those located some distance from the centre of tourism activity. However, this need not always be the case as accessibility is also a determining factor in defining the periphery (Lew, 2000). A visitor attraction located a considerable distance from the centre of tourism activity, but offering easy access, may be described as near periphery according to access criteria, while a site located near a major centre but that is difficult to access may also be termed medium periphery based on access but not distance. To take an Australian example, Uluru (formerly known as Ayres Rock) is located almost in the middle of the continent but is easily accessible by air and may be regarded in one sense as located on the near periphery if defined by access criteria but the far periphery if defined on distance criteria. Conversely, King Island located in Bass Strait is near Melbourne but difficult to access and, therefore, occupies a peripheral location based on access criteria but not necessarily distance. Access is a critical factor and a major potential barrier to travel (Prideaux, 2000). The cost of travel is also significant and influences consumers in their selection between substitute attractions. This concept is developed in greater detail later in this chapter.

Part of the answer to defining the periphery is provided by tourists. Interesting attractions located far from major tourism transit routes usually fail to attract the number of visitors that a similar attraction would draw if it were located adjacent to a major tourism transit route, thereby indicating a measure of peripherality from the tourist's perspective. A further part of the question of definition is supplied by investors who must judge viability as a major investment criteria because viability in the periphery may be more problematic than in the core for similar types of attractions.

Tourism in peripheral areas

The extraordinary interest in tourism development and the apparent panacea-like qualities ascribed to tourism's ability to save many rural areas otherwise in decline, have clouded issues that should be considered as part of any feasibility study into proposals for construction and ongoing operation of visitor attractions. The success of tourism in the periphery in the first order of magnitude is largely dependent on two factors: the presence of something worth visiting and the accessibility of the attraction. These factors are co-dependent. The manner in which such resources are developed, managed and marketed will be discussed later in this chapter. If hasty decisions to establish visitor attractions are made, there is a strong possibility that the fundamental economic axioms of demand and supply may be ignored, leading to projects that become financial drains on sponsoring communities. Other issues classed as being of second-order magnitude include community participation, local infrastructure and the willingness of the public sector to bear some of the costs of establishing tourism as an industry. In the latter case, costs may include provision of education and training opportunities in the community, upgrading infrastructure and offering financial support.

Visitor attractions

Visitor attractions are a complex sector of the tourism industry and are not well understood, yet they are one of the more important components of the industry (Lew, 2000; Swarbrooke, 1995). While a number of definitions have been suggested for attractions (Swarbrooke, 1995), the definition suggested by Walsh-Heron and Stevens (1990) appears the most comprehensive. According to this definition, a visitor attraction is a feature in an area that is a place, venue or focus of activities and does the following:

- sets out to attract visitors
- is a fun and pleasurable experience and is developed to realize this potential
- is managed as an attraction to provide satisfaction to its customers
- provides appropriate facilities
- may or may not charge for admission.

Visitor attractions may range in size from very small to the enormous (Disneyland-sized theme parks), be free of charge for admission (a national park) or expensive (some theme parks), and include natural or built features or a combination of the two. Moreover, attractions may be grouped into clusters, be isolated, be located on a touring circuit or be located in urban or rural settings. Lew (2000) suggests that attractions can also be classified into cognitive or perceptual categories including educational, recreational, authentic and adventurous. The presence of a visitor attraction acts as a lynchpin for the local tourism industry providing the reason for the visit, as well as the reason for parallel investment in associated infrastructure. Large, well-known attractions create visitor interest in an area and may constitute the primary driver for tourism visits. By increasing this pulling power, Bull (1991) argued, well-known attractions may create a degree of obligation on the part of tourists to visit the attraction as well as conferring bragging rights upon the tourist.

Swarbrooke (1995) has written extensively on the subject of visitor attractions and suggests that the factors which experience would suggest as being critical to the success of visitor attractions are the organization and its resources, the product, the market and the management of the attraction. Additional factors suggested in Leask and Yeoman (1999) include quality, productivity, management of supply and demand, visitor management and technology, although the categories listed by Swarbrooke are arguably sufficiently inclusive to encompass these factors. Surprisingly, community participation has largely been ignored, although this element of the social and economic environment in which attractions operate is important, particularly in small communities. Peripheral areas face a unique set of problems in first establishing and then successfully operating visitor attractions. Accordingly, guidelines that may apply to an attraction located in the vicinity of a large urban area do not necessarily apply in the periphery, irrespective of size.

Factors affecting success of attractions in peripheral areas

Of all first- and second-order magnitude factors, four that stand out as being critical for the ongoing success of attractions in peripheral areas are location and access factors, community support, operating economies and management of the attraction, and supporting tourism infrastructure in the surrounding area. This section addresses these factors in relation to developing successful visitor attractions in peripheral areas and their relevance is illustrated by the development of Burra in South Australia as a heritage attraction located in a peripheral position.

Location and access factors

Rapid technological advancement in the transport industry has reduced the cost, discomfort and time of travel, bringing once peripheral destinations into or near the core. Air travel has removed the Caribbean from the distant periphery of European tourism in the 1940s and 1950s, into the near periphery of the 1990s. High-speed rail has achieved a similar reduction in the size of the periphery in Europe. Where automobiles remain the dominant form of transport, distance and travel times continue to define the location and scale of the periphery. Figure 4.1 examines the role of transport as one of the factors determining travel patterns, and thereby defining the scale of the periphery in terms of access and location.

In Figure 4.1, the vertical axis represents costs associated with travel while the horizontal axis represents the distance of travel. Point A represents a visitor origin point, a city for example, while points B, G and F represent attractions that are located at increasing distances away from the origin point. For the purposes of

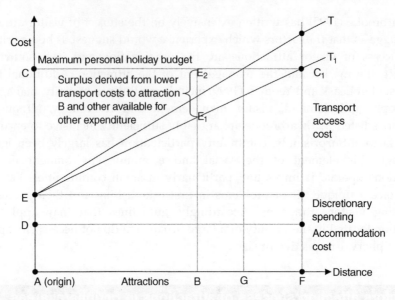

Figure 4.1 Impact of travel cost on demand for attractions in peripheral areas
Source: adapted and modified from Prideaux (2000)

this chapter, B represents a coastal attraction, G a near hinterland attraction and F an attraction located in the periphery. Travel is assumed to be on an overnight basis. Accommodation cost is represented by AD while DE represents discretionary expenditure. In reality, a tourist may substitute between these categories of expenditure, perhaps trading superior standard accommodation for more money to spend on tours or entertainment (discretionary expenditure). Transport costs, which lie between E and C, can also be dissected into three categories:

■ time taken to travel from the origin to the attraction
■ the fare cost
■ the cost of comfort (an example in air travel is first class air versus economy seats).

Transport costs are treated as a variable because they increase with distance from the origin point. Figure 4.1 also assumes that travellers have a fixed personal holiday budget represented by CC_1. It is further assumed that travellers have a choice of transport modes, with ET being the most expensive and ET_1 being the least expensive (ET may be air transport, while ET_1 may be by private vehicle). Funds saved by changing the mode of transport can be reallocated to other classes of expenditure or used for travel to a more distant attraction. Figure 4.1 also illustrates the inverse relationship between transport and other costs using the location of attraction B relative to attractions G and F. Irrespective of which transport option is selected, travel to B is less expensive than to G or F. If when travelling to B, transport option ET_1 is taken, the surplus (E_1E_2) will consist of the lower fare based on distance plus the lower cost of ET_1 relative to ET. Regardless of the transport option selected, a decision to visit B will generate a surplus from the original travel budget. The surplus is then available for other purposes. If the traveller opted to visit attraction F, the surplus E_1E_2 will be reduced to zero as transport costs rise with distance. In the case of attraction F, transport access cost ET will force travellers to choose between a series of alternatives:

- use transport mode ET_1 in preference to mode ET, or
- reduce anticipated expenditure on discretionary items and/or accommodation if continuing to travel to F by transport mode ET, or
- amend travel plans and only travel as far as attraction G.

In peripheral areas the impact of transport factors is critical and is likely to be one of the keys to success, particularly where the scale of the attraction is small or if it does not exhibit some level of iconic value. As the distances from visitor origin points increase, attractions must exert a proportionately larger pulling power to overcome negative distance and access factors. This is unlikely to occur if attractions merely replicate similar attractions closer to the core. Uniqueness is likely to be the single most important factor in creating the degree of interest needed to overcome the problems of isolation and access.

The community

Community support is generally required for the success of visitor attractions, particularly where financial or in-kind assistance is required on an ongoing basis. Evidence by McKercher (2001) suggests that where public money is available to build an attraction, ill-conceived projects and hasty decision-making may lead to financial disaster. Commenting on the Queensland Heritage Trails Network, Prideaux (2002) observed that some of the projects funded under the A$110 million programme were arbitrarily allocated funding in the absence of an initial request for funds, the absence of a steering committee and the absence of a specific project. To overcome problems of this nature, Prideaux (2002) identified a seven-step approach to establishing a rural heritage attraction in Queensland, Australia, based on the experiences of the small farming community of Gatton attempting to develop a rural attraction as the cornerstone for local tourism development. The approach, outlined in Figure 4.2, illustrates the process adopted by the farming community over the course of the project that it sponsored.

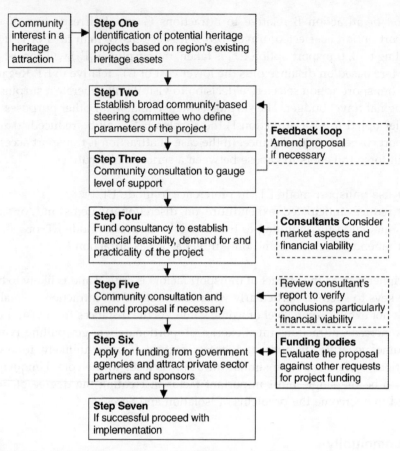

Figure 4.2 Seven-step approach to establishing a rural attraction
Source: Prideaux (2002)

The strength of the approach outlined in Figure 4.2 is that it establishes the sponsoring community's willingness to support the project and verifies financial sustainability through independent consulting advice and subsequent review of that advice. A further important element of this process is the selection of a steering committee that will represent the interests of the community yet also includes the technical skills needed to accept, modify or reject consultancy advice and steer the project from inception to completion. A significant quality of the steering committee should be its possession of a capacity to connect with the community, build trust and represent community aspirations adequately. Where the rhetoric of self-interest expressed by community organizations and individual stakeholders is allowed to dominate, process objectivity may be lost and long-term viability jeopardized. In situations where the private sector is providing funding, a modified model of community consultation will be required.

Operating economies of attractions located in the periphery

In a crowded tourism market where there is a growing supply of new attractions careful consideration needs to be given to each new project to ensure that the additional supply created also has an ability to generate additional demand. This applies particularly in peripheral areas where the evidence (Ditton, Loomis and Choi, 1992) suggests that heritage visitors in peripheral areas constitute a specialized subset of visitors described by Light et al. (1994) as those belonging to the middle class, who are middle-aged, have no children, are well educated, are on holiday away from home and have a prior knowledge of history.

If viability is doubtful, the likelihood of government subsidies must also be considered. Tools for assessment of viability include profitability, employment generation, estimation of net multiplier effects, cost recovery and the total community value of a tourism investment versus investment in other forms of infrastructure. Consideration of operating economies need not follow an economic rationalist approach because there are some community aspirations and needs that are not directly measurable and for which there is little common agreement on an implied or ascribed value. If cultural values are high but the chance of financial sustainability is small, there may be a case for requesting a government subsidy in the same way that governments are often petitioned to support the arts. In some cases, where there is no commonality of agreement, decisions may have to be made arbitrarily by the responsible authorities.

Factors that may affect long-term financial viability include:

- scale or size
- uniqueness
- operating model of the attraction (for example, volunteers often reduce costs in not-for-profit attractions that may include parks and heritage attractions)
- the attraction's ability to maintain visitor interest in the long term
- the impact of competitors located either nearby or in other parts of the nation (Bull, 1991)
- the complexity of the range of tourism products that support the attraction
- market segments that may be broad or narrow, and the potential to attract new generations of visitors
- long-term marketing
- size of investment relative to the income that may be generated by target visitors
- transport (Prideaux, 2000).

While the degree of significance of each of these factors may vary according to the size, location and cultural significance of the attraction, the combination of factors will determine if the project is viable in its own right, requires external support from the government or sponsors or is non-viable and in need of restructuring or cancellation. A final consideration for long-term viability is the attraction's ability to reinvent itself periodically so as to attract repeat visitors and win new customers.

Supporting tourism infrastructure

Two types of infrastructure are required to support the establishment and nurturing of a tourism industry: physical infrastructure and tourism product infrastructure. Physical infrastructure includes hardware such as transport, communications, water, sewerage, health facilities, and services that include law and order, public health and education. Tourism product infrastructure is defined as the fabric of supporting tourism-orientated businesses that include visitor attractions, accommodation, food and beverage services, shopping, recreation, entertainment, festivals and sites of tourism interest. Without supporting tourism product infrastructure, attractions face a difficult task in attracting visitors, particularly where distance is a major consideration. However, the expense of providing both forms of infrastructure increases with distance from the core, driving up operating costs and creating a barrier that can only be surmounted either by passing on additional costs to the visitor or attracting public sector subsidies. In the former case, the attraction is likely to suffer diminished competitiveness vis-à-vis attractions located near the core.

Burra, South Australia: a case study

Capitalizing on its rich mining heritage the town of Burra (population 980 in 2000) has developed into a heritage attraction of national importance. Located 160 kilometres north of Adelaide, Burra, first surveyed in 1845, was for a time the world's richest copper mine and by 1851 was Australia's largest inland town. After the cessation of mining in 1877, the town declined rapidly and pastoralism replaced mining. By the 1960s many of the town's significant sites were in an advanced state of decay. Realizing that urgent action was required to arrest the loss of the town's built heritage, local residents established a branch of the National Trust in 1965 to preserve the community's mining heritage. In the same year the newly established local branch of the National Trust, Australia's key private sector institution for the preservation of the nation's heritage, acquired the Redruth Goal and the

Old Dugouts as Trust properties. In 1966 the Burra National Trust was given an old residence and shop that was restored and reopened as a museum, providing the Trust with a headquarters and a source of income.

In subsequent years the Trust acquired a number of other buildings, properties and sites that enabled it to develop the town as a unique heritage attraction. Controlling access to a large number of sites was solved in the early 1970s, when the Burra branch of the National Trust enlisted the assistance of the local Apex Service Club and the District Council of Burra Burra to develop a self-guided tour of the Redruth Goal and the Miners' Dugouts using a key-hire system. This system was expanded as new properties and sites were added, and in 1988 the Burra Heritage Passport Scheme, incorporating the original key hire system, was introduced. By 2001 the Burra Heritage Passport Scheme system had expanded to enable visitors to gain access to eight locked heritage sites and forty-seven other sites with interpretation throughout an 11 kilometre heritage trail. Approximately 33 per cent of all visitors to the Burra Tourist Information Centre participate in the passport scheme indicating that the A$15 charge is a significant deterrent to many visitors.

Community involvement has been the key driving force behind the long-term success of the Burra branch of the National Trust in preserving the town's mining heritage and simultaneously developing the town as a heritage attraction of national importance. Community support has included service clubs, volunteers who work in the information centre and museum, individuals who have given items ranging from personal memorabilia to major properties and buildings, as well as the efforts of public officials employed by local and state governments. By 2000 the town was attracting 30 000 visitors per year (Kenyon and Black, 2001), serviced by a number of accommodation providers including caravan parks, bed and breakfast establishments, farm stays and motels, as well as gift and souvenir shops, and restaurants.

In the totality of South Australia's tourism industry, Burra occupies a relatively minor place, being overshadowed by wine tourism in the Barossa Valley, other heritage attractions in towns near Burra, the Flinders Ranges and coastal resorts. For marketing purposes, Burra is included in the Clare Valley region which attracted 5.6 per cent of South Australia's intrastate overnight visitors, 2.1 per cent of interstate overnight visitors and 2.9 per cent of international visitors arrivals in South Australia in 2000 (SATC, 2001). Even in the Clare Valley, Burra is overshadowed by Martindale Hall, a stately country manor house, which attracted 21 000 visitors in 2000 compared with 6800 heritage passports sold to visitors in Burra (SATC, 2001). Nor is Burra's heritage as a copper mining area unique. The coastal town of Moonta, also located 160 kilometres from Adelaide, receives a higher number of visitors, primarily because of the town's association with Cornish migrants, its reputation as a 'little Cornwall' and large annual festivals. Forecasts by the Tourism Forecasting Council (2001) that visitation to Australia's peripheral areas will only grow by 1.1 per cent per annum in the period 2000–4 afford attractions located in the periphery little scope in the near future to increase revenue significantly through increased visitor numbers.

While community involvement has been high and the operation of the attractions grouped together under the Burra Heritage Passport Scheme generated a profit of A$130 000 (Kenyon and Black, 2001) in 2000, Burra remains a relatively minor attraction, overshadowed by other mining attractions (Moonta), wine tourism and festivals. Located just over two hours' drive from Adelaide, the town is arguably too distant for Adelaide's day-trip market but too small and lacking other significant attractions to support a large accommodation sector, particularly in the face of the popularity of wine tourism in other parts of the Clare Valley and in the Barossa Valley.

In terms of the core–periphery argument, Burra occupies an interesting position being able to be described according to a number of peripheral locations relative to its tourism-generating markets. In the South Australian market, the town is located on the near periphery, with Adelaide being just over two hours' drive from the Burra. On a national scale, the town occupies a more peripheral position in terms of the large national market located in Sydney and Melbourne. Both peripheries fit Weaver's (1998) notion of a domestic periphery. Internationally, the town is located on the international periphery.

Location and the composition of the town's tourism product have exercised a significant influence on the character and structure of the town's tourism industry. Burra's lack of non-heritage attractions, competition from other heritage sites in South Australia and lack of significant supporting tourism infrastructure will ensure that Burra remains a relatively small attraction. However, given that tourism is a significant employer and that the funds generated are sufficient to ensure viability, Burra can be classed as a successful peripheral tourism attraction. The success of Burra has also demonstrated the need for strong community support and that resources allocated to developing an attraction must match the benefits that are derived from that investment.

Conclusion

Creating viable visitor attractions in peripheral areas is a major task. Many challenges need to be surmounted, including overcoming access factors, coping with competition and gaining local community support. As the isolation factor increases, the scale of the attraction becomes increasingly important, as does the attraction's ability to achieve and maintain viability. This chapter has highlighted many of the issues facing the supporters and managers of attractions in peripheral areas, demonstrating that problems can be overcome, but also highlighting that if viability is an important criterion, the number of candidate attractions will decline as the degree of isolation increases. This was demonstrated by Burra, which, although a nationally significant site, attracts a relatively small number of visitors. However, because of strong local community support and a relatively modest investment in the structure of the attraction, it can be considered viable.

Several areas for future research that would benefit communities and investors contemplating construction and operation of attractions in peripheral localities are the related issues of long-run viability and the creation of supporting tourism product infrastructure. If the countryside is not to be littered with increasing numbers of publicly funded but poorly conceived attractions, built to encourage rural tourism, the blowtorch of viability must first be applied. Moreover, tourists need to be encouraged to make the additional effort required to travel to the periphery by the provision of complementary attractions, visitor services and quality facilities that reward their efforts with unique experiences not found in the core.

References

Bull, A. (1991). *The Economics of Travel and Tourism*. Pitman.

Ditton, R., Loomis, D. and Choi, S. (1992). Recreation specialization: re-conceptualization from a social worlds perspective. *Journal of Leisure Research*, **24**, 33–51.

Kenyon, P. and Black, A. (eds) (2001). *Small Town Renewal: Overview and Case Studies*. Rural Industries Research and Development Corporation.

Leask, A. and Yeoman, I. (1999). *Heritage Visitor Attractions: An Operations Management Perspective*. Cassell.

Lew, A. (2000). Attractions. In *Encyclopaedia of Tourism* (J. Jafari, ed.) pp. 35–37, Routledge.

Light, D., Prentice, C., Ashworth, G. J. and Larkham, J. (1994). Who consumes the heritage product? Implications for European tourism. In *Building New Heritage: Tourism, Culture and Identity in the New Europe* (G. J. Ashworth and P. J. Larkham, eds) pp. 90–116, Routledge.

MacCannell, D. (1976). *The Tourist: A New Theory of the Leisure Class*. Schocken Books.

McKercher, B. (2001). Attitudes to a non-viable community owned heritage tourism attraction. *Journal of Sustainable Tourism*, **9**, 29–43.

Oppermann, M. (1993). Tourism space in developing countries. *Annals of Tourism Research*, **20**, 535–556.

Prideaux, B. (2000). The role of transport in destination development, *Tourism Management*, **21**, 53–64.

Prideaux, B. (2002). Creating rural heritage visitor attractions: the Queensland Heritage Trails Project. Unpublished research paper. University of Queensland.

Richards, G. (1996). Production and consumption of European cultural tourism. *Annals of Tourism Research*, **23**, 261–283.

SATC (2001). *Tourism Research: Clare Valley (Mid North) Tourism Profile*. South Australian Tourism Commission.

Swarbrooke, J. (1995). *The Development and Management of Visitor Attractions*. Butterworth-Heinemann.

Tourism Forecasting Council (2001). *Forecast Report*. No. 11. Tourism Forecasting Council.

Wall, G. (2000). Centre–periphery. In *Encyclopaedia of Tourism* (J. Jafari, ed.) p. 76, Routledge.

Walsh-Heron, J. and Stevens, T. (1990). *The Management of Visitor Attractions and Events*. Prentice Hall.

Weaver, D. (1988). The evolution of a 'plantation' tourism landscape on the Caribbean Island of Antigua. *Tijdschrift voor Economische en Sociale Geografie*, **79**, 319–331.

Weaver, D. (1998). Peripheries of the periphery tourism in Tobago and Barbuda. *Annals of Tourism Research*, **25**, 292–313.

5

Visitor attraction development in East Asia

Joan Henderson

Aims

The aims of this chapter are to:

- identify recent trends in the development of visitor attractions in East Asia and the relative importance of traditional and modern attractions
- compare the attractions base, and marketing and development strategies, of Hong Kong and Singapore, with specific reference to heritage
- illustrate the social and political significance of heritage attractions in expressing national and cultural identities.

East Asian tourism: an overview

The World Tourism Organization (WTO) defines East Asia and the Pacific in terms of Northeastern and Southeastern Asia and Oceania. The countries making up the Asian regions exhibit similarities and contrasts as destinations, and the range in the scale of their tourism industries is reflected in Table 5.1 which shows international arrivals and earnings at the close of the twentieth century.

China dominates statistically, and Northeast arrivals exceed those of the Southeast as a consequence. East Asia and the Pacific as a whole increased its share of the international tourist market to 14.6 per cent in 1999 from 9.5 per cent in 1985, and accounted for 15.4 per cent of total spending. Outbound travel too has expanded, with tourists from the region representing 15 per cent of the world's total and recording the highest global growth rates (WTO, 2000). Much of this travel has taken place within Asia and has been accompanied by greater

Table 5.1 International tourism in East Asia/Pacific, 1999

	Arrivals (thousands)	Earnings (US$ millions)
China	27 047	14 098
Hong Kong SAR	11 328	7 210
Japan	4 438	3 428
North Korea	130*	N/A
South Korea	4 660	5 623
Macau	4 743	2 700
Mongolia	159	28
Taiwan	2 411	3 571
Total Northeastern Asia	54 928	36 658
Brunei	964*	37*
Cambodia	368	190
Indonesia	4 700	4 045*
Laos	270	103
Malaysia	7 931	2 822
Myanmar	198	35
Philippines	2 171	2 534
Singapore	6 258	5 788
Thailand	8 651	7 000
Vietnam	1 782	86*
Total Southeastern Asia	33 377	20 414*

Note: * Figures for 1998.
Source: WTO (2000)

participation in domestic tourism, made possible by economic advances and the emergence of an affluent middle class. The strong performance of East Asian states is indicative of their popularity and the presence of attractions with considerable appeal. However, the comparatively low volumes of inbound tourism for several countries that have a wealth of resources indicate unexploited opportunities. In many instances there are serious barriers to overcome before such potential can be fully realized, and progress depends upon changes in the economic, political and social environments (Hall and Page, 2000).

Trends in visitor attractions

Traditionally, countries of East Asia have been associated with natural and cultural heritage attractions. The former is represented by climate, beaches and islands, forest and mountain scenery, and plant and animal life. Cultural attractions include built heritage, historic sites, festivals, customs, traditional lifestyles, and arts and crafts. However, modern attributes such as shopping malls, events, theme parks, integrated resorts and casinos are of significance as well as sports and health treatments. The role of sex tourism in certain locations cannot be overlooked and food is another attraction difficult to classify. Attractions are therefore not confined to coastal and rural areas and historic urban zones, but are to be found in specialized centres and the major metropolitan conurbations.

Theme parks have emerged as prominent attractions characterized by their artificiality. They are part of a rapidly evolving entertainment industry driven by mounting regional demand for leisure products. Investment is shifting from Europe and America to Asia and the Pacific Rim where the industry in Japan is already well established. Of the top twenty amusement/theme parks worldwide in 1999, Tokyo Disneyland had the highest attendance of 17.45 million. Three other Japanese parks are on the list and there are now about thirty sites with annual attendance figures of over 1 million, and a further thirty which attract between 500 000 and 1 million. These are based around Tokyo, Osaka and Kobe. Growth in Japan has been stimulated by the success of Tokyo Disneyland after its opening in 1983, large-scale corporate investment, official policies and an enthusiastic population with very high levels of discretionary income. The economic recession in Japan has adversely affected the operation of some parks, with additional problems of poor management, but the concept has retained its popularity. Universal Studios opened its first park outside the USA in Osaka in 2001, when a new DisneySea park also began operation in Tokyo. Elsewhere, major investment is planned in China, Taiwan and South Korea, which currently has two of the world's busiest parks.

In terms of other modern attractions, there is evidence in East Asia of the more universal shift towards 'inclusive, all-weather, mixed retail, entertainment and leisure developments in out of town locations' (Stevens, 2000: 68). This is illustrated by the COEX Plaza in the South Korean capital of Seoul which comprises an aquarium, a multiplex and retailers covering 95 000 square metres. These trends indicate that large, purpose-built facilities, which rely heavily on technology and a central retail component, have an important place alongside more conventional attractions of nature, culture and heritage.

East Asian destinations thus comprise a composite of attractions serving markets of excursionists, domestic tourists, and Asian and Western visitors, which each have their own sets of needs and expectations. What constitutes an attraction is subject to interpretation, and depends on individual and group perceptions. Cultural differences are likely and tourists from the West may be more concerned about certain qualities than their Asian counterparts. For example, Westerners might be expected to have more romantic and idealized notions of the Orient and its inhabitants, who are presented to them as exotic and mysterious in the promotional images employed by the tourism industry. Contrived and sophisticated attractions of a sort they can find at home may be of limited appeal. In order to take advantage of the multiplicity of markets and products, differentiation has been adopted by many national tourism organizations. For example, the Tourism Authority of Thailand has moved from mass marketing to niche marketing, and now concentrates on food, shopping, health, heritage, sports, culture and business travel. Other countries like Cambodia and Mongolia, possessing a more restricted product range, have chosen to focus on particular attributes. Ecotourism, combining natural and social dimensions, is being widely pursued, as is heritage tourism.

The complexities of the relationship between heritage and tourism have been the subject of much debate and are the focus of the remainder of this chapter. Heritage has a dual function as a visitor attraction and as a vehicle for nation building and the expression of identity, giving it a political and social significance in addition to its economic value as a generator of revenue and employment. Many commentators have been critical of the exploitation of heritage by the tourism industry and state authorities, in pursuit of their own interests, but it has also been praised as a guardian of heritage and a positive force for conservation. Such topics are especially relevant in newly independent states and former colonies, or during times of change and uncertainty. These are characteristics of much of Asia. Hong Kong and Singapore, leading Asian destinations which are now emphasizing heritage in their tourism marketing and planning, have been selected as appropriate cases for discussion given their recent histories. Hong Kong became a Special Administrative Region (SAR) of the Communist People's

Republic of China in 1997, after 150 years as a British colony, while Singapore's multiracial population gained full independence in 1965. This required their governments and societies to address questions about the meanings of identity and heritage.

Hong Kong and Singapore compared

Strategic planning, heritage attractions and identity

Hong Kong and Singapore are successful international tourist destinations (Travel and Tourism Intelligence, 1999a; 1999b), which both have strategic plans with the same goal of being principal Asian urban tourism destination (HKTC, 2000; STPB, 1996). These plans necessitate consolidating current strengths, devising innovative products and widening market appeal by adding new attractions and upgrading those already in existence. Heritage has an important contribution to make to the realization of these objectives, and has been given a high priority by the Hong Kong Tourism Commission (HKTC). Buildings and historic and archaeological sites with tourism potential are being identified, and the maintenance of colourful traditions encouraged by a newly formed Heritage Tourism Force. The appeal of heritage and traditional culture has equally been recognized in Singapore, and the current plan proposes specific clusters of heritage and cultural attractions as suitable development zones. Theming of the ethnic area of Chinatown is now being carried out in stages, although the project has generated some controversy about the absence of local participation and the replacement of a living community with a theme park.

The conclusion that heritage tourism in Hong Kong is 'being institutionalised with product enhancement and facilitation' (Travel and Tourism Intelligence, 1999a: 33) may be extended to Singapore. Tourism authorities in the two destinations are well aware of the advantages of heritage as a marketable commodity, and are vigorously promoting it as a result, becoming advocates of conservation at the same time. Hong Kong's tourism literature offers a range of built heritage from the Imperial Chinese and British colonial eras as well as historic sites, heritage trails and traditions and customs. Singapore, too, advertises its physical heritage of monuments, buildings and sites. Much of this dates from the colonial period, but indigenous architecture and manifestations of ethnic cultural heritage are also featured. Both have a variety of museums and galleries devoted to assorted aspects of history and culture.

In addition to commercial gains, there are sociopolitical considerations to take into account regarding heritage tourism, particularly in respect of official interest in heritage and its conservation. This is suggestive of the influence of underlying political agendas. The colonial government in Hong Kong, acting through the Antiquities and Monuments Office, was especially active in the period before the handover. Most listed monuments were approved by the office in the 1980s and mid-1990s, and a heritage trust was formed in 1992 to raise awareness and aid community-organized heritage projects. The British regime also built the Hong Kong Cultural Centre in 1989, an arts venue of striking design on the waterfront, and was responsible for several new museums. These actions can be explained in terms of the assertion of a separate Hong Kong identity and heritage to help assist the territory retain its individuality and remain intact within the larger Chinese state.

The current government stance is one of continued support for heritage with the emphasis on Hong Kong's long Chinese history linked to contemporary achievements and future ambitions. The Hong Kong Museum of History reopened at an enlarged site in 2000, when a Hong Kong Heritage Museum was also founded along with a newly reconstructed Tang dynasty monastery showcasing the Chinese ancestry of the Hong Kong people. Such attractions can be seen as embodying the common origins and shared destiny of China and Hong Kong, strengthening ties and signifying the People's Republic as the motherland. British rule is portrayed as only a temporary interruption, and its legacy recorded as 'memorabilia' and 'British shadows' on the Hong Kong Tourism Association, now the Hong Kong Tourism Board (HKTB), website (HKTA, 2000). Thus heritage sites are a way of delivering political and sociocultural messages about formal constructions of identity, and the heritage from which it is derived, to audiences of residents and external publics as well as tourists.

Whether official representations coincide with popular perceptions is uncertain. While the people of Hong Kong have acquired Chinese nationality, they are still distinct from mainland Chinese, and there are signs of a desire to maintain that distinction and a unique Hong Kong identity. This has led to an exploration of cultural roots and a rediscovery of local heritage among some citizens, with greater interest in conservation. Writing about a popular heritage trail, Cheung (1999: 572) describes a situation of 'government desiring to construct heritage sites, foreign tourists seeking the exotic East, domestic tourists seeking an aspect of themselves'.

Singapore has been following a more conventional journey towards nationhood, and the realization of a sense of shared identity and purpose has been a principal aim of the People's Action Party, in power since the 1960s. This task has been made more difficult by the presence of minorities officially classified as Malays, Indians and others, besides the ethnic Chinese who make up over 75 per cent of the population. Originally the government was concerned mainly with economic advancement and the satisfaction of material aspirations, but there was a subsequent acknowledgement that a nation is determined by its culture and history as well as its economics. Singaporeans must have an appreciation of a common history and destiny based on shared values if the country is to survive and prosper. Alongside this concept of a single national identity, multiculturalism has been fostered to allow the races to live together peacefully as Singaporeans, whilst retaining their own cultures. However, there has also been a desire to prevent race from becoming an overtly political issue.

These policies have been mirrored in attitudes to conservation of the built heritage as Singapore evolved from a colony to a modern state that initially had little regard for the past. Rapid urbanization and industrialization transformed the island, with few people sympathetic towards conserving old buildings, seen as an unproductive use of scarce land and a barrier to progress. Later, heritage was reassessed and accepted as a positive force in both nation building and tourism development. It could symbolize and reinforce a unifying Singaporean spirit and character, transcending other allegiances because 'a nation with a memory . . . gives it a sense of cohesion, continuity and identity . . . a sense of common history is what provides the links to hold together a people who come from the four corners of the earth' (URA, 1991: 24). The presentation of cultural heritage attractions thus serves to promote the vision of an ethnically diverse community living in harmony, thereby obscuring the realities of a degree of racial tension. Conserved monuments display a balanced representation, with Chinese and Indian temples, Muslim mosques and Christian churches featuring in promotional material. The ethnic enclaves of Chinatown, Little India and Kampong Glam, dating from the nineteenth century, have been conserved in schemes that incorporate redevelopment and adaptive reuse. Multiculturalism is further demonstrated in the official tourist guide by the country's food, traditions, festivals and cultural events.

Heritage and its conservation have assumed a new relevance in Singapore, and heritage sites presented as visitor attractions for both residents and tourists can be interpreted as constituting a narrative of nationalism, unity and pride in attainment. Hegemonic motives appear to inform many of these decisions, the government portrayed as the protector of the core values essential to the country's well-being which are expressed in tourist images and sites. Heritage attractions in Hong Kong and Singapore therefore have a political and social function relating to pressing questions of national and cultural identity and government legitimacy, indicative of wider trends in the region. Many other parts of East Asia still confront the demands of nation building with governments determining the role of heritage, employing attractions to communicate identity, history and contemporary conditions. Consensus may not exist, and conflicts arise, although there is sometimes little scope for contesting official versions.

More modern attractions

Notions of heritage and identity are also affected by globalization and related social changes, which often encourage cultural homogeneity. Hong Kong and Singapore display signs of such internationalization, but they have had a history of exposure to outside influences and an ambivalent culture has emerged, which is neither wholly Asian nor Western. There is perhaps a constant interaction of international, national, ethnic (in the case of Singapore) and local (in the case of Hong Kong) layers of identity, which further complicates the quest for understanding.

Such ambivalence is reflected in the tourism resource bases of the two locations, combining heritage and modern attractions, and in promotional images of sophisticated cities with a fascinating mix of East and West. In juxtaposition to heritage attractions, facilities of ultra-modern hotels, shopping centres, conference venues and transport are highlighted, and opportunities for shopping, fine dining and enjoying the arts and world-class events are advertised. Family fun at Ocean Park maritime theme park and Madame Tussaud's Waxworks is another selling point for Hong Kong, while Singapore markets the island of Sentosa as a holiday playground, comprising an assortment of specially created attractions.

The HKTB marketing campaigns are intended to convey vibrancy and diversity, enriching the Hong Kong brand conceptualized as a marriage of the traditional and contemporary. The Singapore Tourism Board also depicts a modern, progressive and cosmopolitan city state, epitomized by the New Asia-Singapore brand which was introduced in 1996. The brand's personality traits are cosmopolitanism, youthfulness, vibrancy, Asian modernity, reliability and comfort, and there are clear parallels between the Hong Kong and Singapore exercises in content and execution.

Looking to the future, modern attractions are central to strategic planning in Hong Kong and Singapore, exceeding heritage in importance if measured by levels of actual and planned investment. Hong Kong favours large-scale facility and attraction projects, the HKTC recommending a new cruise terminal, another conference and exhibition centre, an international performing arts venue and a multipurpose stadium. Innovations agreed on or already started are Hong Kong Disneyland, a wetland park and an extension to Ocean Park. Under review are two cable-car systems linking attraction sites, a San Francisco-style Fisherman's Wharf and an entertainment corridor on Lantau Island. Government commitment to large-scale tourism development is confirmed by its financial support for Hong Kong Disneyland, examined in a case study at the end of this chapter. This provides an interesting example of Chinese political and cultural sensitivities over Westernization giving way to commercial imperatives.

Singapore, which had some ambitions to be the location of Disney's second Asian theme park, has already invested heavily in expensive tourism infrastructure and superstructure, and is at a more advanced stage in the implementation of its strategy. For example, there is a third S$200 million conference centre and The Esplanade-Theatres on the Bay performing arts complex will be completed by 2002 at a cost of approximately S$600 million. The latter plays a part in another campaign to turn Singapore into a global arts centre, and there are attempts to draw world-class sporting competitions and other major events, again in competition with Hong Kong which positions itself as the events capital of Asia.

Given the promise of an exciting fusion of West and East, and old and new, there is perhaps a danger in these initiatives of an overemphasis on international-style attractions and a loss of perceived and actual distinctiveness. Development may follow a common path to create a uniform tourism landscape of contrived attractions, promoted in a way that reinforces similarities. Problems arise of maintaining a balance between the past and present and ensuring that aspects of heritage, such as the built environment and cultural traditions, are not overwhelmed by excessive development and the race to modernize and globalize. Heritage thus assumes an additional dimension whereby its conservation can help to maintain a unique sense of place and difference, intrinsic merit and commercial appeal, as a means to secure an advantage over rivals.

This argument extends to natural heritage, and green tourism is a second important strand in strategic planning. Resources include Hong Kong's nature parks, which occupy 40 per cent of the total land area of 1097 square kilometres (almost double that of Singapore), the rural hinterland of the New Territories, and numerous small islands, beaches and upland scenery which support a diversity of outdoor activities. Some of Singapore's offshore islands, besides Sentosa, have been designated for recreation. Indeed Singapore does have several small nature sites, advertising itself as a clean and green garden city.

Case study: Hong Kong Disneyland

After lengthy negotiations, in November 1999 Disney selected Hong Kong as the site for its third theme park outside the USA. The park is planned to open in 2005, on reclaimed land at Penny's Bay on Lantau Island where the new airport is located. It will be about 12 kilometres from central Hong Kong and linked to the city by road, high-speed rail and ferry.

The Hong Kong government and Walt Disney Company formed a joint venture company named Hong Kong International Theme Parks Ltd to build and operate the park. The estimated building cost is US$14.1 billion, comprising US$8.4 billion in debt and US$5.7 billion in equity. The government will initially own 57 per cent of the shares and inject US$3.25 billion of the total equity. The debt component is made up of a US$5.6 billion government loan to be repaid with interest over twenty-five years (6.75 per cent for the first eight years, declining thereafter) and the remainder from commercial sources. In addition, the government is to spend US$13.6 million on infrastructure such as roads, two ferry piers, police, fire and ambulance stations, drainage and sewage systems and preparing the 280-hectare site. There will be an irrigation reservoir serving as a water recreation centre, and the area will be appropriately landscaped. The authorities have maintained that such heavy expenditure would have been necessary anyway as the site had been designated for recreation development.

Disneyland and related hotel and catering, retailing and entertainment outlets will occupy up to 126 hectares initially, with the possibility of extending to 180 hectares at a later stage. The park will be of traditional American Disney style, and Chinese influences are likely to be limited to food and official languages. Disney has already vetoed early government proposals for the infrastructure and periphery designs which sought to incorporate a Chinese and Hong Kong flavour (China Online, 2000).

The government has estimated a 5.2 million attendance figure in the first year, most of these from mainland China, which will double after fifteen years. Of this total, 3.4 million in Year 1 will be incoming tourists who will spend an additional US$8300 million; by Year 15 these figures will have increased to 7.3 million and US$16 800 million respectively. The net economic benefit of the project will be US$148 billion over forty years with 18 400 new jobs created on opening and 35 800 over twenty years. Nearly all employees will be from Hong Kong, graduating from a local Disney University, and thirty-five will be trained to take over from an original expatriate management team of forty. More conservative scenarios were also presented based on lower numbers, generating a revised net economic benefit of between US$80 000 and US$128 000 million.

The government has argued that:

> Hong Kong Disneyland will herald a new era for Hong Kong's tourism industry, and enhance Hong Kong's image as a vibrant and cosmopolitan international city. Disney's choice of Hong Kong for its third international theme park is a vote of confidence in our city and our future by the world's best known and most prestigious theme park and entertainment corporation. (HKVAR, undated)

There have been some criticisms, however, about the extent of government commitment and over-optimistic forecasts (Asiaweek, 1999). Concerns have also been expressed about environmental impacts on marine life, such as the Chinese white dolphin, and the further Americanization of Hong Kong culture by a group called 'Beware of Mickey'.

Singapore's Haw Par Villa

Haw Par Villa was created by the Aw brothers in 1937, and became known as Tiger Balm Gardens, the family making its fortune from the ointment of that name. In addition to the house itself, demolished after the Second World War, it was famous for a collection of brightly coloured statues and displays illustrating tales from Chinese folklore and mythology mixed with Confucian ideology and religion. As many as 1000 figures and 150 tableaux were installed between 1937 and 1954. These were intended to impart moral lessons and promote values such as good over evil and filial piety. Entrance to the grounds was free (Teo and Yeoh, 1997).

Over time, the gardens became outdated and rather neglected, and the family gave the site to the state in 1985 in the hope that it could be restored to life. The lease was taken up by the Singapore Tourism Board (STB) which believed it had the potential to be a major attraction. Private sector tenders for initiatives combining redevelopment and preservation were invited and International Theme Parks Pte Ltd (ITP) successfully secured a forty-year lease in 1988. The park reopened as Dragon World in 1990 after a S$80 million refurbishment. Modern facilities such as indoor AV theatres, a flume ride, a 60-metre dragon containing a boat ride through the Ten Courts of Hell (depicting the punishments awaiting sinners after death and before reincarnation), an amphitheatre, and catering and retail outlets, had all been added. It was marketed as a marriage of modern technology and Chinese tradition with an entrance fee of S$11 which later rose to S$16.50.

While initially attracting new interest and more visitors, attendances then started to fall. A new general manager sought to reverse the decline with a series of changes which highlighted the authenticity of The Original Tiger Balm Gardens, as they were renamed (Legends, 1995). These efforts proved unsuccessful and the park had recorded losses of S$31.5 million by 1998, when admission was reduced to S$5. ITP opted out of the lease in early 2000, continuing to manage the gardens for another year while the STB explored alternatives involving local and international organizations. Walt Disney and Universal Studios were even mentioned at one stage. Then the STB announced in late 2000 that it would be returning the park to its original form in recognition of its 'cultural and historical significance' for many Singaporeans (STB, 2000). The decision was based on public feedback and would require reducing the area from 9.8 hectares to its 4-hectare core, using the remaining land in ways to support the central Chinese mythological theme.

A tender was raised for a project consultant to help in the process of consolidation through land parcelling, reconfiguration, space planning, landscaping and other aspects of infrastructure. Following this exercise, another tender in early 2001 would seek operators to manage the park within the guidelines set. The park was due to close from March 2001 at the end of the ITP contract, reopening at the beginning of 2002. However, it was revealed in April 2001 that a new operator (Orient Management Pte Ltd) would be keeping it open and offering free admission. Renovations by skilled craftsmen would be completed in stages with minimum inconvenience to visitors. The company had a two-year contract and it was anticipated that its overheads would be reduced significantly because of the more limited scale of operation, sufficient income being generated by food and beverage and retail sales.

According to the STB, the attraction will be positioned as a place where visitors can:

> learn about the Chinese heritage and mythology, rather than as a Western-styled entertainment centre which its previous formulation entailed. Our challenge is to entice more visitors to the park so that they can appreciate how valuable the park is as a cultural asset that gives insight not just into Chinese mythology, but also into the life and times when the park was built. (STB, 2001)

Conclusion

These are interesting times for East Asian tourism, and exploration of the evolving pattern of attractions in Hong Kong and Singapore reveals some of the problems and opportunities which lie ahead as all destinations strive for recognition and growth in an increasingly competitive tourism industry, exposed to internal and external change. Hong Kong and Singapore have responded to the challenges faced by pursuing comparable tourism strategies in terms of product enhancement, innovation and marketing, directed at almost identical objectives of pre-eminence as an Asian city destination, with similar types of attraction. Policies are being followed with great energy by tourism agencies, actively supported by governments, and it would be surprising if they did not meet with some success in the new millennium. Central to such policies is heritage tourism, recognized as a unique selling point of considerable commercial potential.

This chapter has shown that the promotion of heritage attractions is not dictated by economics alone. Heritage attractions are also employed in the exploration, discovery and expression of national and cultural identities. Meanings of identity and the heritage from which it is derived may, however, be disputed, and the state acts as a key decision-maker and mediator, often following an essentially hegemonic agenda in matters of interpretation, presentation and conservation. Tourism thus becomes a medium for the transmission of official messages, and possibly an exploiter of heritage, although its potential as a benefactor and guardian must also be acknowledged. Hong Kong and Singapore illustrate some of these processes, as well as important features of the relationship between identity, heritage and tourism. Heritage visitor attractions have become a political issue in both locations, as well as elsewhere in the region, and this chapter suggests that such attractions are best studied and understood within their broader political and social context.

References

Asiaweek (1999). Making a magic kingdom. *Asiaweek*, 11 December.

Cheung, S. C. H. (1999). The meanings of a heritage trail in Hong Kong. *Annals of Tourism Research*, **26**, 570–588.

China Online (2000). Back to the drawing board. 9 September. http://www.chinaonline-.com, accessed 25 April 2001.

Hall, C. M. and Page, S. (eds) (2000). *Tourism in South and Southeast Asia: Issues and Cases*. Butterworth-Heinemann.

HKTA (2000). Hong Kong – heritage – culture and heritage. East versus West. http://www.discoverhongkong.com, accessed 20 November 2000.

HKTC (2000). *Hong Kong Tourist Development Action Programme*. Hong Kong Economic Services Bureau.

HKVAR (undated). Hong Kong Disneyland. Press release. http://info.gov.hk/disneyland, accessed 20 November 2000.

Legends (1995). Newsletter from Haw Par Villa.

STB (2000). Haw Par Villa to retain old charms. Press release, 13 December.

STB (2001). Haw Par Villa goes back to Tiger Balm Garden roots. Press release, 2 April.

Stevens, T. (2000). The future of visitor attractions. *Travel and Tourism Analyst*, **1**, 61–85.

STPB (1996). *Tourism 21: Vision of a Tourism Capital*. Singapore Tourist Promotion Board.

Teo, P. and Yeoh, B. (1997). Remaking local heritage for tourism. *Annals of Tourism Research*, **24**, 192–213.

Travel and Tourism Intelligence (1999a). *Hong Kong*. City Reports No. 3. Travel and Tourism Intelligence.

Travel and Tourism Intelligence (1999b). *Singapore*. City Reports No. 1. Travel and Tourism Intelligence.

URA (1991). *A Future with a Past: Saving our Heritage*. Urban Redevelopment Authority.

World Tourism Organization (2000). *Tourism Highlights*. World Tourism Organization.

6

Public transport as a visitor attraction

Derek Robbins

Aims

The aims of this chapter are to:

- investigate the relationship between transport and tourism, including the requirement to travel to the tourist destination, and the requirement for mobility at the destination itself
- analyse the impact of tourism transport on the environment and explore the case for sustainable transport policies
- evaluate how and why the transport service, and in particular the vehicle, sometimes becomes the visitor attraction
- analyse the impact of seasonality on the profitable operation of the transport visitor attraction
- utilize a case study of Guide Friday, the world's largest operator of specialist sightseeing bus tours, to illustrate the operational issues.

Introduction

Transport impinges on the visitor attraction sector at four different, but not mutually exclusive levels. Most obviously there is the role of accessibility. Visitors need to be able to get to visitor attractions, so transport services are an essential component of the overall product offer. The journey itself may well be a pleasurable experience and may even be a significant contributor to the overall enjoyment of the visit to a visitor attraction. Perusal of current television advertisements for cars demonstrates that many manufacturers still perceive driving as a pleasurable experience, which may be regarded by some as a leisure activity. Nevertheless, the journey to a visitor attraction is neither the sole purpose or even the dominant purpose of the trip and to that extent it is not undertaken for its own sake (it is in effect a derived demand). Furthermore, it will not be a pleasurable activity for many visitors to attractions. In this role, transport is a complementary industry to visitor attractions, an essential prerequisite.

The second level is where transport itself (usually transport heritage) is the central focus of the visitor attraction. Many attractions have static transport exhibits, although occasionally the attraction has working vintage vehicles or sometimes replica vehicles.

The third level is where the vehicle itself has become a visitor attraction and yet retains the principal function of providing transport services, often to the local population more than to visitors.

The final level is where the journey itself has become the visitor attraction and transport is principally undertaken for its own sake. This chapter will, however, demonstrate that the distinction between these latter two levels can become blurred.

Transport for accessibility (a complementary industry)

Visitors need to be able to get to visitor attractions, so transport services are an essential component of the overall product offer. In the developed world of Western Europe and North America where levels of car ownership are high, the car dominates accessibility, particularly in respect of visitor attractions that are heavily dependent on the non-staying day-visitor market.

The car offers huge advantages over public transport for the visitor. While the cost of acquiring a car can be high, approximately 70 per cent of motoring costs are fixed annual charges. This means that the cost of travel 'at the point of use', excluding all the fixed costs of annual road tax, depreciation and insurance, is very low, perhaps as little as 16 pence per mile (AA, 1998). Attendance at visitor attractions is a social activity usually undertaken by groups of friends or relatives. The car is an ideal unit for groups of four to five people as there is no significant incremental increase in the cost of travel for each person until the vehicle is at full capacity. The average car occupancy for day visits and tourism trips is 2.3, markedly higher than the occupancy level of 1.2 for the journey to work (DETR, 1998a). Therefore those households which have acquired a car primarily for other purposes, such as the journey to work, will often find the additional cost of making leisure journeys by car the cheapest option.

The car also offers greater flexibility than public transport. It does not operate to fixed routes and fixed timetables, and it is widely accepted that the growth of car ownership and car use has brought huge advantages in individual mobility. In the words of the UK's 1998 White Paper on transport, 'Cars in particular have revolutionised the way we live, bringing great flexibility and widening horizons' (DETR, 1998b). The increased opportunities are especially important for both holiday trips and leisure day-trips. In the case of day-trips, car ownership creates opportunities for impulse journeys. This was noted as far back as 1973, when in an essay 'Some thoughts about the motor car', Colin Buchanan[1] eloquently described the impact of car ownership on the quality of life:

> I have never managed to make much money, and for the most part, in my half century of motoring, I have made do with second-hand cars. But what an enrichment of life has resulted! Marvelous holidays – camping, caravanning, much of Europe at our disposal in a three week vacation. Short visits in infinite variety – to relatives and friends, to the sea, out into the country, to great houses, gardens, zoos and parks. Spur of the moment trips – it is a fine day so out we go. Why cannot we be less hypocritical and admit that a motor car is just about the most convenient device that we ever invented, and that possession of it and usage in moderation is a perfectly legitimate ambition for all classes of people.

It is difficult to ascertain the exact modal split for travelling to visitor attractions in the UK, but it is clearly dominated by the car. Some 86 per cent of all UK passenger kilometres undertaken for all journey purposes are undertaken by car (DETR, 2000). Table 6.1 shows the dominance of the car for making holiday trips. Unfortunately, collated data on day-visits, which make up such a high percentage of the visitor attraction market, is contradictory. The National Travel Survey (NTS) combines holiday travel with day-visit leisure travel, but shows a car share of 77 per cent. Meanwhile the United Kingdom Day Visitor Survey, 1998 (UKDVS) (Costigan, 1999) shows that 56 per cent of all leisure day-trips were taken by car – a figure much lower than that suggested by the NTS. *Sightseeing in the UK*

Table 6.1 Transport used to travel on holiday, 1995 (percentage)

Holiday type	Car	Bus and Coach	Rail	Other	Source
Holiday 4+ nights	78	10	7	4	UKTS
Holiday under 3 nights	83	7	6	5	UKTS
All holidays	80	8	7	4	UKTS
Holidays 4+ nights	77	13	7	3	BNTS
Holidays/day-trips	77	9	6	8	NTS

Sources: UK Tourism Survey (1996), British National Tourism Survey (1995), National Travel Survey (1995/97)

(BTA/ETB, 1998) estimates the proportion of visitors arriving at attractions by coach at 9 per cent in 1997, with visits to workplaces (20 per cent) and visits to historic properties (13 per cent) showing the highest coach shares, which also makes the UKDVS figure seem low. The evidence from surveys undertaken at specific visitor attractions is also mixed, although the car share does seem to vary with the type of area. The public transport share of the market is at its lowest for rural areas. The 1994 survey of visitors to all national parks (Centre for Leisure Research, 1996) showed no fewer than 91 per cent of visitors arriving by car, van or camper van. The share increases for visitor attractions in urban areas, which are traditionally better served by public transport, and particularly those attractions sited in historic towns which attract a significant share of overseas visitors (Table 6.2). The highest public transport share is achieved in large cities, with dense public transport networks often including urban rail, light transit systems or tram services in addition to the traditional bus network, which itself demonstrates

Table 6.2 Mode of travel by visitors to UK historic towns (percentage)

Destination	Car	Train	Bus/Coach	Other	Total
York (1989)	67	20	13	0	100
Chester (1990)	62	13	23	2	100
Bath (1986)	59	17	21	3	100
Cambridge (1994)	55	17	23	5	100
Stratford-upon-Avon (1987)	53	10	34	3	100
Oxford (1991)	48	16	33	3	100

Source: Grant, Human and Le Pelley (1995).

much greater frequency of service. Heavy traffic congestion combined with restricted parking capacity (which is also often very expensive) all add to the merits of public transport. Public transport market share is at its highest for those visitor attractions in large cities where overseas visitors form a high percentage of visitors, and at its lowest for destinations dominated by the domestic market. Surveys indicate that over 90 per cent of day visitors to Bournemouth arrive by car (Godsall, 1998).

Overall, it is important for visitor attractions to collect market research information, including the mode of transport used by their visitors. Although many elements of access are beyond the control of the visitor attraction (such as the capacity of the local road network), the attraction needs to establish its infrastructure requirements, most notably car parking facilities. Furthermore, accessibility may well influence, indeed constrain, future development and expansion through the planning process.

A number of countries are beginning to develop sustainable transport policies in response to environmental concerns generally, and in particular the car's contribution to greenhouse gases (especially carbon dioxide). In response to these concerns, a number of visitor attractions outside major city centres which have traditionally been dominated by car access have introduced innovative projects in an attempt to reduce their dependence on the car. These projects mostly involve the introduction of reduced price admission for those travelling by public transport either on the production of a valid ticket or sometimes in the form of a combined single ticket. For instance, over forty attractions and catering establishments in the North York Moors National Park offer significant discounts to users of the Moorsbus network (Breakwell, 2000), while Legoland, Windsor, introduced a discounted entrance ticket combined with a rail ticket including a free shuttle bus from the station. The impact was very marginal with a mere 3 per cent of arrivals utilizing the discount (Oswin, 1999). It would seem that the advantages of arrival by car outlined above remain very strong.

Transport as a visitor attraction

Museums and theme parks

Transport itself can form the central focus of the visitor attraction. There are a number of museums and theme parks that incorporate the history or development of a range of modes of transport as their central focus. Table 6.3 lists the main transport museums in terms of visitor numbers in the UK. In addition, other major national museums such as the Science Museum in South Kensington, London, which attracts in excess of 1.5 million visitors per annum, incorporate a

Table 6.3   Visitor numbers to transport museums in the
UK, 1998

	Visitors
National Maritime Museum, Greenwich	609 000
National Railway Museum, York	430 000
Museum of Transport, Glasgow	400 000
National Motor Museum, Beaulieu	355 000
Merseyside Maritime Museum, Albert Dock	291 378
National Motorcycle Museum, Bickenhill	220 000
London Transport Museum, Covent Garden	214 000
British Road Transport Museum, Coventry	140 000

Source: BTA (2000)

significant collection of historical transport vehicles. While the bulk of these attractions consist of static exhibits, a number do incorporate the opportunity to ride on either vintage or replica vehicles.

The vehicle becomes part of the attraction

There are degrees to which transport vehicles are a visitor attraction. At one level, there are many instances where the vehicle has become synonymous with the destination, a form of icon in effect. The most obvious examples are from large cities with high media and film exposure such as the double-decker red bus (London), black taxi cab (London), yellow taxi cab (New York) or the street cable cars (San Francisco). The degree to which tourists identify with the vehicle is clear from much anecdotal evidence, with the sale of model buses and taxis in gift shops, to the widespread use of the images on postcards and posters. However, both tourists and the local population require mobility around the tourist destination area, and the principal function of such vehicles is transport. While the vehicles may well contribute to the overall tourist experience, there is no strong evidence that tourists make additional journeys on these vehicles merely for a pleasure activity.

The development of transport services into a visitor attraction is not confined to destinations benefiting from widespread media attention. In Malta, public transport is provided by a fleet of 508 vintage buses, of which 300 are over thirty years old, and a few are over fifty years old. The fleet structure emerged as a result of a prolonged lack of investment and not as a deliberate policy. Indeed, the government still has its replacement by a fleet of modern vehicles as a key policy objective. However, this fleet has developed into a popular visitor attraction and tourists contribute approximately 12 per cent of all trips taken on the network (around 5 million trips per annum) (Robbins, 1996a). The ageing fleet is less of an attraction to the local population, who make up the majority of passengers. If significant fleet replacement becomes a reality, there is significant scope to retain older vehicles on specific routes with high tourist use. Malta has a very high population density (1139 people per square kilometre) and so a large-scale switch from public transport to the private car (including car hire by tourists) would be very problematic. Elsewhere, the scope to use vintage vehicles to attract people from their cars to public transport has been tried as a more deliberate policy with some success. The Trossachs Trundler operated a May–September season in the Callander area in Scotland between 1992 and 1999 using a 1950s' vintage bus with a Duple Vista body, offering a scheduled service designed to attract tourists out of their cars. This approach begins to change the nature of the transport service and one may question whether the principal function remains mobility for the tourist, or whether the journey itself has become the visitor attraction. However, very heavy maintenance costs incurred in difficult hilly operating terrain led eventually to the withdrawal of the vintage vehicle.

The transport journey as the visitor attraction

For the purposes of this chapter, a transport visitor attraction is defined as one where 'the journey is undertaken primarily for its own sake and the pleasure derived from riding on the vehicle is the principal motivation of the visitor'.

Boat cruises

Tourist destinations located on a river or coast will include short sightseeing trips by boat as a visitor attraction. In mass tourist locations these can attract mass tourism figures. For instance, in the popular Lake District region of the UK, Windermere Lake Cruises attract in excess of 1 million visitors per annum (and Mersey Ferries Leisure Cruises over 600 000).

Steam railways

The most common form of land transport attraction in the UK is the preserved railway, using mostly, although not exclusively, steam locomotives. There are 103 preserved railways in the UK, many dating from the late 1960s or early 1970s, and often using redundant track and rights of way which were closed when the national railway network contracted as a consequence of the influential yet controversial Beeching Report (British Railways Board, 1963). Around 75 per cent of these preserved railway lines have opened since 1970 (49 per cent since 1980) (BTA/ETB, 1998). Due to the complexity of running a railway, including a range of highly technical and complex safety and other regulatory requirements overseen by the Railway Inspectorate, many preserved railways are now operated as private limited companies. However, they employ a relatively small full-time staff and remain heavily reliant on the activities of volunteer enthusiasts. For instance, the Swanage Railway is operated by a limited company (The Swanage Railway Company Ltd), which is responsible for the publication of the timetable and for the safe operation of the railway. In addition the Southern Steam Trust shares the same address and is a registered charitable organization with various forms of membership. The trust raises funds and is actively involved in volunteer recruitment for what it describes as a 'volunteer-run railway'.

There are a number of variations of rail attractions. The most common are standard gauge railway lines, although there are a number of successful narrow gauge railway lines and other specialist services such as the Snowdon Mountain Railway. Steam railways form a separate category within UK visitor attraction statistics and account for around 5 million admissions per annum. Table 6.4 shows the visitor numbers for the ten most visited lines.

A closer examination of the steam railway market illustrates that some lines are developing a wider role. A number are well located to serve other well-established visitor attractions such as the Swanage Railway, which has a station at the National Trust property, Corfe Castle, or the Keighley and Worth Valley Railway, with a station at Haworth serving the Rectory (the birthplace of the Brontë sisters and now a visitor attraction). This offers the preserved railway the

Table 6.4   Visits to steam railways, 1998

	Visitors
North Yorkshire Moors Railway	275 000
Severn Valley Railway, Shropshire	212 439
Ffestiniog Railway, Porthmadog	211 627
Bluebell Railway, Sussex	176 671
Paignton and Dartmouth Steam Railway	161 864
Lakeside and Haverthwaite	160 000
Swanage Railway, Dorset	147 243
Romney, Hythe and Dymchurch Railway	146 867
West Somerset Railway, Minehead	144 160
Snowdon Mountain Railway	141 000

Source: BTA (2000)

opportunity to undertake collaborative marketing and sales, including combined rail and admission tickets. The journey itself no longer remains the sole purpose of the day out but it is still a significant part of the overall leisure package.

There are increasing ambitions for some lines to upgrade from their role as a visitor attraction to an all-year-round public transport service serving a number of functions for the local population. For instance, some lines with stations conveniently located to serve schools have tendered to operate special schools' services as an alternative to special bus services.[2] A published aim of the Southern Steam Trust, in the Swanage Railway 2001 timetable, is 'the restoration of the rail link between Swanage and Wareham and the re-establishment of a daily service to connect with main line trains'.

The transition from a seasonally dominated, volunteer-operated leisure visitor attraction, to a scheduled operator of daily services all the year round, is a giant step that can only be viable in a limited number of cases where specific circumstances prevail. However, it does serve to illustrate further the blurring of the distinction between transport infrastructure and the visitor attraction, as well as the aspirations of some operators to bridge that gap.

Settle to Carlisle railway line

The Leeds, Settle and Carlisle railway is one of a relatively small number of rural railway lines in the UK to escape the Beeching cuts of the 1960s. As a poorly performing line requiring public subsidy, the then British Rail filed for closure of the line in the mid-1980s. However, the line retained one huge attribute – a scenic railway line, which crossed the Pennines and incorporated several spectacular and well-known features, most notably the Ribblehead Viaduct, a phenomenal piece of Victorian engineering. Once closure had been refused, British Rail relaunched the line as a visitor attraction with considerable success. They did not introduce old rolling stock, and although a proposal to operate steam trains for special leisure services was briefly considered this was quickly rejected, not least because there was a shortage of essential infrastructure for coal and water. In fact British Rail took an alternative approach, with large-scale investment in new Sprinter trains. So in contrast with previous examples, the vehicle did not become a visitor attraction, although the scenic nature of the railway line did emerge as a visitor attraction. The line still serves the local population for a range of activities; yet, due to the dramatic growth in passenger numbers, internal surveys show that in excess of 50 per cent of passengers per annum use the line purely for leisure purposes. It attracts over 30 per cent of its passengers from outside the local area, including overseas visitors. There is a clear distinction between this piece of transport infrastructure and the steam railways discussed above, and yet there are also similarities. Just as some steam lines are seeking to develop from pure visitor attractions into having a wider transport function, this line has a wider transport function but now serves purely as a visitor attraction for a significant number of passengers, for whom the journey itself has become the principal purpose of the trip.

Open-top bus tours

Open-top bus tours have been a feature of the transport system in Central London for many years. Initially, this was a monopoly market for the then publicly owned London Transport, but the Transport Act 1980 deregulated this market and at its height over twelve operators were competing. This has now settled down to four main operators. The competitive nature of the market makes calculation of its total size difficult, although past consultancy undertaken by the author indicated around 28 per cent of overseas visitors to London take a tour. The market was well suited to London as there are many historic buildings of which the open-top vehicle offers excellent views (and photo opportunities). Furthermore, with around 20 per cent of overseas arrivals in the off-peak months of January to March, the peak season is not too peaked, offering operating companies the opportunity to operate all the year round. Over time the product has evolved to allow passengers to get on and off the vehicle as they please and, hence, combine the tour with visits to various attractions. However, mobility around London is offered by London Underground (the tube) and bus networks utilizing an off-peak travel card, and visitor surveys show over 90 per cent of visitors use the tube and 70 per cent the bus. Hence, the tour itself, rather than mobility at the destination, is the prime motive for the journey.

Operators are able to serve a wider range of language commentaries and handle several nationalities on the same tour by using taped commentaries. The disadvantage of taped commentaries is that the road conditions can vary significantly, influencing the average speed of the vehicle, and it can prove difficult to keep the commentary in sequence with the tour. A number of operators therefore opt for the more personal approach of using a guide.

More recently the concept of the open-top bus tour has been developed in many other more seasonal locations pioneered by a company called Guide Friday (see the case study in this chapter).

The concept of tours following fixed routes has been extended beyond the bus. The use of Second World War amphibious landing craft was developed in a number of American cities (such as Boston) under the product name of Duck Tours. This has recently been copied in London. The nature of the vehicle enables a small part of the tour to be conducted on water, with entry to the water as a featured highlight.

Case study: Guide Friday open-top bus tours

Guide Friday is the largest open-top sightseeing bus operator in Europe, with over 1000 tours daily throughout Britain, Ireland and Europe during the peak season. The company was founded in 1975 and based in Stratford-upon-Avon, where it first operated tours. As the company expanded it acquired its first double-decker bus in 1977. Operations were extended to Cambridge and Edinburgh in 1986, shortly followed by Bath, Oxford and York. From humble beginnings, the company has expanded rapidly. Today it operates in over thirty destinations (see Table 6.5), carrying over 3 million passengers per annum on a fleet in excess of 200 vehicles and employing (during the peak season) 750 staff.

Guide Friday introduced the concept of the open-top sightseeing tour that had seen considerable success in London to provincial towns. It made the decision to avoid entry into the already highly competitive London market and, instead, sought to introduce the product to alternative destinations, which in itself was innovative. Until then, the conventional wisdom was that the product would not succeed outside London, the principal barrier being seasonality (see Chapter 9 for a more in-depth discussion on seasonality). While London itself has a peak season, there are significant visitor numbers during the winter months, which enabled the services to operate all the year round, albeit at reduced frequency during the winter months. In contrast, Table 6.5 shows that Guide Friday operates an all-year service in only six of its twenty-nine UK destinations, although these are the first group of destinations served by the company. The length of the season in the remaining twenty-three locations is variable. While some destinations such as Brighton justify a season from March to early October (seven months) others are operational for three months. Furthermore the pattern of demand in the six 'all-year' destinations is highly seasonal and the peak summer season frequency of a departure every six or seven minutes (Oxford) is not matched in the winter months. Consequently, the summer pattern of supply of 1000 tours per day in twenty-nine UK destinations is contrasted by fewer than 100 tours per day in six destinations in the winter, with a number of variations during the shoulder months. How can this pattern of demand be served profitably?

Clearly there is low, even non-, utilization of much of the fleet of 200 vehicles during the winter months. However, Guide Friday took an interesting approach to this problem. Essentially, it purchased old, second-hand vehicles at a relatively low cost so, although the assets themselves achieved low utilization, the actual depreciation of those assets was also very low. To illustrate this point, the very first double-decker vehicle acquired by the

Table 6.5   Guide Friday destinations, 2001

Destination	Partner	Season	Length of Tour	Commentary	Peak frequency
Bath	First Badgerline	All year	60 mins	Guide	10 mins
Bournemouth		13 Apr–07 Oct	45 mins	Taped	30 mins
Bourton on the Water		13 Apr–23 Sept	35 mins	Guide	45 mins
Bristol		17 July–02 Sept	50 mins	Guide	60 mins
Brighton		24 Mar–28 Oct	50 mins	Guide	20 mins
Cambridge		All year	60 mins	Guide	15 mins
Cardiff		17 Apr–28 Oct	55 mins	Guide	30 mins
Chester	Chester City Trans	07 Apr–28 Oct	60 mins	Guide	15 mins
Dover		05 May–30 Sept	60 mins	Taped	60 mins
Eastbourne		13 Apr–07 Oct	45 mins	Taped	30 mins
Edinburgh		All year	60 mins	Guide	15 mins
Glasgow	First Glasgow	24 Mar–28 Oct	80 mins	Guide	30 mins
Hastings		21 Apr–24 Sept	60 mins	Guide	30 mins
Inverness		05 May–30 Sept	80 mins	Guide	45 mins
Leicester		30 June–02 Sept	60 mins	Guide	60 mins
Lincoln	Road Car Co.	13 Apr–23 Sept	50 mins	Guide	30 mins
Llandudno	Alpine Travel	26 May–23 Sept	60 mins	Guide	30 mins
Loch Ness		05 May–30 Sept	3 hours	Guide	twice daily
Margate		26 May – 02 Sept	75 mins	Taped	90 mins
Oxford		All year	60 mins	Guide	10 mins
Perth	Stagecoach	26 May–02 Sept	55 mins	Taped	60 mins
Plymouth	Plymouth Citybus	07 April–21 Oct	45 mins	Guide	30 mins
Portsmouth		05 May–30 Sept	60 mins	Taped	20 mins
Stirling	Stirling Council	13 Apr–30 Sept	70 mins		40 mins
Stonehenge	Wilts and Dorset	13 Apr–29 Oct	2 hours	Guide	three times daily
Stratford-upon-Avon		All year	60 mins	Guide	15 mins
Torquay		23 June–30 Sept	55 mins		40 mins
Windsor		17 Mar–28 Oct	55 mins	Guide	15 mins
York		All year	60 mins	Guide	10 mins

Note: European locations are Cork, Dublin, Galway, Berlin, Madrid, Paris and Seville.

company in 1977 was over fourteen years old on purchase and cost a mere £300. The company operated it for a further nineteen years, thus demonstrating negligible depreciation. This approach can work for two reasons. First, the older-looking vehicle can add a 'heritage feel' to the tour. Second, the maintenance and operational costs of utilizing older vehicles are not prohibitively expensive, not least because of the low annual mileage undertaken by each vehicle. Although there are exceptions, the majority of tours last between forty-five and sixty minutes, with an average tour length of seven to eight miles, producing a daily mileage for most vehicles of less than 100 miles. With a season lasting no longer than seven months, and allowing some downtime for routine maintenance, it is difficult to envisage average annual mileage exceeding 15 000 miles per vehicle.

The other major issue surrounding seasonality is, of course, staff. Table 6.5 shows that, in the majority of destinations, commentary is provided by tour guides rather than a tape. Traditionally, tour guides are self-employed and, although the company has found that the 'Blue Badge' guide qualification overseen by regional tourist boards covers too wide an area and has therefore undertaken 'in-house training', the employment of guides on seasonal contracts has proved viable. However, the majority of drivers are also only required on a seasonal contract. During periods of relatively high unemployment there has been a pool of appropriately qualified drivers available and the seasonal contract has proved particularly popular to recently retired drivers who wish to supplement their income without returning to full-time, year-round employment. However, over recent years bus companies have found it increasingly difficult to recruit full-time drivers (Robbins, 1996b)[3] and this may prove the most difficult operational issue for Guide Friday in the coming years.

A second approach to deal with seasonality is to operate in a limited number of destinations in partnership with a local operator. Hence some, if not all, of the vehicle and staff requirements can be provided by the partner operator for whom the summer is not always the peak period of demand and who therefore has underutilized assets available for the venture.

The choice of destinations is also interesting. Guide Friday required destinations that attracted significant numbers of visitors, as clearly the open-top bus tour is not a major trip attractor but will attract impulse purchases from a captive market. The destination also requires buildings or landscapes of historical, architectural or scenic interest, which are easily accessible for the bus.

Guide Friday initially selected historic towns as destinations and one such destination, Canterbury, has proved unsuccessful because the town's road structure, with a ring road and significant pedestrianization, did not allow good bus access and views of the key sites. It has since diversified into scenic tours and resorts, and operates in many sensitive environmental areas. Despite the ageing structure of its fleet, Guide Friday has converted over 10 per cent of the fleet to operate on liquid petroleum gas (LPG), which enhances local air quality by the reduction of volatile organic compounds (VOCs), which are widely linked to rising incidences of asthma and other respiratory diseases

(Royal Commission on Environmental Pollution, 1994). The use of LPG also reduces greenhouse gas emissions (particularly carbon dioxide).

Arguments as to the wider environmental impacts of sightseeing buses are less clear cut. On the one hand, the majority of tours enable passengers to 'get on and off as you please', with tickets valid all day. It can then be argued by the operators that their service offers mobility around the destination to the visitor and, in the case of UK passengers, may well be serving as a substitute to the private car (which can be parked outside the historic centre) and thereby bringing environmental benefits. Nevertheless, while the vehicles technically have a capacity of seventy-eight seats, the lower deck is predominantly unused and so, in terms of environmental measurements, the emissions per passenger are somewhat higher than one might expect (and much higher than average emissions per seat). Furthermore, if the vehicle itself is the visitor attraction, then a large number of passengers are making optional leisure journeys rather than substituting the bus for another mode of transport. Finally, a phenomenon first noted in the earliest days of competition in London was the role played by the vehicle itself in promoting the service. Guide Friday estimate that only half of its passengers pre-book (often in joint promotions such as with the BritRail pass), while the remaining half are impulse buyers (the percentage of impulse buys is at its highest in seasonal destinations where the domestic market is dominant). Operators like to have a vehicle on the stop for much of the time at the main departure points, and therefore try to delay dispatch of a new tour until a vehicle is ending its tour and can replace the departing vehicle at the stop. This holds greater importance for those destinations where there is more than one operator competing for the tour business (Oxford, York, Edinburgh and Bath all have rival operators). This can be considered by some as visually obtrusive.

Conclusion

The future prospects for transport as a visitor attraction are mixed. Certainly operators indicate that they attract relatively low levels of repeat business. Once a journey has been undertaken and enjoyed, then for all but the enthusiast there is no great incentive to undertake it again. Hence future growth is heavily dependent on a significant pool of potential first-time customers. Some preserved railway lines attempt innovative marketing with theme weeks (such as Thomas the Tank Engine trains or Santa Specials) in an attempt to vary the product. However, by and large it is a consistent product year on year with only minor variations possible, for example, to the route (for bus tours) or to the vehicles. One cannot match the scope to develop new elements to the attraction in the way theme parks or museums can. This is perhaps reflected in the visitor numbers to preserved railways over the last ten years (1989 to 1998), where the growth of 7 per cent is lower than the overall increase in attendance at visitor attractions (10 per cent) (BTA/ETB, 1999). Transport as a visitor attraction seems unlikely to increase its overall market share.

On the other hand, there is scope for developing transport services as attractions in their own right in order to contribute to a more sustainable approach to tourism growth. For example, in the UK there is a potential conflict between a transport policy aimed at slowing down road traffic growth (DETR, 1998b) and a tourism strategy aimed at accelerating tourism growth (DCMS, 1999). The car dominates UK domestic tourism trips, including trips to visitor attractions, and a policy that reduces overall levels of road traffic growth may also reduce growth or even visitor numbers to attractions. However, tourists can be persuaded to travel around a destination by public transport even if they travelled to the destination by car. A recreational transport network operating in the North York Moors National Park (Moorbus) has attracted significant growth in passenger numbers and surveys demonstrate that 50 per cent of users are from car-owning households (Breakwell, 2000). This transfer to public transport can be further increased by making the transport vehicle part of the visitor attraction. The use of vintage vehicles (for example, the Trossachs Express near Stirling or vintage buses in Malta) or open-top vehicles – in Bournemouth 100 000 passengers are carried on the predominantly tourist coastal route in a twelve-week season – has achieved some success. The further development of specialist services will, in the author's view, become increasingly used as a strategy to reduce dependency on the car in sensitive destinations while preventing an overall reduction in tourism. However, although many of these services will serve a dual role of accessibility and visitor attraction in their own right, as preservation railways themselves have shown, they are likely to remain seasonal. The gap between seasonal visitor attraction and all-year scheduled service is huge.

Notes

1 The quote is taken from a 1973 essay 'Some thoughts about the motor car' by Colin Buchanan, a leading light in Transport Planning in the 1960s, and Chair of the influential 1963 Government Working Party 'Traffic in Towns'. Parts of the essay are reproduced in both AA (1997) and Adams (1993).

2 Note that, in the UK, the local education authority is obligated to provide free transport for children required to travel a distance of over 3 miles.

3 Drivers' wages have fallen considerably in relative terms over the last fifteen years. Prior to the privatization of the National Bus Company and the deregulation of bus services under the Transport Act 1985, wages were close to the national average. By 1998 the national average wage was £384 per week in contrast to drivers' wage levels of £272.30. Following periods of high economic growth, bus companies, particularly in London and the South East, have found it increasingly difficult to recruit full-time staff, and this will have knock-on effects to employers of seasonal labour.

References

AA (1997). *Living with the Car*. Automobile Association Policy.

AA (1998). *Technical Information – Motoring Costs 1998*. Automobile Association Policy.

Adams, J. (1993). No need for discussion: the policy is now in place. In *Local Transport Today and Tomorrow* (P. Stoneham, ed.) pp. 73–78, Local Transport Today.

Breakwell, B. (2000). Delivering integrated transport. Paper presented to Countryside Recreation Conference: Delivering Sustainable Transport to the Countryside, Cardiff.

British National Tourism Survey (1995). *Digest of Tourist Statistics*. No. 20. British Tourist Authority.

British Railways Board (1963). *The Reshaping of British Railways*. HMSO.

BTA (2000). *Digest of Tourist Statistics*. No. 23. British Tourist Authority.

BTA/ETB (1998). *Sightseeing in the UK 1997*. British Tourist Authority/English Tourist Board.

BTA/ETB (1999). *Sightseeing in the UK 1998*. British Tourist Authority/English Tourist Board.

Centre for Leisure Research (1996). *1994 All Parks Visitor Survey*. Vol. 12. Herriot-Watt University.

Costigan, P. (1999). *UK Leisure Day Visits Survey: Technical Report 1998*. National Centre for Social Research.

DCMS (1999). *Tomorrow's Tourism: A Growth Industry for the New Millennium*. Department of Culture, Media and Sport, and The Stationery Office.

DETR (1998a). *Focus on Personal Travel*. Department of the Environment, Transport and the Regions, and The Stationery Office.

DETR (1998b). *A New Deal for Transport: Better for Everyone*, Cmnd 3950. Department of the Environment, Transport and the Regions, and The Stationery Office.

DETR (2000). *Transport Statistics Great Britain*. Department of the Environment, Transport and the Regions, and The Stationery Office.

Godsall, S. (1998). Bournemouth tourism planning. Paper presented to Bournemouth Transport Strategy Conference, The Crossroads, Bournemouth, 3 April.

Grant, M., Human, B. and Le Pelley, B. (1995). Tourism and park and ride. *Insights*, **7**, A95–A99.

National Travel Survey (1995/97). In DETR (1998). *Focus on Personal Travel*. November. Department of the Environment, Transport and the Regions, and The Stationery Office.

Oswin, J. (1999). The role of tourism operators in increasing public transport use. Paper presented to Journey to Success, English Tourism Council Conference, Regents College, London, April.

Robbins, D. K. (1996a). A sustainable transport policy for tourism on small islands: a case study of Malta. In *Sustainable Tourism in Islands and Small States* (L. Briguglio, R. Butler, D. Harrison and W. Leal Filho, eds) pp. 180–198, Pinter.

Robbins, D. K. (1996b). *Performance Trends in the Bus and Coach Industry*. Lloyds Bowmaker Limited.

Royal Commission on Environmental Pollution (1994). *Transport and the Environment.* Eighteenth report, Cmnd 2674. HMSO.

UK Tourism Survey (1996). *The UK Tourist – Statistics 1995*. August. English Tourist Board, Northern Ireland Tourist Board, Scottish Tourist Board, Wales Tourist Board.

Part Three

The management of visitor attractions

Part Three of the book focuses on the operational and strategic management of visitor attractions, with a particular emphasis on the fundamental inter-dependencies involved in managing the various components of the visitor attraction product. Managing visitor attractions successfully requires the effective integration of a wide range of complex and interrelated management considerations arising both from within and outside the visitor attraction sector. In this respect, the management of the visitor attraction sector can be seen as a microcosm of the wider tourism industry. The challenge for visitor attractions is to achieve this integration with what is frequently a very limited resource base.

A constant challenge for many attractions, particularly those of a heritage or cultural genre, is that of maintaining the authenticity of the attraction. This theme is examined in Chapter 7, where Philip Feifan Xie and Geoffrey Wall introduce the concept of authentication as it applies to ethnic tourism experiences and ethnic visitor attractions, and discuss the management challenges involved. Tourism has often been accused of having a negative impact on the authenticity of indigenous cultures. Visitor attractions are, however, often perceived as the most appropriate vehicle for protecting and promoting specific cultural identities through 'good' tourism, despite frequent pressures on attractions to 'commodify' or otherwise 'pollute' the visitor experience. With detailed case studies of ethnic visitor attractions in Hainan, China, Feifan Xie and Wall examine the relationship between ethnic and cultural tourism and explore the potential benefits to be derived from the development of ethnic visitor attractions.

The need for heritage and culture-based visitor attractions to maintain their authenticity also features in Chapter 8, which looks at the management of visitor impacts. In this chapter, Brian Garrod examines the role visitor attractions play in advancing the objectives of sustainable development and identifies some of the main impacts that the development and operation of visitor attractions can have on the natural and built historic environments. Garrod then goes on to explore what impacts visitors to visitor attractions exert on the fabric of the attraction itself and, more importantly, how these impacts might best be managed. A number of tools for the management of visitor impacts are introduced, and discussion of their suitability – and indeed their desirability – then follows. The findings of a study of visitor impacts at attractions in Scotland then go part way to assessing the viability of some of the main tools available to managers of visitor attractions for addressing visitor impacts.

As is the case across much of the tourism industry, and particularly in the temperate climatic zones, one of the biggest challenges to operators of visitor attractions is that of seasonality. A large number of visitor attractions experience a relatively short peak season, with attendant implications for staffing, transportation and accommodation, among many other issues. In Chapter 9, Philip Goulding reviews what is understood by the concept of seasonality and investigates the operational implications of seasonality for visitor attractions, both as revenue centres in their own right and more widely as part of the local tourism economy. Within the context of seasonality being interpreted as a broad and complex phenomenon, Goulding assesses the range and possible management responses to the realities of a seasonal market and evaluates their likely degree of overall effectiveness. Despite the fact that visitor attractions are often at the mercy of the seasonal nature of market forces, Goulding argues that through their operational policies, attractions can collectively, and sometimes individually, contribute to, reinforce or combat patterns of seasonality in a tourism destination. This is particularly the case where major attractions or groups of attractions play a catalytic role in promoting and sustaining the destination of which they form part.

In many destinations around the world, religion-based attractions serve as the principal draw for tourists. Perhaps more than any other genre of visitor attraction, however, religion-based attractions typically face a range of strategic objectives with considerable potential for conflict among stakeholder groups. In Chapter 10, Myra Shackley illustrates the diversity of religion-based attractions and identifies the management trends and manifold challenges confronting them. For example, how are competitive and operational strategies developed successfully to accommodate divergent organizational goals and how can the operational management of religion-based attractions accommodate the divergent needs of different visitor and user groups? One of the most controversial issues facing religion-based attractions is that of charging for visitor entry. Shackley develops this theme in a case study which explores the charging for entry to cathedrals in England. The case study also serves as a vehicle to examine the broader themes of visitor management and access.

The final chapter in Part Three, by Sandra Watson and Martin McCracken, analyses the role of human resource management in visitor attractions. The human resource is increasingly becoming a critical success factor for visitor attractions, particularly in respect of frontline staff. Management challenges revolve around the successful recruitment, training and retention of staff, and staffing is now viewed as a vital ingredient of effective competitive strategy. Not only do Watson and McCracken discuss how the relationship between human resources and competitive strategy can be strengthened, but they also explore key issues including labour intensity, service quality, and competitive environments and their influence on human resource management practices. In particular, Chapter 11 examines the people management skills required by visitor attraction managers and looks at how these can be implemented effectively by studying a case study of good practice.

7

Authenticating visitor attractions based upon ethnicity

Philip Feifan Xie and Geoffrey Wall

Aims

The aims of this chapter are to:

- introduce the concept of authenticity as it applies to ethnic tourism experiences and ethnic visitor attractions, and to suggest that authenticity is a negotiated rather than a fixed attribute
- suggest that the process of authentication provides a tractable way of examining aspects of authenticity at visitor attractions
- provide a framework that identifies key stakeholders and five dimensions of authenticity that can be used to guide data collection and its interpretation at visitor attractions
- illustrate the utility of the framework through application to ethnic visitor attractions in Hainan, China.

Introduction

Tourism involves the movement of people outside their normal places of work and residence. As such, it provides participants with novel experiences, often bringing them into contact with unaccustomed places and people. For many tourists this is a search for the 'other', this being judged in relation to the 'self' and one's usual behaviours and settings. Thus, tourism brings into contact people who are not only strangers to one another, but who may also be members of different ethnic groups. Sometimes, the presence of minority peoples is a visitor attraction in itself. However, even in such places, specific tourism businesses may be created to provide opportunities for tourists to experience aspects of ethnicity. This chapter is concerned with visitor attractions of this type. In particular, it addresses some of the tensions and trade-offs that should be addressed if such attractions are to meet the goals of the diversity of stakeholders with interests in their operation.

The development of cultural tourism and, in particular, ethnic tourism, which can be viewed as a specific form of cultural tourism, has brought to prominence a number of important questions:

- What is an authentic ethnic visitor attraction and how should such ethnic tourism experiences be provided?
- Can indigenous cultures survive the impacts of tourism?
- Will ethnicity be polluted and ultimately destroyed, or is it possible that tourism can actually nurture a cultural renaissance?
- How can indigenous groups benefit from cultural tourism at acceptable costs?

An understanding of these and related research questions is essential if high-quality tourism experiences based on expressions of ethnicity are to be made available in a sustainable manner.

There is a substantial and growing literature on cultural tourism and ethnic tourism (Cohen, 1988; MacCannell, 1984; Picard and Wood, 1997; Smith, 1989; Wall, 1996; Walle, 1998). Most of these works focus upon the normative issue of whether tourism is beneficial or detrimental to its hosts (Wood, 1998). However, the traditional 'impact' paradigm tends to oversimplify situations, ignoring the fact that tourists and investments in tourism are not always imposed but are often sought, that residents respond and adapt to changing circumstances and that tourism has such longevity and is so pervasive in some destinations that it is virtually impossible to visualize that place and its people in the absence of tourism. Further issues, such as authenticity of experience and commodification of culture, have been hotly debated but little research has paid attention to the concept of authentication, which refers to the identification of those who make claims for authenticity and the interests that such claims serve (Jackson, 1999).

This chapter will elucidate relationships between tourism and culture, particularly in relation to the issue of ethnicity. Terms associated with ethnic tourism will be defined and described, and the state of current knowledge will be assessed. An example of ethnic visitor attractions from Hainan, China, will be presented. It will be concluded that assessment of authentication rather than authenticity may provide a more practical way of addressing quality issues in ethnic visitor attractions.

Cultural tourism and ethnic tourism

Cultural tourism can be viewed from a variety of perspectives. From an ethnographic perspective, cultural tourism can be defined as 'a genre of special interest tourism based on the search for and participation in new and deep cultural experiences, whether aesthetic, intellectual, emotional, or psychological' (Reisinger, 1994: 24). From an anthropological perspective, culture is much more than the rituals, ceremonies and dances residents might perform for tourists at cultural centres or visitor attractions. The richer meaning of culture refers to those activities associated with many private and unknown traditions that are part of the local person's daily life (Fridgen, 1996). Mathieson and Wall (1982) suggested that culture comprises the conditioning elements of behaviour as well as the products of that behaviour. Therefore, ethnic tourism is defined as the absorption by tourists of features resembling the lifestyles of societies observed through such phenomena as house styles, crafts, farming equipment and dress (Smith, 1989). The underlying motivation for ethnic tourism emphasizes understanding contrasting ways of life and the associated interchange of knowledge and ideas (Pigram, 1993). Thus, cultural elements such as handicrafts, gastronomy, traditions, history, music, dance and architecture, whether unmanaged or staged specifically for visitors, can be major visitor attractions.

Ethnic tourism is part of cultural tourism, which is 'a form of recreation combining cultural and natural resources that is marketed to the public in terms of "quaint" customs of indigenous and often exotic peoples' (Smith, 1989: 2). However, the nature of ethnicity is more complex than it might seem at first sight. In the field of anthropology, ethnicity does not constitute a new domain of research but tourism is a challenge to the adequacy of conventional cultural theory (Cohen, 1978). There are two basic perspectives regarding the relationship between ethnicity and culture: primordial and situational (Hitchcock, 2001). The former views cultures as static and leads to the assumption that any change

109

imposed by contact with a politically dominant state must result in irreversible acculturation. The situational perspective, on the other hand, involves understanding the process by which ethnic identities and boundaries are created, modified and maintained (Barth, 1969). Wood (1980) indicates that culture should not be viewed as being a concrete entity acted upon by forces from outside but, rather, as sets of symbols, or as webs of significance and meaning. Culture is not a thing, but a process. Ethnic identity is a feeling 'subject to ebb and flow' (Poole, 1997: 133).

Cultural tourism has long been regarded as a mild oxymoron by some researchers. According to anthropologists, tourists are generally ill-prepared to visit other cultures. Tourists tend to lack information about ethnic cultures and are usually naive about what to expect and how to behave (Fridgen, 1996). The prevailing assumption is that any attempt to use cultural elements to accommodate tourists will cheapen or trivialize the presentation and interpretation of ethnic arts and heritage (Kelly, 1994). Tourism research related to ethnicity has concentrated upon describing and understanding the impacts of tourism on host societies (Moscardo and Pearce, 1999). A number of studies have concluded that ethnic tourism is in danger of consuming the phenomena on which it is based (see, for example, Altman, 1989; van den Berghe and Keyes, 1984). Ethnic tourism practice may destroy the host's culture or may calcify a culture into a 'frozen' picture of the past. Cultures are named and stereotyped. The visitors seek to see representations of the culture and the host society provides access to the expected symbols.

On the other hand, research on ethnic tourism also unveils positive impacts: tourism can promote the restoration of arts, revitalize skills, foster creativity and provide a platform for communities to present themselves positively (Cohen, 1988; Graburn, 1984; Pitchford, 1995). McKean (1973), writing on cultural tourism in Bali, Indonesia, stimulated a reshaping of common perceptions. He concluded that tourism was strengthening the arts in Bali and that, as a result of tourism, there were more dancers, musicians, wood carvers and other crafts persons than there otherwise would have been. Furthermore, he suggested that the Balinese were quite successful in maintaining the boundary between what belonged to their culture and what could be presented to tourists. 'Cultural involution' was proposed as a term to indicate that culture is mutable and that tourism infuses new meanings for local cultures, adding value both economically and psychologically to cultural expressions previously largely taken for granted. Another example is Esman's (1984) study of Louisiana, which suggests that tourism has led to the re-creation of Cajun identity and helped perpetuate an ethnic boundary that might otherwise have disappeared due to acculturation.

The terms 'touristic culture' and 'touristification' were proposed by Picard (1990) in reference to situations where tourism is so pervasive that it has become an integral part of everyday life. In such situations, the interaction with tourists may be a central component in the definition of ethnic identity. Picard (1995) showed that the Balinese have come to objectify their culture in terms of the arts and to evaluate tourism impact in terms of whether the arts are flourishing or not. The convergence of tourism and culture in the late twentieth century was presented by Richards (1996: 12) as a pragmatic *fait accompli*, and Richards went on to suggest that 'in spite of reservations about the potential negative impacts of tourism on culture, it seems that tourism and culture are inseparable'.

Authenticity and commodification

Authenticity can be defined as 'a desired experience or benefit associated with visits to certain types of tourism destinations. It is presumed to be the result of an encounter with true, uncommercialized, everyday life in a culture different than that of the visitor' (Smith, 1989: 31). It has become a major public concern and a topic that has received increasing attention across the social sciences over several decades. The relationship between history and heritage (Lowenthal, 1985; 1996), the portrayal of aboriginal peoples in Canada (Butler and Hinch, 1996; Li and Hinch, 1998) and Australia (Altman, 1989), and the contested interpretations of the significance of place (Tunbridge and Ashworth, 1996) are three examples among many. In tourism research, perspectives have varied from those of Boorstin (1964), who saw tourists as being duped and seduced to visit contrived attractions, to MacCannell (1976), who viewed tourists as modern pilgrims in search of the authentic, to Wang (1999), who argued that there are different types of authenticity, to Cohen (1988), who suggested that authenticity is of differing importance to different market segments. Authenticity is, therefore, a slippery and contested term. Handler and Linnekin (1991) proposed that the concept of authenticity as 'a red herring', of spurious essentialism, because all culture is mere social construction, constantly re-invented to serve particular purposes. Preston (1999) argued that authenticity is not equal to historical accuracy and that tradition is not equal to truth. The argument challenges the conventional dichotomy that authenticity is conceived either as something objective, passively inherited, embodied and transmitted, or as the purely contemporary product of human self-consciousness. Thus, the authentic is not a fixed property of an object or a situation, but is a negotiated attribute with multiple dimensions whose status is evaluated differently by different assessors.

The term 'commodification' is used to refer to situations in which a price is placed on artefacts or experiences which were previously not for sale so that cultural expressions become marketable tourism products. The commodification of tourism has been criticized as the 'bastardization' and 'pollution' of previously authentic ethnic cultures for the purpose of touristic display (Wood, 1998). Touristic ethnicity, in other words, is phoney ethnicity, as seen in so-called 'airport art' and fake ethnic souvenirs. Such tourism is seen as being a 'development which has the power to dilute unique and authentic traditions with standardised stereotypes tailored to the exotic yearnings of the Western traveller' (Oakes, 1992: 3).

Recent studies suggested a more complex perspective: that commodification and authenticity are not a dichotomous pair of concepts. Commodification does not necessarily destroy the meaning of cultural products, either for the locals or for the tourists (Cohen, 1988). Commodification of cultural expressions can be interpreted as a means of marking identity and a step in the finding of the true self through the appropriation of heritage. Furthermore, if hosts are to benefit economically from tourism, it is essential that money is extracted from their visitors.

One of the most notable deficiencies in the existing literature is a lack of attention to the concept of authentication. In other words, there is a dearth of research that seeks to understand who authenticates cultural tourism and tourism resources: the indigenous people, governments at various levels, tourists, or other participants in the tourism system? This chapter suggests, by using a case study of ethnic visitor attractions in Hainan, China, that the concept of authentication not only provides a way of avoiding personal value-laden judgements of authenticity, it is also a practical way of addressing issues of authenticity.

Dimensions of authenticity and authentication

Folk villages are purpose-built visitor attractions that provide visitors with access to expressions of folk culture for a fee. They are essentially small theme parks in which the theme is ethnicity. Folk villages constitute one of the most visible manifestations of ethnic tourism in Hainan, and are probably the most common sites of interaction between members of ethnic minorities and tourists. As such, they provide significant and convenient points of access for the investigation of relationships between tourism and ethnic cultures.

Among the many groups of people with interests in tourism in folk villages, four key stakeholders were identified for investigation:

- governments at various levels
- tourism businesses, that is, the folk village managers
- visitors

■ ethnic communities, in this case represented by dancers performing in the folk villages.

Building upon the work of Swain (1989), it is suggested that stakeholders, in their evaluation and attribution of authenticity, may be assessed according to their positions on five continua:

1 *Spontaneity versus commercialism*: this is essentially an indicator of the degree of commodification (Wood, 1997).
2 *Economic development versus cultural preservation*: development implies change and although many changes may be desired, not all changes are desirable. This dimension thus suggests a possible tension and trade-off between economic enhancement and cultural maintenance.
3 *Cultural evolution versus museumification (the 'freezing' of culture)*: dynamic cultures are not static but evolve. Thus, although there are signs and symbols with strong associations with particular ethnic groups, this perspective suggests a more 'situational' view of culture (Hitchcock, 2001; Rex, 1986), with ethnicity being continually renegotiated.
4 *Ethnic autonomy versus state regulation*: in the case of ethnic minorities, this dimension contrasts the common desire of minority peoples to control their own destinies in the face of the power that is commonly vested in the majority and the state (Oakes, 1992; 1998);
5 *Mass tourism versus sustainable cultural development*: this dimension contrasts a desire to seek tourism development at almost any cost against a perspective that sees tourism as one possible means of contributing to the well-being of communities, economically, environmentally and socially.

These continua constitute paradoxes and tensions within cultural tourism, and they occur because of the inherent contradictions between stability and change that are found in processes of development. The situation is further complicated by the fact that vibrant cultures are not static but evolve through time. For example, the concepts of spontaneity and commercialism appear to be antithetical. However, it can be countered that commodification may actually be a mechanism that can be used to protect cultural resources and revitalize indigenous cultures. Furthermore, fees may be charged for some cultural experiences and not for others. Destinations that selectively transform cultural resources into tangible products, including visitor attractions, not only facilitate the exchange of cultural experiences for a financial return, but they also have the potential to create a situation in which sustainable development can be promoted through the careful management of resources. Although ethnic communities may be highly vulnerable to the commercial exploitation of their culture, this does not mean that all commercialism is undesirable. In fact, even though there are risks, ethnic communities stand to benefit significantly from tourism through the associated economic development.

Standardization of ethnic culture through state regulation can lead to the production of staged events such as folk dance performances and costumed photo sessions. However, a focus on the ethnic minority as a tourism resource may also serve as a basis for negotiations between the state and minority communities. Thus, cultural tourism may provide minority groups with a forum for making claims about themselves that may eventually be turned into enhanced local autonomy.

Tourists often expect ethnic minorities to be quaintly traditional in a state of 'museumification'. While some social and cultural changes are likely to result from tourism and may even be desired, economic development may act as a catalyst for cultural preservation through the enhanced values that are accorded to traditional ways. Thus, at the same time, economic benefits may enhance local standards of living and contribute to the conservation of aspects of ethnic culture.

Mass tourism may cause environmental degradation and a potential clash between cultures. However, selectively choosing or excluding expressions of culture for presentation to tourists may keep sacred or special aspects of culture from being denigrated by mass tourism. Furthermore, staged performances in purpose-built tourist villages or other predetermined locations, may relieve pressures of mass tourism on places that are culturally or environmentally sensitive (Buck, 1978; MacCannell, 1973).

As is implied by the above discussion, the five dimensions in the framework are neither distinct nor easy to quantify. Furthermore, it is not suggested that any one of these dimensions or any particular polar position is inherently superior to another. However, it is suggested that together they provide a more tractable way of approaching authenticity. These components are presented in the form of a conceptual model in Figure 7.1. In this chapter, these dimensions are used to organize the perspectives of the stakeholders in cultural tourism in Hainan folk villages.

The data for the study were collected in summer 1999 using a variety of research methods. They can be briefly summarized as follows:

1 Locations of folk villages were identified by examining tourism brochures and interviewing tourism authorities.
2 All folk villages were visited, photographed and inventories of their tourism offerings were made (a total of twelve villages, three of them had

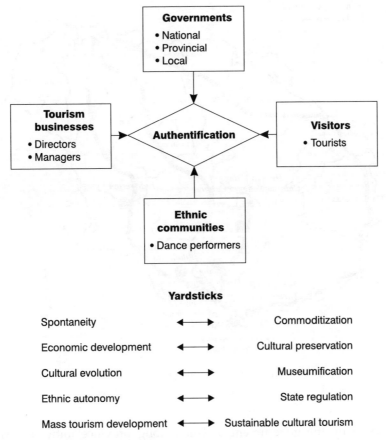

Yardsticks

Spontaneity	◄——►	Commoditization
Economic development	◄——►	Cultural preservation
Cultural evolution	◄——►	Museumification
Ethnic autonomy	◄——►	State regulation
Mass tourism development	◄——►	Sustainable cultural tourism

Figure 7.1 A conceptual framework for authentification

gone out of business). A map was constructed of the distribution of villages. Managers of the folk villages were interviewed to ascertain information on their perceptions of authenticity.

3 Interviews were conducted with employees of folk villages and, for three sites, with visitors. A total of 139 employees in the folk villages were interviewed (the majority were dance performers). A survey was conducted with visitors to three selected villages and a total of 586 surveys were completed and returned.

Ethnic tourism in Hainan

Hainan is a large tropical island located off the southern coast of China. It has a total land area of 33 900 square kilometres (Figure 7.2). The island was

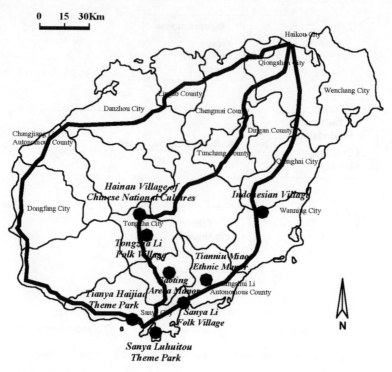

Figure 7.2   A map of Hainan and the folk villages

administered by the government of Guangdong province until 1988 when it became a province. As a special economic zone (SEZ), Hainan is more readily accessible to investors and travellers than most parts of China. While SEZ status has resulted in mixed success with respect to economic development, the ready access to both people and investments that this designation affords is advantageous to tourism. Hainan's tropical climate, splendid beaches, spas, attractive landscapes, cuisine and cultural diversity constitute a solid base on which tourism can be built. Indeed, tourism is already an important economic sector in Hainan. There is a substantial complement of excellent hotels and supporting infrastructure, such as highways and airports. The number of visitors and total visitor expenditures have been expanding annually, the former having grown substantially from just over 750 000 in 1987 to nearly 5 million in 1996 (Chen, 1998) and over 7 million in 2001.

Nonetheless, the Hainan tourism industry faces many challenges. Most visitors come from mainland China and the number of international visitors continues to be small. While the number of domestic visitors has increased, occupancy rates in hotels have declined and many, if not most, hotels operate at a loss. There is a difficulty in finding skilled labour in Hainan and migrants from the mainland take many tourism positions. Members of ethnic minorities, who could make an important and distinctive contribution to tourism, are minimally employed in tourism except for some involvement in the informal sector. Thus, while Hainan has great tourism potential, this potential has yet to be realized.

There are fifty-five ethnic minorities in China that are officially recognized by the Chinese government. They make up 8 per cent of the population, totalling about 96 million people and occupying about 65 per cent of China's total area (Sofield and Li, 1998). While minorities are usually accorded low status in China, tourism has become the most promising industry for Chinese ethnic community development (Swain, 1993).

In Hainan, the Li minority numbers more than 1 million people. Hainan is also home to other ethnic groups, including Miao and Hui with a population of approximately 60 000 and 10 000 respectively (Hainan Tour Atlas, 1997). Minority populations are concentrated in the south-central part of the island, in the Li and Miao Autonomous Prefecture. The prefecture covers an area of 1169 square kilometres and has a population of 100 000, 59 per cent of whom are Li (Hainan Tour Atlas, 1997). In addition, there are locations in Hainan with Hui (Muslim) and Indonesian Chinese minorities. Although minority populations are not

Figure 7.3 The gate of Hainan folk village in Baoting County

heavily involved in tourism, their existence is widely publicized in tourism brochures. A number of folk villages have been established where song and dance performances, the enactment of ceremonies, and the availability of ethnic foods and souvenirs provide opportunities for visitors to become acquainted with ethnic cultures (Figure 7.3).

Key issues in the authentication of ethnic tourism in Hainan

Space does not permit the full reporting of all the findings of the research project. Some highlights of the results will be presented for each of the four main stakeholder groups across most of the five continua identified in the framework. In this way, differences in the positions of the stakeholders with respect to ethnic tourism, particularly at folk village attractions, will be revealed.

Governments

National, provincial and local governments all play a part in tourism. At the national level, because national unity is the major guideline when developing ethnic tourism, control is an important issue in the presentation of culture. The national government plays a dual role in authenticating the cultural resources. On the one hand, it supports cultural distinctiveness for economic development, particularly of tourism. On the other hand, it suppresses any 'true' autonomous rights. In terms of commodification, the national government standardizes ethnic markers to fill a symbolic and commercial niche for public gaze. Ethnic attractions, such as tourist folk villages, have been commodified with the support of state policies. In terms of cultural evolution, the policies of the national government seek to 'fossilize' certain aspects of cultural tradition, drawing distinct boundaries around local customs, fixing them in time and space, and ensuring they remain encased as exhibits for the modern tourists to observe and appreciate. State policies also encourage the Li to be more 'developed' and 'modernized'. The direction of evolution can be seen as a process of 'Hanification' in which the Li minority is subsumed into the Han majority. The national government places great emphasis on job creation, therefore, cultural tourism is viewed as one of the best ways to minimize the high unemployment rate in ethnic communities. Economic functions have been given precedence and cultural preservation has not received much attention from the national government.

At the provincial level the focus has also been on economic development and tourism has been identified as Hainan's leading economic sector. The rapid development of tourism holds out the prospect of substantial benefits to the Li communities. Although Li folk villages have been built in response to increased interest from domestic tourists, most administrative positions are occupied by Han people who generally have little knowledge of Li culture. The provincial government pays little attention to the negative sides of commodification and museumification of ethnic cultures. Instead, mass tourism is highly encouraged by the provincial government. Although sustainable development plans for Hainan have been proposed by the provincial government, it is not clear how these will be implemented.

In the past, agriculture was essentially the only source of income for the Li communities. Tourism is, therefore, a novel idea for the local government and the impacts on the aboriginal communities have yet to be appreciated. Local government plays a passive role in finding a balance between culture and commodification.

Tourism businesses

Village managers pay more attention to attracting and satisfying the tourists than to presenting authentic aspects of Li culture. The management of the folk villages insists on 'livening things up' so that the visitors will not get bored. They have reduced the length of the 'traditional' dance and incorporated a visitor participation programme at the end. Some employees in the newer villages who wear Li clothing are not of Li origin and, for some, ethnic clothing has become a business uniform and the 'traditional' dance performances have become 'manufactured' routines. Ethnic presentation is in a state of 'museumification', portraying traditional aspects of Li culture as ancient, exotic and fossilized.

Since the business hinges upon the number of tourist arrivals, mass tourism is used to exploit ethnicity for economic purposes. Although tourism businesses could play a key role in balancing cultural preservation and economic development, profit is the major concern. Folk villages have become a combination of ethnic presentations and sales outlets from the numerous vendor stands. The manipulation of ethnic dance programmes and other ethnic cultural events to serve economic interests has resulted in the loss of authenticity and educational value. Spectacle and entertainment are emphasized and authenticity appears to be a flexible notion in folk villages. The concept of sustainable cultural tourism is not widely appreciated or applied.

Visitors

Almost all the tourists (98 per cent) come from mainland China and visit folk villages as part of organized tours. Direct contact with the ethnic minority is limited and tourism businesses almost always play an intermediary role. Their stop at a folk village is only one of many places visited on a three- or four-day excursion.

Although tourists are interested in ethnic cultures, the majority have little knowledge of ethnicity. They usually lack the time and the depth of experience to understand the more complex and intricate aspects of ethnic culture. They are not well prepared for a tour of a village and their knowledge on ethnicity is generally superficial. As such, it is more appropriate to see them as 'coincidental' cultural tourists rather than as true cultural tourists.

Although tourists expect to see non-commercial and non-contrived aspects of ethnic presentation in the villages, the place they visit is, in fact, a highly commercial attraction. Most visitors enjoy their experiences as the villages endeavour to satisfy the touristic gaze and turn ethnicity into 'hyper-reality'.

Ethnic communities

In this research, attention was focused upon dancers as community representatives. In fact the performances are spectacles and the dancers are a young, beautiful and predominantly female subset of Li people. Their performances emphasize romantic aspects of the Li lifestyle and, as such, cannot represent Li culture in its entirety. Nevertheless, dancers are appropriate individuals to consult concerning the authenticity of cultural tourism because they share aspects of their culture with tourists, interact with tourists, are positioned on the interface between tourism and culture on an ongoing basis and have familiarity with the compromises and trade-offs required to provide an attractive tourism product.

Economic matters are most important for dance performers, and skills in ethnic dancing are turned into a good way to make money. They are paid relatively well and the village proprietors strive to make a profit: they are asked to perform for as long as tourists visit the village. Mass tourism is seen by dancers as being an optimal strategy since the business prospects for dance performers hinge upon the number of tourist arrivals.

Conclusion

This chapter has provided an overview of the diverse perspectives concerning authenticity of experience as applied to ethnic tourism in general and visitor attractions in particular. It has been suggested that authenticity is not an attribute that is inherent to a place or product, such as a tourist destination or visitor attraction. Rather, it is a status that is ascribed externally. Nevertheless, although authenticity is difficult to define, managers of cultural visitor attractions will be expected to provide authentic experiences as judged by many of their visitors, and failure to do so may result in a reduced level of visitor satisfaction. However, the visitors themselves may have divergent views on authenticity and these may differ from those held by other stakeholders, including members of the ethnic group whose culture is being shared with the visitors. As such, the process of authentication merits much more attention than it has hitherto received.

A conceptual framework has been presented, and its utility illustrated through application to ethnic visitor attractions in Hainan, China. It has been shown that different stakeholders exhibit different positions with respect to the various paradoxes associated with authenticity. These positions serve different interests. Thus, for example, in the case of Hainan folk villages, managers have predominantly commercial concerns and strive to make a profit, governments see tourism as a means to stimulate economic development and the employees of the villages welcome economic opportunities in a poor area where job opportunities are few. The tourists do not have high expectations and are largely not in Hainan primarily as cultural tourists. They generally enjoy their visits but would welcome more detailed explanations of the culture that they experience and, in some cases, the availability of more interesting souvenirs. Culture is presented as a series of spectacles and only limited concern appears to exist at present for cultural conservation or for sustainable tourism development more broadly conceived. Although conflicts appear to be few at present, it would be a constructive step to encourage dialogue between representatives of the differing stakeholder groups, perhaps through the organization of 'round tables' so that they can appreciate each other's positions, perhaps leading to an enhancement of their mutual interests.

Is the Li culture as portrayed in the folk village attractions of Hainan authentic? This seemingly simple question does not have a simple answer. On the evidence that has been presented, strong cases can be made for both an affirmative and a negative response. Authenticity is not a one-dimensional concept that lends itself to simple interpretation. Nevertheless, it is possible to explore the issues that underpin authentication, as has been done in this chapter. Authenticity is elusive (and often illusive): the investigation of authentication offers a tractable way forward.

References

Altman, J. (1989). Tourism dilemmas for aboriginal Australians. *Annals of Tourism Research*, **16**, 449–456.

Barth, F. (1969). *Ethnic Groups and Boundaries*. Norwegian University Press.

Boorstin, D. (1964). *A Guide to Pseudo-Events in America*. Harper and Row.

Buck, R. (1978). Boundary maintenance revisited: tourist experiences in an Old Order Amish community. *Rural Sociology*, **43**, 195–207.

Butler, R. and Hinch, T. (1996). *Tourism and Indigenous Peoples*. International Thomson Business Press.

Chen, Y. (1998). South China's legendary island. *China Tourism*, **2**, 6–7.

Cohen, E. (1988). Authenticity and commoditization in tourism. *Annals of Tourism Research*, **15**, 371–386.

Cohen, R. (1978). Ethnicity: problem and focus in Anthropology. *Annual Review of Anthropology*, **7**, 379–403.

Esman, M. (1984). Tourism as ethnic preservation: the Cajuns of Louisiana. *Annals of Tourism Research*, **11**, 451–467.

Fridgen, J. (1996). *Dimensions of Tourism*. Educational Institute of American Hotel and Motel Association.

Graburn, N. (1984). The evolution of tourist arts. *Annals of Tourism Research*, **11**, 393–449.

Hainan Tour Atlas (1997). *Hainan Tour Atlas*. Measurement Publishing Ltd.

Handler, R. and Linnekin, J. (1984). Tradition, genuine or spurious. *Journal of American Folklore*, **97**, 273–290.

Hitchcock, M. (2001). Anthropological reflections on the study of tourism. In *Contemporary Perspectives on Tourism* (G. Wall, ed.) pp. 109–128, University of Waterloo.

Jackson, P. (1999). Commodity cultures: the traffic in things. *Transactions of the Institute of British Geographers*, **24**, 95–108.

Kelly, R. (1994). The cultural tourist: friend or foe? *Focus on Culture: Statistics Canada*, **6**, 1–3.

Li, Y. and Hinch, T. (1998). Ethnic tourism attractions and their prospects for sustainable development at two sites in China and Canada. *Asia Pacific Journal of Tourism Research*, **2**, 5–17.

Lowenthal, D. (1985). *The Past is a Foreign Country*. Cambridge University Press.

Lowenthal, D. (1996). *The Possessed by the Past: Heritage Crusade and the Spoils of History*. Free Press.

MacCannell, D. (1973). Staged authenticity: arrangements of social space in tourist settings. *American Journal of Sociology*, **79**, 589–603.

MacCannell, D. (1976). *The Tourist: A New Theory of the Leisure Class*. Schocken Books.

MacCannell, D. (1984). Reconstructed ethnicity: tourism and cultural identity in Third World communities. *Annals of Tourism Research*, **11**, 375–391.

Mathieson, A. and Wall, G. (1982). *Tourism: Economic, Physical, and Social Impacts*. Longman.

McKean, P. (1973). Cultural involution: tourists, Balinese, and the process of modernization in anthropological perspective. PhD thesis, Brown University.

Moscardo, G. and Pearce, P. (1999). Understanding ethnic tourists. *Annals of Tourism Research*, **26**, 416–434.

Oakes, T. (1992). Cultural geography and Chinese ethnic tourism. *Journal of Cultural Geography*, **12**, 2–17.

Oakes, T. (1998). *Tourism and Modernity in China*. Routledge.

Picard, M. (1990). Cultural tourism in Bali: cultural performances as visitor attraction. *Indonesia*, **49**, 37–74.

Picard, M. (1995). Cultural heritage and tourist capital: cultural tourism in Bali. In *International Tourism: Identity and Change* (M. Lanfant, J. Allcock and E. Bruner, eds) pp. 44–66, Sage Studies in International Sociology.

Picard, M. and Wood, R. (1997). *Tourism, Ethnicity, and the State in Asian and Pacific Societies*. University of Hawaii Press.

Pigram, J. (1993). Planning for tourism in rural areas: bridging the policy implementation gap. In *Tourism Research: Critiques and Challenges* (D. Pearce and R. Butler, eds) pp. 156–174, Routledge.

Pitchford, S. (1995). Ethnic tourism and nationalism in Wales. *Annals of Tourism Research*, **22**, 35–52.

Poole, M. (1997). In search of ethnicity in Ireland. In *In Search of Ireland: A Cultural Geography* (B. Graham, ed.) pp. 151–173, Routledge.

Preston, R. (1999). Reflections on culture, history, and authenticity. In *Theorizing the Americanist Tradition* (L. Valentine and R. Darnell, eds) pp. 150–162, University of Toronto Press.

Reisinger, Y. (1994). Tourist-host contact as a part of cultural tourism. *World Leisure and Recreation*, **36**, 24–28.

Rex, J. (1986). *Race and Ethnicity*. Open University Press.

Richards, G. (1996). *Cultural Tourism in Europe*. CABI.

Smith, V. (1989). *Host and Guests: The Anthropology of Tourism*. University of Pennsylvania Press.

Sofield, T. and Li, F. (1998). Tourism development and cultural policies in China. *Annals of Tourism Research*, **25**, 362–392.

Swain, M. (1989). Developing ethnic tourism in Hunnan, China: Shilin Sani. *Tourism Recreation Research*, **14**, 33–39.

Swain, M. (1993). Women producers of ethnic arts. *Annals of Tourism Research*, **20**, 32–51.

Tunbridge, J. and Ashworth, G. (1996). *Dissonant Heritage: Management of the Past as a Resource in Conflict*. Wiley.

Van den Berghe, P. and Keyes, C. (1984). Introduction: tourism and re-created ethnicity. *Annals of Tourism Research*, **11**, 343–352.

Wall, G. (1996). Perspectives on tourism in selected Balinese villages. *Annals of Tourism Research*, **23**, 123–137.

Walle, A. (1998). *Cultural Tourism: A Strategic Focus*. Westview Press.

Wang, N. (1999). Rethinking authenticity in tourism experience. *Annals of Tourism Research*, **26**, 349–370.

Wood, R. (1980). International tourism and cultural change in Southeast Asia. *Economic Development and Cultural Change*, **28**, 561–581.

Wood, R. (1997). Tourism and the State. In *Tourism, Ethnicity, and the State in Asian and Pacific Societies* (M. Picard and R. Wood, eds) pp. 1–34, University of Hawaii Press.

Wood, R. (1998). Book review. Bali: cultural tourism and touristic culture. *Annals of Tourism Research*, **25**, 770–772.

8 Managing visitor impacts

Brian Garrod

Aims

The aims of this chapter are to:

- identify the importance of the notion of sustainability to visitor attractions
- highlight the relevance of visitor impacts to the issue of sustainability
- outline the major impacts of visitors on visitor attractions
- examine a range of tools for managing visitor impacts
- discuss the findings of a study of visitor impacts at Scottish visitor attractions.

Introduction

It is widely acknowledged that visitor attractions play an important, perhaps even pivotal, role in the world tourism industry. Large, often purpose-built visitor attractions are increasingly being employed as instruments of economic regeneration, particularly in run-down urban areas and in locations where traditional seaside tourism has been in decline. Even larger, destination-style, so-called 'mega-attractions' are also now appearing all over the world. These are often linked to the aspirations of governments to establish 'growth poles' in relatively underdeveloped areas (Disneyland Paris being a good example). Then there is the growing number of World Heritage sites, representing the 'crown jewels' of the world's natural and cultural heritage, and forming the mainstay of the tourism industry of many countries. At the other end of the scale, meanwhile, is a multitude of smaller visitor attractions, many of which are independently owned and operate almost on a casual basis. Such attractions often represent a major factor in drawing tourists to a particular destination. Visitors to the UK, for example, typically cite the desire to experience the nation's unique heritage and culture as the most important reason for their trip, and visitor attractions are clearly an important medium of such experiences.

Yet the visitor attractions sector currently faces the unenviable problem of being pulled between contradictory demands. On the one hand, many visitor attractions are based on specific natural, built, manufactured or cultural assets, the uniqueness and quality of which forms the core of their 'products'. Opening such sites to visitors carries with it the risk of exposing them to a range of potential visitor impacts, the consequence often being that visitors compromise the very things that they are coming to see. Even in purpose-built attractions, negative visitor impacts such as overcrowding and traffic congestion can serve to reduce the quality of the visitor experience. As with any other form of business, unless customers receive a product that satisfies their expectations, they will not return to purchase it again or recommend it to others.

On the other hand, it is axiomatic that visitor attractions need visitors in order to achieve their objectives, whether they are attempting to make profits for their owners, earn revenues to pay for the continuing protection and conservation of the site, educate the public or fulfil a wider social function. For many visitor attractions, particularly those that are purpose-built, opening to visitors is their fundamental *raison d'être*. For others, being open to the public for at least limited periods of the year is a feature of their ownership, especially when they are owned by membership organizations such as the National Trust in England and Wales. For others again, receiving paying visitors represents an economic lifeline, as without these visitors the assets the visitor attraction is based upon would inevitably have to be sold, converted to alternative uses or allowed to fall into disrepair.

The dilemma for visitor attractions is that, generally speaking, the greater the exposure of the site to visitors, the greater is the potential for negative visitor impacts to arise. The incidence of such impacts not only serves to threaten the continued economic viability of the visitor attraction as a commercial concern, but also raises serious questions about the sustainability of the attraction. At the core of the sustainability concept is the requirement that things of value should not be squandered by the present generation, but maintained for the benefit of future generations. If today's visitors damage the things they come to see, then those things will simply not be available for future generations to appreciate, enjoy and learn from.

Visitor impacts often pale into insignificance in comparison with the wider environmental threats that are faced by visitor attractions (Shackley, 1998). Historic buildings, for example, are under constant threat from the natural elements, the effects of pollution, the risk of fire and the ravages of time. Visitor impacts can, however, seriously exacerbate such problems. For example, the structural integrity of Craigeivar Castle in Scotland has been compromised literally by the weight of visitor numbers, whose unrelenting passage through the upper floors has left them unsafe for continued public access (Croft, 1994). Meanwhile, the growing volume of visitors to the Valley of the Kings near Luxor, Egypt, is thought to have been responsible for a major roof collapse in the tomb of Seti I. The presence of visitors at such fragile sites is clearly a mixed blessing in terms of achieving and maintaining sustainability. While visitors bring the revenues that many sites so badly need to fund their conservation and restoration efforts, they also bring with them impacts that can make the need for such efforts all the more real and urgent.

Sustainability requires that these contradictory demands are effectively tackled, and that a means is found of enabling both access to visitors and the effective protection of the site and its contents from being damaged by those visitors. Typically the response of visitor attractions has been to introduce some form of visitor management, the aim being to moderate the impacts of visitors while still enabling them to come onto the site, interact with whatever is to be found there and achieve a satisfying experience from their visit.

Types of visitor impact

Visitor attractions are subject to a wide range of negative visitor impacts. A report by the English Tourist Board (ETB, 1991) suggests that visitor impacts tend to fall into the following categories: overcrowding, wear and tear, traffic-related problems, impacts on local community and the impacts of visitor management itself on the authenticity of visitor attractions.

Overcrowding

The problem of overcrowding is highly dependent on the capacity of the site to receive visitors. When a visitor attraction becomes overcrowded, visitors begin to get under each other's feet, the result being that everyone finds it increasingly difficult to move around the site. Once visitors are no longer able to keep moving, queues will begin to form at bottlenecks. Typically such pressure points tend to make themselves evident in the admissions area, near popular exhibits or at particular locations such as shops, refreshment areas and toilets.

Overcrowding might therefore occur either at the level of the site as a whole or in particular parts of it. It can also be a persistent problem or, more usually, be restricted to particular times of the day and days of the year. A famous example of a visitor bottleneck was at the Jewel House of the Tower of London, where long queues would form at busy times as visitors attempted to view an impressive selection of British crown jewels. The problem has recently been addressed by a £10 million scheme involving 'travelators' that are switched on at busy times and allow each visitor only a fixed time to see each exhibit before they are whisked onwards (Shackley, 1999).

The impacts of overcrowding are typically evidenced by visitors feeling that they are unable to appreciate the character or ambience of a site, a reduced opportunity for visitors to see and do everything they want to and a consequent negative impact on visitor satisfaction. Of course, overcrowding is a highly subjective issue. What feels overcrowded to one person may not seem overcrowded to another, while what is considered to be too long a queue for one person will be perfectly acceptable to another and they will happily wait in it.

Wear and tear

This group of visitor impacts includes trampling, handling, humidity, temperature, pilfering and graffiti. Trampling involves visitors walking on sensitive parts of the site, ranging from carefully manicured lawns to antique carpets in stately homes, to the very fabric of ancient monuments. A good example of the latter is the erosion caused by visitors walking along the top of Hadrian's Wall, the remains of a Roman defensive structure in northern England. Trampling may be deliberate or accidental, and is especially likely when the site becomes congested. Handling, on the other hand, is more likely to be a deliberate act on the

127

part of the visitor who cannot resist putting sticky or moist fingers on fragile items, even when they are requested not to do so.

Humidity and temperature, meanwhile, are always unintentional on the part of the visitor; however, they are often unavoidable if the site is to be opened to visitors in significant numbers. The problem is not generally the levels of humidity and temperature themselves, which can quite easily be controlled, but the rapid changes in environmental conditions that tend to occur as visitors move around the site. A good example of the impact of humidity on a visitor attraction is the damage caused to the ancient wall paintings in the tomb of Queen Nefertari in Egypt. The presence of visitors in the tomb raises the level of humidity significantly, causing the paint to flake away from the limestone surface of the inner walls of the tomb. The effect has been so severe that a limit of only 150 visitors per day has been set, with visitors taken into the tomb in small groups, each permitted to stay inside for a maximum of sixteen minutes.

Pilfering and graffiti, meanwhile, are intentional acts on the part of the visitor. Pilfering can range from petty theft in the gift shop or cafeteria, to the theft of valuable exhibits. While the former might be considered a relatively minor problem in terms of the protection of the site, it may nevertheless have important implications for the cash flow and general financing of the attraction. Similarly, graffiti can range from being a minor blemish on the ambience of the site to becoming a very real issue in terms of the protection of the site. For example, several of the stones comprising Stonehenge, a prehistoric monument in southern England, have been daubed with paint that has proved impossible to remove without further damaging the stones. The paint will take many centuries to be weathered away by the natural elements.

Traffic-related problems

Most visitors arrive at visitor attractions by car or by coach. Yet many sites pre-date the invention of the automobile and were not therefore designed to cope with the traffic generated by visitors. Others are located within city centres, where visitor-generated traffic may exacerbate existing traffic problems. Traffic-related problems include traffic congestion, pollution from vehicle exhausts, the increased risk of accidents, damage to verges and lawns due to poor parking, the restriction of access by thoughtlessly parked cars and coaches, and vibration damage to buildings. Traffic problems may be persistent or merely occasional, evidencing themselves only at peak times. They may also be restricted to the site itself or, particularly if the attraction has only a limited amount of parking space, spill over into the locality.

Small historic cities are particularly vulnerable to traffic-related visitor impacts, with relatively small and enclosed city centres being swamped by visitors in the high season. Canterbury in south-east England is a good example of a small historic city beleaguered by visitors, many of whom arrive as part of a coach party. Before a series of traffic management measures were introduced during the 1980s and 1990s, traffic in the city centre was increasingly being brought to gridlock by coaches trying to set down and pick up passengers (Curtis, 1998).

Impacts on the local community

Many visitor impacts can spill out into the local community. The potential for poorly parked cars and coaches to restrict access to neighbouring areas has already been mentioned. Another possible impact on the local community may result from the thoughtless and antisocial behaviour of visitors. This may range from visitors unwittingly trespassing on private property, to loutish behaviour by visitors who have consumed too much alcohol in the visitor attraction bar. Visitors may be accused of rudeness towards local people, treating them without due respect or even as curiosities laid on as part of the visitor attraction experience. Visitors in large numbers can also cause congestion in local facilities, such as shopping areas or leisure centres. As a result the local community can come to feel besieged by visitors and perceive them to have a negative influence on the local community.

At the same time it is possible to envisage impacts running in the opposite direction, that is, local people having a negative impact on the visitor experience. For example, visitors may feel unwelcome in the vicinity of the visitor attraction because of the way they are treated by the local residents.

Impacts of visitor management on the authenticity of the attraction

Interestingly, the ETB report also identifies the potential of visitor management itself to have damaging impacts on the authenticity of the visitor attraction and the experience it offers. These impacts may take the form of:

- the provision of visitor facilities (for example, direction signs or handrails) that may have a detrimental effect on the ambience of the attraction
- adaptations made in order to enhance visitor flow around the site that may be considered architecturally inappropriate or felt to compromise the architectural integrity of the site
- adaptations made to enable access by disabled visitors (for example, lifts or ramps) that may necessitate the use of inappropriate equipment or materials

129

- the need to take measures to ensure visitor health and safety that conflict with the conservation objectives of the site
- a tendency towards intrusive interpretation or interpretation that is not faithful to the history of the site.

These types of impact might be considered even more invidious than those outlined above, since they raise the possibility that taking action to remedy visitor impacts might actually result in a worse situation than that which would have arisen in the absence of such efforts. The dilemma for visitor management, then, becomes not simply *how* to manage visitor impacts but *whether* to manage them.

Techniques for managing visitor impacts

The techniques of visitor management can be divided into those that are designed to regulate supply and those that are designed to manage demand for the visitor attraction.

Supply-side techniques

This group of techniques attempts, in a number of different ways, to increase the capacity of the site to receive visitors without being unduly damaged or the visitor experience otherwise being impaired.

Queue management

When the demand for the visitor attraction exceeds the capacity of the site to receive visitors, queues will begin. Typically these take the form of pedestrian queues outside admission points or lines of motor vehicles outside of the main gate. Queues can have a number of adverse impacts on the visitor experience (Barlow, 1999):

- Visitors may feel that their enjoyment of the experience offered by the attraction is impaired because they have had to spend a considerable amount of time in queues, either to enter the attraction or to see specific parts of it.
- Some potential visitors may turn away when they see the length of the admission queue; others may join the queue but become bored by its slowness and find something else to do instead.
- Other potential visitors may be put off from visiting the attraction because it has gained a reputation for lengthy queues.

- In order to try to eliminate the queues, staff may be forced to spend less time with each visitor; certain time-consuming features or services may have to be abandoned entirely.
- Staff may become demoralized because they have insufficient time to meet visitors' needs and provide a high-quality experience for every visitor.

Queue management is often the first response to the problem of excess demand, since most other visitor management techniques will take more time to implement. Queue management techniques include:

- snaking the queues, so that they appear to move faster
- providing literature and displays (perhaps audiovisual) to distract visitors while they queue
- bringing the queues further into the property, so that visitors can experience its ambience while they wait
- entertaining the visitors while they wait in the queue.

None of these measures will reduce the size of the queue: they will merely make waiting in the queue more bearable. As such, queue management cannot realistically be viewed as a long-term remedy to the problems of overcrowding and congestion.

Making capacity more flexible

Given a sufficient length of time, visitor attractions can take a number of measures to make their existing capacity more flexible. This can help to reduce or even eliminate queues. Techniques include:

- extending opening hours, or opening for more days of the year
- opening more admission tills when demand is high, and closing these off when demand subsides
- increasing staffing levels in periods of high demand, enabling visitor needs to be met more effectively when the site is busy
- opening additional areas within cafeterias and other facilities during busy times
- offering or prescribing certain routes, thereby facilitating the free flow of visitors around the site
- cross-training staff so that they can work in the busiest areas of the attraction according to demand.

Such measures can be highly effective. However, in the case of many smaller, heritage-based attractions, making capacity more flexible can be extremely problematic. Physical restrictions in the entry hall, for example, may limit the number of admission tills that it is possible to operate.

Increasing capacity

In the longer term, visitor attractions may seek to address the problem of persistent excess demand by investing in additional physical capacity. This can range from building an extension to the gift shop, to constructing an additional building to house particular parts of the collection or visitor activities. The danger, however, is that such efforts may serve to reduce the authenticity of the site, reducing the quality of the visitor experience and potentially compromising efforts to conserve the resource base of the attraction for future generations.

Site hardening

Other impacts, particularly various forms of wear and tear, are traditionally addressed through the use of 'site hardening' techniques. These include:

- employing security people and room stewards (often volunteers at heritage-based attractions) to provide a physical presence at sensitive locations
- roping-off vulnerable parts of the site
- the use of glass, perspex or other materials to encase artefacts or divide off certain areas
- strengthening footpaths
- covering carpets with protective materials
- use of prohibitive notices.

At the extreme, site hardening can even take the form of the removal of originals and their replacement with facsimiles. For example, visitors to Hereford Cathedral in western England get to see a facsimile of the ancient and fragile Mappa Mundi, which they can examine closely before they get to see the original which is safely cocooned in its purpose-built but less accessible display area.

Site hardening techniques can be extremely sophisticated, for example, the 'travelator' system installed at the Tower of London mentioned earlier. However, the problem with almost all site hardening is that it risks compromising the authenticity of the site. This may be a particular problem at heritage-based attractions, where a major element of the visitor experience may be to gain an insight into how the property may have looked in its heyday. The excessive use of such techniques may also run counter to the conservation objectives of the owners of the site.

Restrictive ticketing and quota systems

Perhaps the most extreme of the supply-side measures available to manage visitor impacts is ticketing that restricts the time of entry (requiring pre-booking), the length of stay, the size of groups, the number of visitors permitted per day, or some combination of these. Such measures may be introduced to try to combat overcrowding or address particular forms of wear and tear (such as trampling or visitor-induced humidity). An example is the tomb of Queen Nefertari in Egypt, referred to previously, where a daily quota of visitors has been set along with a maximum dwell time for each party. Visitor attractions are typically reluctant to introduce such measures since they tend to discourage certain types of visitor, particularly the independent visitor and small groups. The casual visitor, meanwhile, can be excluded entirely. Many managers of heritage visitor attractions, however, prefer such measures to the use of price incentives, which are widely considered to be even more distasteful.

Demand management techniques

This group of techniques aims to influence the number or behaviour of visitors in order to moderate their impact on the site and/or its associated artefacts.

Price incentives

One possible pricing technique for managing visitor impacts would be to use elevated admission prices to moderate overall levels of demand. Reducing the pressure of numbers could help to address problems such as overcrowding of the site, traffic congestion or trampling damage to footpaths. The use of elevated admission prices would also accord with the 'user pays' principle, which states that those responsible for using resources that are vulnerable to damage should be required to pay for the remediation of any user-induced impacts. Increased admission prices can also raise much needed revenue to fund the attraction's wider strategic goals, such as conservation of the site or public education.

A potential problem with using price incentives to manage overall levels of demand is that while the demand for visitor attractions tends to be relatively price elastic (responsive) at low prices, as admission prices rise above 'token' levels, demand tends to become increasingly price inelastic. In many cases, therefore, elevated admission prices would appear to be a rather blunt instrument in attempting to moderate demand in general.

Charging elevated prices for admission is also highly unpopular among visitor attraction managers. Indeed, to many in the heritage establishment, charging for admission at all is considered repugnant. Among the main reasons offered for this standpoint are that:

- charging elevated admission fees may conflict with the wider objectives of the visitor attraction, such as equality access to all social groupings or public education
- attractions do not have a legal right to charge for access to public land or public buildings, or a moral right to charge for access to one's own heritage
- charging for admission may lead to a bias of concern for those elements of our heritage that can most easily be 'sold' to visitors
- the cost of collecting admission charges may in some cases outweigh the revenues collected
- high admission charges may act as a disincentives for impulse, casual and repeat visitors
- secondary spend may fall if high admission charges are introduced
- charging may also reduce spending elsewhere in the local economy.

Even if raised admission charges are considered objectionable in respect of managing overall levels of demand, they may still be useful tools for managing the nature of demand. For example, price variations might be used to encourage demand at off-peak times and discourage it during the peaks. Special prices can be offered to certain types of visitor. Encouraging school groups, for example, might encourage further visits by their families (Barlow, 1999). It has also been argued that the level of admissions price can help to determine visitors' perceptions of the importance of the site and therefore their behaviour. If visitors pay a relatively high admission price they may be led to understand that they are visiting a particularly unique, pristine or spectacular site, and will need to behave respectfully towards it in the course of their visit (Fyall and Garrod, 1998).

Marketing

Other elements of the marketing mix than price can also be used to manage demand. Visits at off-peak times can be promoted through advertising or joint-ticketing arrangements; heavily used sites can be de-marketed and less intensively used sites marketed as alternatives. It might even be desirable to develop new visitor attractions to deflect pressure from more sensitive sites. This has been the strategy adopted by Canterbury in England, for example, where new purpose-built attractions have been developed outside of the city centre in an attempt to reduce the level of pedestrian overcrowding caused by visitors to the cathedral (Curtis, 1998).

Education and interpretation

Education and interpretation also have the potential to serve as tools for managing visitor impacts. Experience has shown that educating visitors about the negative impacts of certain forms of behaviour, informing them how to behave appropriately, and encouraging them to act accordingly, can have a critical influence on their behaviour both during and after the visit (Bramwell and Lane, 1993). The following advantages of this approach have been identified:

- People tend to react more positively to requests to refrain from certain forms of behaviour when they know and understand the reasons.
- Visitor impacts can be reduced by offering visitors a more engaging experience which not only informs them about how to act responsibly but also encourages them to act accordingly.
- Visitor movement both in time and space can be influenced, for example, by drawing attention to alternative routes around the sites, substitute attractions or different visit times.
- Raising the public's conservation ethic may pay longer-term dividends for the visitor attraction in terms of contributions to charities and other good causes related either directly or indirectly to the work of the visitor attraction.
- Educational and interpretive facilities can bring local economic benefits by employing local people, selling local products (such as local handicrafts), providing services (such as refreshments) and helping to diversify the local economy.
- Local community participation can also be enhanced through the provision of education and interpretation. For example, local people can help decide what to educate visitors about and what to interpret.

Education and interpretation would in many ways appear the ideal solution to visitor impacts. The major difficulty with this approach, however, is that the demand for visitor attractions is typically based on recreational rather than educational motivations. While it is true that some visitors will be motivated by the desire to learn about the things they are coming to see, the principal motivation for the typical visitor will be to relax, and to have fun with friends and family. Indeed, going to visitor attractions has been said to be more akin to window shopping than a learning experience. Under such circumstances it will probably always be difficult to influence visitors' behaviour by means of education and interpretation.

Case study: visitor impacts at Scottish visitor attractions

Visitor attractions are a critical component of the Scottish tourism industry. While only a small proportion of inbound tourists come to Scotland with the specific intention of visiting an attraction, once they have arrived a much larger proportion do so. Meanwhile, the relatively dispersed pattern of visitor attractions across Scotland is thought to help tempt tourists away from the 'honey pots' of the central belt, enabling the benefits of tourism to be spread to more peripheral areas (Smith, 1998). Visitor attractions also help to combat the problem of seasonality, increase secondary spending and provide wet weather facilities for tourists. At the same time, the Scottish visitor attraction sector is thought to be particularly vulnerable to visitor impacts, the sector comprising a large proportion of cultural and heritage attractions, with relatively few large, purpose-built, general leisure attractions.

With the aim of identifying the perceived range and severity of visitor impacts in Scottish visitor attractions, a postal survey of all 510 paid admission attractions was undertaken during the summer of 1999. The preliminary findings of the survey were then explored through interviews with a number of key informants, including representatives of the two largest owners of visitor attractions in Scotland, Historic Scotland and the National Trust for Scotland. Table 8.1 illustrates some of the main results of the survey. Statistical analysis was then performed to determine whether there was any relationship between the severity of various visitor impacts on the one hand, and characteristics of the visitor attraction, such as attraction type and visitor numbers, on the other.

A notable feature of Table 8.1 is the relatively low importance accorded to traffic-related problems. There would seem to be at least two possible explanations for this. The first relates to the large proportion of visitor attractions located in the more peripheral parts of the country, where population densities are lower and traffic problems are generally less problematic. A second possibility is that traffic-related impacts are more easily disregarded by visitor attractions, particularly during times when competition for visitors among attractions is intense, as has been the case in Scotland in recent years. Cars and coaches contain visitors, who are indisputably the lifeblood of visitor attractions. There is also an evident tendency among visitor attraction owners and managers to associate success with high or growing visitor numbers, rather than with more qualitative indicators such as educational impact or visitor satisfaction.

The behaviour of locals toward visitors registered the highest level of importance of any of the categories of impact included in the survey. This finding might be considered of real concern given that the reputed warmth of welcome shown by the Scottish people is often cited as a major strength of Scotland's tourism industry (Scottish Executive, 2000). It may also suggest

Table 8.1 Visitor impacts at Scottish visitor attractions*

Type of impact		Not/quite important (%)	Very/extremely important (%)
Occasional overcrowding	Whole site	67.8	32.2
	Parts of site	58.0	42.0
Persistent overcrowding	Whole site	64.1	35.9
	Parts of site	61.5	38.5
Wear and tear	Trampling	60.4	39.6
	Handling	56.4	43.6
	Humidity	56.0	44.0
	Temperature	57.5	42.5
	Pilfering	55.0	45.0
	Graffiti	63.7	36.3
Occasional traffic-related congestion	On-site	73.2	26.8
	In locality	75.0	25.0
Persistent traffic-related congestion	On-site	73.6	26.4
	In locality	72.5	27.5
Other traffic-related problems		63.5	36.5
Visitors' behaviour towards locals		57.9	42.1
Locals' behaviour towards visitors		41.8	58.2
Visitor management compromising authenticity of site		42.5	57.5

Note: * Figures exclude 'don't know' and nil responses.

that the traditional concern for the impacts of the behaviour of visitors towards locals may be misplaced, the more significant impacts in fact running in the opposite direction.

The potential for visitor management itself to have adverse impacts on the authenticity, ambience or character of the site registered the second highest degree of importance by respondents. This opens out a new dimension in the practice of visitor management, in that the task becomes complicated by the need to identify 'second-best' solutions to the problems faced. Because visitor management can itself have adverse impacts on the visitor attraction site, the task of visitor management becomes one of balancing the benefits and side effects of visitor management, rather than simply applying increasingly strict visitor management measures until visitor impacts are reduced to acceptable levels.

Visitor impacts by attraction type

Visitor impacts varied significantly by attraction type only in four cases: trampling, humidity, temperature and occasional overcrowding of parts of the site. Trampling was particularly associated with castles, gardens and historic houses, while humidity and temperature were associated mainly with historic houses, followed by museums and galleries, and then castles. These relationships would seem to make intuitive sense, given that these are the types of attraction that are most likely to contain fragile artefacts (such as the carpets of historic houses or certain exhibits in museums).

Occasional overcrowding of parts of the site was significantly more problematic in castles, with museums and galleries being among the least likely to experience such problems. That historic castles should be especially prone to overcrowding is not particularly surprising, since they tend to have been designed specifically to impede the flow of people around them rather than promote it. Museums and galleries, meanwhile, are often purpose-built, with the free flow of large numbers of visitors in mind.

No other visitor impact demonstrated a significant relationship with particular types of attractions, which would tend to suggest that no particular type of visitor attraction is entirely invulnerable to any of these impacts. The message here is that managers of visitor attractions should aim to address the full range of visitor impacts, including those that would not normally be considered important to their particular type of attraction.

Visitor impact by visitor numbers

Visitor impacts varied significantly by visitor numbers only in two instances: occasional overcrowding of parts of the site and occasional traffic congestion in the locality. In both cases the perceived severity of impact increased along with visitor numbers. These relationships would seem intuitive, in that they suggest that larger visitor volumes, being more difficult to manage, tend to be associated with more severe visitor impacts.

In all other cases, however, no significant relationship between visitor impacts and visitor numbers was found. One possible explanation for this perhaps surprising result could be that different attractions manage their visitors with different degrees of success, depending on factors such as how visitor management is funded or the degree of commitment to managing visitor impacts. This would mean that even attractions with a small volume of visitors can experience severe visitor impacts if visitor management is poorly done. The opposite may of course also be true, in that even visitor attractions receiving large volumes of visitors can minimize the impacts of those visitors if they manage them effectively. The key message here is that rather than attempting to regulate overall visitor numbers, managers of visitor attractions would do better to refocus their attention on the impacts *per visitor*. The role of educating visitors about their potential impacts on the attraction, and what they can do to minimize these impacts, is clearly paramount in such efforts.

Conclusion

Visitor attractions play an important role in the tourism industries of many countries. They also have an important role to play as stewards of the cultural and natural heritage of many countries. These roles often conflict, and one important source of conflict is the potential for visitors to compromise, through a variety of impacts, the very things that they come to see. Visitor attractions are required to walk a fine line between enabling the public to interact with the various elements of their cultural and natural heritage on the one hand, and protecting those elements from the negative impacts of those who come to visit them on the other.

References

Barlow, G. (1999). Managing supply and demand. In *Heritage Visitor Attractions: An Operations Management Perspective* (A. Leask and I. Yeoman, eds) pp. 157–175, Cassell.
Bramwell, B. and Lane, B. (1993). Interpretation and sustainable tourism: the potential and the pitfalls. *Journal of Sustainable Tourism*, 1, 71–80.
Croft, T. (1994). What price access? Visitor impacts on heritage in trust. In *Cultual Tourism* (J. M. Fladmark, ed.) pp. 169–178, Donhead.
Curtis, S. (1998). Visitor management in small historic cities, *Travel and Tourism Analyst*, 3, 75–89.
ETB (1991). *Heritage Sites Working Group: Report to the Touirsm and Environment Task Force.* English Tourist Board/Employment Department Group.
Fyall, A. and Garrod, B. (1998). Heritage tourism: at what price? *Managing Leisure*, 3, 213–228.
Scottish Executive (2000). *A New Strategy for Scottish Tourism*. Scottish Executive.
Shackley, M. (1998). Conclusions. In *Visitor Management: Case Studies* (M. Shackley, ed.) pp. 194–205, Butterworth-Heinemann.
Shackley, M. (1999). Visitor management. In *Heritage Visitor Attractions: An Operations Management Perspective* (A. Leask and I. Yeoman, eds) pp. 69–82, Cassell.
Smith, R. (1998). Visitor attractions in Scotland. In *Tourism in Scotland* (R. MacLellan and R. Smith, eds) pp. 187–208, International Thompson Business Press.

9

Seasonality: the perennial challenge for visitor attractions

Philip Goulding

Aims

The aims of this chapter are to:

- examine and review what is understood by the concept of 'seasonality' in tourism
- examine the operational implications of seasonality to visitor attractions, both as revenue centres in their own right and as part of the wider local tourism economy
- assess the range and possible management responses to the phenomenon of a seasonal market.

Scotland's tourist industry and visitor attractions are the context of many of the findings and analysis in this chapter, including a case study relating to the seasonality of visitor attractions in the Scottish Borders. A broad view of what constitutes an 'attraction' is adopted in this chapter.

Introduction

The significance of visitor attractions in local, regional and even national tourism economies has been well documented. In Scotland, Leask, Fyall and Goulding (2000), Fyall, Leask and Garrod (2000) and Scottish Enterprise (cited in Fyall, Leask and Garrod, 2001) have recorded their ability to stimulate market development and overall visitor spend, interpret and present aspects of cultural heritage and create local honey pots. Meanwhile Smith (1998) noted their ability to underpin tourism-dependent businesses in remote locations. Many attractions include all-weather facilities, and as such have the potential to generate tourist trips or excursions throughout the year. Despite this, seasonality remains endemic in the visitor attraction sector, particularly in the temperate climatic zones, within which a sizeable part of the world's tourism activity takes place. In fact, visitor attractions play a dual role in seasonality. They are typically at the mercy of the seasonal nature of market forces. Yet through their operational policies they can collectively, and sometimes individually, contribute to, reinforce or combat patterns of seasonality in a tourism destination. This is particularly the case where major attractions, or groups of attractions, play a key role in promoting and sustaining the destination of which they are part.

Toward an understanding of seasonality

'Seasonality' has been a facet of tourism since the emergence of the mass movement of people for leisure purposes and the growth of a range of service-based sectors to serve their needs. The seminal works of Blass Nogueira et al. and Bar On in the 1960s and 1970s illustrated two significant issues of seasonality for tourism development. The first is that understanding temporal patterns of human movement is key to understanding the role of tourism in destination development. This, in turn, clearly impacts on the development and fortunes of many visitor attractions, which depend on the well-being of tourism in their locality or region. The second significant issue is that the effects of such temporal imbalances are commonly experienced in many parts of the world, given the interconnectedness of demand and supply (Bar On, 1975; Blass Nogueira et al., 1968). Bar On's longitudinal study of sixteen countries over a ten-year period provided ample evidence of the universality of seasonality in tourism, even though the actual patterns varied from place to place.

While 'seasonality' in a tourism context is usually understood to refer to temporal imbalances in the market, definitions reveal different approaches. Grant, Human and Le Pelley (1997) refer to the peaks and troughs of visitor numbers during a calendar year, while Holloway (1998) includes 'periodicity' under the umbrella of temporal imbalances – that is, shorter-term fluctuations in demand (from day-to-day, weekday-to-weekend and week-by-week variations). Within the UK and European context, presentation of tourism seasonality data by public authorities is generally done with some resonance to the natural seasons, often in the form of monthly trip or occupancy data aggregated to three-monthly (quarterly) periods. This simplifies the task of year-on-year trend analysis. However, presentation of seasonal tourism data in such formats may mis-represent individual operators, whose market performance varies significantly from the overall destination, regional or national norms within any given quarter of the year.

Moreover, there is an inherent vagueness in the terminologies applied to seasonality. The term 'shoulder period' is used extensively in tourism to denote a period of time linking 'peak' demand and periods of least demand, though there is little evidence of criteria used to denote the characteristics of the 'shoulder period'. Similar vagueness applies to the terms 'off peak', 'high season', 'mid-season' and 'low season'. This is especially pertinent, given the market peculiarities of individual attractions, when public agency intervention or destination-wide collaborative initiatives are used to promote seasonal extension policies, 'low season' market growth, seasonal employment and so on. The 'twin peaks' or 'multi-peaking' effect of demand may indeed render concepts of a defined 'shoulder' or 'low season' obsolete.

Seasonality is thus generally accepted to be a demand-driven phenomenon. The view is that the vagaries of the market dictate opening and closing patterns of tourism businesses and facilities, and the levels of service provided at certain times of the year. However, Goulding and Hay (2001) note that a reliance on demand patterns to explain seasonality is an oversimplification. A summary of their examination of four distinct perspectives of seasonality is shown in Figure 9.1. Their findings indicate, in addition to demand-led market forces, the role of causal factors, of supply-side decisions and of wider resource implications as factors that collectively determine the seasonal nature of tourism to a location and its attractions.

The above perspectives span the wider tourism system, including generating and destination areas, intermediaries and transport modes; hence the complex-ity of deconstructing seasonality to a purely 'demand management' phenom-enon. Butler (2002) and Allcock (1995) in their respective surveys of seasonality, share the view that a multidimensional approach is necessary to understand patterns of seasonality. Butler's (2002: 5) definition of seasonality provides a broad approach: '[a] temporal imbalance ... which may be expressed in terms of dimensions of such elements as numbers of visitors, expenditure of visitors,

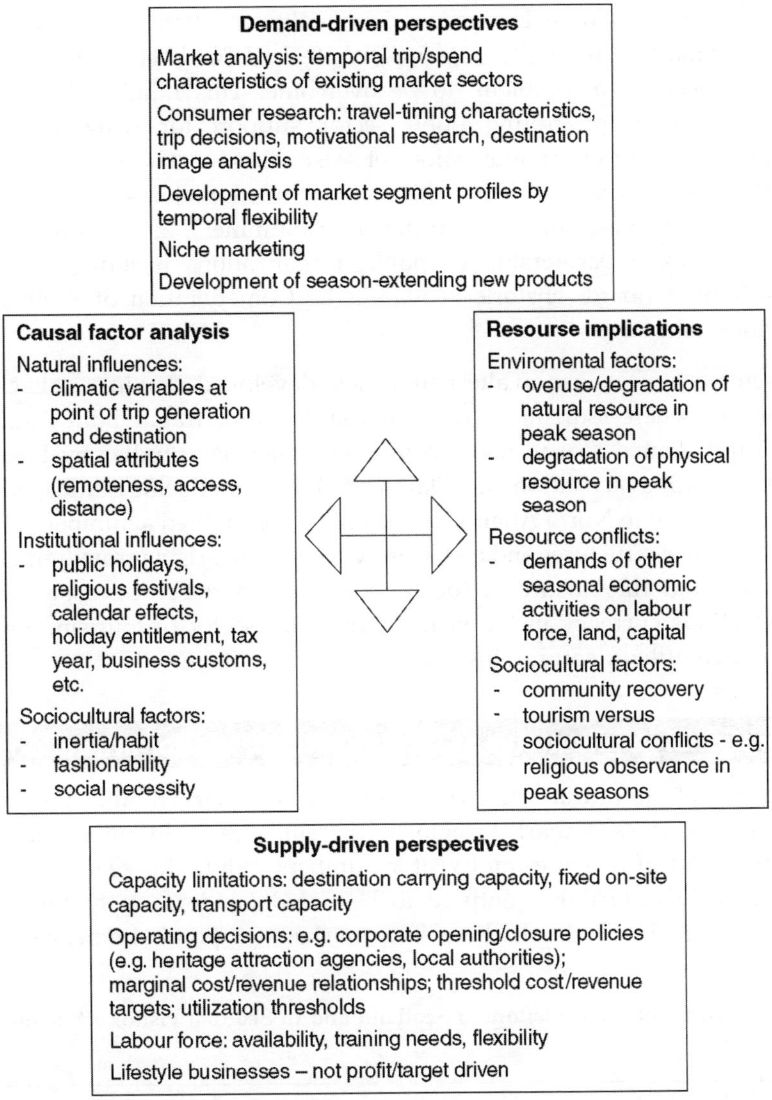

Demand-driven perspectives

Market analysis: temporal trip/spend characteristics of existing market sectors

Consumer research: travel-timing characteristics, trip decisions, motivational research, destination image analysis

Development of market segment profiles by temporal flexibility

Niche marketing

Development of season-extending new products

Causal factor analysis

Natural influences:
- climatic variables at point of trip generation and destination
- spatial attributes (remoteness, access, distance)

Institutional influences:
- public holidays, religious festivals, calendar effects, holiday entitlement, tax year, business customs, etc.

Sociocultural factors:
- inertia/habit
- fashionability
- social necessity

Resourse implications

Enviromental factors:
- overuse/degradation of natural resource in peak season
- degradation of physical resource in peak season

Resource conflicts:
- demands of other seasonal economic activities on labour force, land, capital

Sociocultural factors:
- community recovery
- tourism versus sociocultural conflicts - e.g. religious observance in peak seasons

Supply-driven perspectives

Capacity limitations: destination carrying capacity, fixed on-site capacity, transport capacity

Operating decisions: e.g. corporate opening/closure policies (e.g. heritage attraction agencies, local authorities); marginal cost/revenue relationships; threshold cost/revenue targets; utilization thresholds

Labour force: availability, training needs, flexibility

Lifestyle businesses – not profit/target driven

Figure 9.1 Perspectives of seasonality
Source: adapted from Goulding and Hay (2001)

traffic on highways and other forms of transportation, employment and admissions to attractions'.

Until the 1990s, temporal variations in tourism were overwhelmingly considered, both in the literature and by public policy makers at large, to be a negative condition for the development of tourism, both at national or destination levels and for individual businesses. Seasonality is often identified as a key symptom of market failure (Bull, 1995; SQW, 1997; STCG, 1994; Wanhill, 1998) and as such is seen as a 'problem' to be overcome. This mindset has played a significant role in prompting public-sector support for struggling tourism economies wherever the manifestations of seasonality have been seen to be acute. In Scotland since the mid-1990s this has included major seasonal extension marketing initiatives, notably 'Spring into Summer' and 'Autumn Gold', spearheaded by a partnership of public organizations including the former Scottish Tourist Board, Historic Scotland, the Confederation of Scottish Local Authorities, and others.

Only in recent years has an alternative view developed: that in certain contexts, for example, where tourism utilizes environmental or fragile built resources, a defined and limited season may actually be beneficial. Studies by Flogenfeldt (2002) in Scandinavia, Britton and Clark (1987) in South Pacific islands and Baum and Hagen (1999) in North Atlantic islands have highlighted a number of benefits to labour market structures and community well-being arising from limited levels of demand and the closure of tourist amenities in the 'off season'. Such an argument finds currency in the visitor attractions sector of tourism, where the core resource utilizes natural, historic or cultural heritage.

Operational implications of seasonality for visitor attractions

The nature of an attraction's composite visitor market, and the seasonal characteristics of each market segment therein, clearly influence the overall seasonal spread of revenues and visitor numbers. While this seems to state the obvious, many attractions continue to be overdependent on highly seasonal market sectors. In Scotland, there is a marked temporal difference between

Table 9.1 Distribution of visitors to Scotland and to Scottish visitor attractions, by quarter, 1999

Quarter	UK visitors' holiday trips (%)	Overseas visitors' holiday trips (%)	Visits to attractions (all visitor markets %)
January–March	16	5	14
April–June	23	28	31
July–September	33	57	40
October–December	28	10	15

Source: STB (2001)

144

overseas and domestic holiday visits, as illustrated in Table 9.1. Around 70 per cent of visits to attractions occur between the months of April and September, influenced significantly by the summer-oriented overseas visitor holiday market. In less accessible peripheral areas of Scotland, the degree of seasonal concentration of overseas visitors is more acute.

The 2000 Visitor Attraction Monitor (STB, 2001) identified 116 Scottish attractions as operating for less than six months of the year, approximately one-sixth of the Scottish total. These included such primary regional attractions as Balmoral Estate (Grampian), Cawdor Castle (Highlands), Dryburgh Abbey (Borders), Mount Stuart House and Gardens (Isle of Bute) and the Skye Museum of Island Life (Isle of Skye). The most prevalent – and overrepresented in terms of seasonal attractions – were privately owned and managed attractions. In contrast, Scotland's two largest attractions' estates, Historic Scotland and the National Trust for Scotland, have relatively few seasonal attractions in their respective portfolios, reflecting their commitment to Scotland's national tourism seasonal extension campaigns.

Irrespective of the forms, causes or manifestations of seasonality, there are some fundamentally universal implications for seasonal attraction operators. Two of the main ones are labour-related and capacity utilization issues.

Labour force issues

A seasonally defined tourism destination can create instabilities in the local labour market, especially in tourism-dependent rural or peripheral locations. In their analysis of tourism in peripheral regions of northern Europe and maritime Canada, Baum and Hagen (1999) noted the negative impact on the quality of service delivery caused by the short tourism season, which in turn reduced the competitive edge of amenities and visitor attractions in those places. A number of contributory issues were identified, including the following:

Recruitment of staff
The disproportionate cost to the organization of hiring staff for relatively short periods (as little as ten weeks in some cases) inhibits the development of progressive remuneration packages for those employees. Moreover, short seasonal working contracts may limit the pool of local labour willing and able to undertake such work. Citing the case of the Swedish island of Gotland, Baum and Hagen noted the dependence of operators on school and university students to fill vacancies. The end of the island's tourism season is determined as much by the flight of labour at the start of the academic year (15 August) as by consumer demand.

An additional recruitment issue for some heritage attractions is that highlighted by Deery and Jago (2001). They note the specialist craft skills required by some attraction operators to authenticate the visitor experience. Such skills, for example, working as a wheelwright or operating coal or textile machinery, may be unique to a particular attraction and in short supply in the local workforce, which are in turn more inclined to take up permanent posts than seasonal ones.

Cost of training and development

Given that this is spread over a shorter time span, attractions may be less willing to invest in training and development for their seasonal staff, particularly where the work pattern is predominantly part time. The Association of Scottish Visitor Attractions (ASVA) encourages its members to demonstrate commitment to raising service quality through extending training opportunities to all staff, both seasonal and permanent.

Commitment of seasonal workers to the operation

Although it is accepted that an element of the labour force will prefer short-term contracts of either a full- or part-time nature, for other job starters there remains an issue of commitment to the organization. Faced with competition from other service sectors offering the prospect of more permanent employment (for example, retail, hospitality, call centres), seasonal attractions may have to carry the costs associated with relatively high staff turnover rates. Little in the way of structured, comparative research has been done into the retention and turnover of seasonal staff in the attractions sector.

Heritage attractions and those operated by trusts often rely to a significant degree on volunteer staff. Table 9.2 shows the degree of prevalence of volunteer

Table 9.2   Seasonal employment in Scottish visitor attractions, 2000

Employment type	Male (%)	Female (%)	Total employees
Full-time permanent	48	52	100% = 2080
Part-time permanent	24	76	100% = 1089
Full-time seasonal	39	61	100% = 953
Part-time seasonal	29	71	100% = 1128
(Unpaid volunteers)	44	56	100% = 2752

Source: STB (2001)

staff in Scotland's visitor attractions. Jago and Deery (2001) note the increasing complexity of volunteers' motivations in heritage attractions and the ascendancy of personal development as a desired unremunerated reward. Accordingly, seasonal attractions relying on such staff may increasingly find themselves having to address volunteer management and development to ensure their commitment to return the following season.

Loss of skills and experience at the end of the season

Interlinked with commitment is the problem of consistency, where valued, skilled staff are unavailable for the following season. Given that the essence of visitor attraction service delivery is often the interactions between staff and customers (Laws, 2001), consistency in service quality from year to year may depend on continuity of the skills, experience and personal qualities of frontline staff.

Capacity utilization

Although 'problems' associated with seasonality are most often considered in terms of underutilization, demand peaking can be just as problematic for visitor attractions, manifesting itself in short-term overutilization of the attraction.

Symptoms of peak season overutilization include:

- congestion, including overflowing car and coach parks, on-site traffic congestion, exceeding natural or built carrying capacity and visitor bottlenecking
- wear and tear on the core resource and its ancillary infrastructures, including degradation of the physical fabric of the resource resulting from the volume of visitor throughput. This may be compounded by a deficiency in the level of visitor management and control at peak times
- diminished visitor satisfaction from the experience: excess queuing, limited dwell time in popular areas, limited access to guides or other on-site staff, diminished service in retail or catering units, limited access to toilets, childcare facilities and so on, all contribute to lower satisfaction levels
- externalities (community costs) including off-site parking and traffic congestion and resultant costs of extra traffic management to the local community, increased levels of litter, noise and other forms of pollution.

Bull (1995) suggests that visitor attractions can employ supply-rationing methods to overcome capacity constraints during periods of peak demand, most typically including queue management, cordoning car parking and limiting access once carrying capacity is reached.

Characteristics of seasonal underutilization include:

1 Perishability of the unit of production. Goulding and Leask (1997) identified various aspects of this, including: the element of permanency in the physical structure of attractions means that most attractions are relatively inflexible in adapting to lower scales of operation during quiet periods; underachievement of revenue-earning potential during much of the operating season; and seasonal demand or closure patterns in core attractions render ancillary revenue-generating components perishable (for example, on-site catering, garden centres, retail sales outlets). There is a clearly defined inventory in cost and revenue generating terms in many attractions (e.g. preserved railways, theme park rides, special exhibitions), the contributions of which can be seasonally measured.
2 Cash flow, revenue and profit contribution concentrated into a short operating period and subsidizing fixed and variable costs over the full operating period. Findings from studies undertaken by Goulding and Leask (1997) and Leask, Fyall and Goulding (2000) into Scotland's visitor attractions indicated that these financial considerations were key reasons for attractions operating seasonal closures or restricted opening patterns during parts of the year.
3 Opportunity costs of idle space, equipment and staff for much of the operating period, where the attraction is operating below its fixed capacity to produce (Goulding and Leask, 1997).
4 Capital investment: the income-concentrating effect of seasonality can deter capital investment in tourism infrastructures and at destinations generally. For private-sector attraction operators, the shorter the season, the greater are the risks in recouping investment costs and the longer the payback time required.

In the increasingly competitive and uncertain national and international market place for leisure and tourism, overcoming the issues outlined above requires ever more resourceful and imaginative measures. Some of the main management responses to seasonality are discussed in the next section.

Management responses to seasonality

First, there are arguments that maintaining current seasonal market conditions and trading patterns is a valid option. Hartmann (1986) was among the first to advocate the cause for dormant periods in tourism being necessary for the recovery of social and ecological environments, many of which may be heritage-based resources. Flogenfeldt (2002) takes the view that many season-extending tourism initiatives are of limited success, are resource intensive, given the fickleness and competitiveness of the marketplace, and are thus of questionable sustainability.

One approach to 'dealing with' seasonality is what might be termed the 'level of response continuum', whereby attractions can take one of the following actions:

1 Accept prevailing seasonal structures: in which case they either maintain the operational status quo or concentrate their response efforts on redeploying resources more efficiently. This could involve:
   (a) devoting more effort to visitor management in peak periods
   (b) attempting to shift demand within existing peak periods (for example, through extending daily opening and/or closing times, negotiating with groups to vary arrival and dwell times as appropriate)
   (c) tackling some of the implications of seasonal employment as discussed above
   (d) optimizing the use of the 'low season' or non-trading period for such tasks as maintenance and repair, trade fair attendance, training, business planning, marketing, inventorizing, recuperation, and so forth.
2 Employ tactical responses to seasonal extension. These usually focus on marketing mix elements, including:
   (a) product extension and development. Typical among these elements in the context of historic houses are the staging of *ad hoc* events, where space permits, such as seasonally themed horticultural shows, classic vehicle rallies, food and drink demonstrations, craft fairs, antiques fairs, farmers' markets. Such events have the advantage of utilizing otherwise unemployed ground space that can be sublet for events. Several of the seasonal properties in the Scottish Borders, for example, use the winter and early spring 'downtime' for non-touristic revenue-generating activities, such as promoting themselves as filming locations, hosting seminars and extended corporate hospitality events. Museums, galleries and themed commercial attractions can develop educational and community events to coincide with shoulder or low season periods, around the school curriculum or with local businesses, media and charities, for example hosting fundraising activities.

      Seasonal product-extension initiatives may focus on the non-core features of the attraction, for example, retailing and food/beverage provision, where these are seen as viable revenue centres in their own right.

(b) pricing: in their respective surveys of revenue management in Scottish visitor attractions, Goulding and Leask (1997) and Leask, Fyall and Goulding (2000) found seasonal pricing techniques to be an under-utilized tool among attraction operators. This was largely influenced by the policies of multiple-attraction operators (chiefly the larger local authorities and the two large heritage attraction operators) for whom pricing policies tended to be centrally set with little discretion given to site managers. Customers' perception of value for money is known to be an issue here (Wanhill 1998), resulting in many attraction operators keeping seasonal price differentiation narrow, while concentrating instead on offering additional product benefits in non-peak periods. For example, entry to temporary exhibitions, craft demonstrations or ancillary on-site attractions can be included in the gate price in shoulder or low season periods.

'Periodic' pricing is increasingly employed as a reward for early morning or late afternoon arrival during quieter periods of the year, to encourage greater spread in visitor flows. However, where time-differentiated pricing is used, the main objective is often to shift existing demand away from peaks rather than to create additional off-peak demand.

A current pertinent issue for private commercial attraction operators in the UK is the perceived threat of loss of market share resulting from government policies to extend free entry attractions in the public sector. To survive such a threat, commercial operators will have to employ ever more creative seasonal pricing policies designed not simply to meet fixed cost contributions or other financial targets, but as importantly to encourage repeat visitation and customer loyalty in the longer term.

3 Take a strategic view of seasonal extension, which might include:
   (a) market diversification: as an example, the Scotch Whisky Heritage Centre (SWHC) in Edinburgh has successfully developed lucrative corporate hospitality, meetings and small functions markets. Initially on the back of its core attraction, these have become self-sustaining and separate markets in their own right.
   (b) having a greater sensitivity to the needs of increasingly disparate market sectors and targeting under-represented social groups in off-peak periods. Following the example of the Disney Corporation, Alton Towers, part of the Tussauds Group, targeted the gay and lesbian market for a day during late September 2001. Perceived to be a relatively leisure-oriented, high discretionary spend group, this market is also less bound by the traditional school holiday calendar.

(c) investment in facilities, interpretation and service. To achieve the above market diversification, the SWHC invested in converting office space into prestigious meetings rooms.

(d) adopting yield management philosophies as creatively as in other sectors, such as hotels, budget airlines, car hire. Though the cost structures of most attractions reflect high fixed to variable cost relationships, there is plenty of scope for attraction operators to be more responsive to seasonal revenue contributions.

Collective responses

On a broader front, it is increasingly recognized that attractions need to be proactive in destination area market development and adopt a more commercial outlook, where once a curatorial outlook pervaded (especially in public-sector attractions). While this may seem difficult to achieve in practice for small, independent attractions, initiatives to improve management development opportunities for attractions managers are gaining pace throughout the UK. In Scotland, the enterprise networks, Tourism Training Scotland and the ASVA have taken the lead, while in England the ETC is co-ordinating similar management development initiatives with partners including the Training and Enterprise Councils and Business Links (ETC, 2000). Meanwhile, adoption of benchmarking by the Association of Independent Museums, the Association of Leading Visitor Attractions and the Cultural Heritage National Training Organization, is intended to enable comparison of performance indicators and best practice (ETC, 2000).

There are, as Fyall, Leask and Garrod (2001) discuss, a number of collective response channels available to visitor attractions. These include themed marketing initiatives within a destination locale or region (such as the Explore Edinburgh initiative of several major scientific attractions); more formalized consortia to enhance collective purchasing power; active involvement in local tourist board seasonal extension marketing campaigns (a most notable recent example of which has been the development and promotion of the Edinburgh Hogmanay Festival); and, particularly in the case of multiple-attraction operators, involvement in national-level season extension strategies.

While the shoulder or low seasons may offer a natural 'space' for collaboration compared with the peak season, commercial sensitivities can limit their effectiveness. For example, collective seasonal extension pricing promotions by locally competing attraction operators can be a double-edged sword. Fyall, Leask and Garrod (2001) noted the reluctance of larger (that is, higher profile)

151

attractions to engage in off-season joint ticketing initiatives, when the risk of reduced dwell time and secondary expenditure by visitors has a greater impact than in peak season periods.

Finally, the role of governments and their public-sector agencies must be considered as part of the overall management response to tourism seasonality. As noted earlier, seasonality has been seen as a symptom of market failure in tourism, and as such forms the rationale for government intervention. The issue has been addressed in a wide range of public policy issues beyond direct tourism initiatives, including proposals to stagger academic holidays (notably by the European Commission; see Commission of the European Communities, 1993), rural development and transport policy. Figure 9.2 identifies a range of public sector as well as attraction specific (supply-side) responses to seasonality, as surveyed by Goulding and Hay (2001) in Scotland.

Attraction responses	Public-sector policy responces
Adoption of seasonal extension policies and practices: - seasonal pricing - market diversification - product extension/diversification - events strategy - promotional activities - participate in collective promotions (e.g. destination marketing initiatives, travel trade incentive visits)	Adoption of season-extension policies and practices: - fiscal incentives - labour force incentives (e.g. training initiatives) - staggering of school holidays - business support services geared to seasonal extension (e.g. marketing, financial advice) - creation, support or participation in seasonal extension programmes
Acceptance of seasonality: - offer reduced capacity in line with resource limitation (e.g. reduced staffing level) - lower service level (e.g. part closure of non-essential amenities) - full seasonal closure of all facilities - temporary closure (e.g. during lowest revenue periods) - restrict opening/closing times	Acceptance of seasonality: - enviromental regeneration initiatives - focus business support on high season initiatives - support off-season community initiatives (e.g. local arts festivals)

Figure 9.2 Supply-side responses to seasonality
Source: Goulding and Hay (2001)

Case study: seasonality Scottish Borders

The Scottish Borders is an inte
adjoining the English border re
peripheral, accounting for around ⸂visitor attractions
from domestic markets and around 1.
overseas visitors (Goulding and Hay, 2

The Borders' economy

Tourism contributes almost £80 million to the Sc
year, employing over 4000 of the region's approxin.
active population (SBTB, 1999). The Borders eco.
agrarian based, with agriculture accounting for 28 per c
product in 1997 (SoSEP, 2000), although along with
manufacturing, tourism provides an important income sourc

Faced with the triple crises during the 1990s, of agricultural de...
closures of textile mills and the sudden closure of the region's large..
electronics factory, the Scottish Parliament awarded the Borders a £3 million
cash injection in 1999 to develop tourism projects, and successfully applied
for European Union Objective 2 status for the area as part of a wider South of
Scotland Objective 2 designation (Goulding and Hay, 2001).

During 2001 the region's agriculture and tourism sectors were further hit,
and hit hard, by the effects of the Foot and Mouth crisis, with much of the
Borders countryside closed to walkers and other outdoor leisure pursuits from
April until near the end of the year.

The Borders tourism product

The basis of Borders tourism has long been its outstanding natural landscape,
including the River Tweed, the Southern Upland hills (easily accessible to
ramblers) and important marine and wildlife reserves, such as the dramatic
coastline with its colonies of breeding seabirds. In recent years, priority has
been given to the development of outdoor activity-based leisure tourism, in
particular for high discretionary spend visitor markets. Hence, hill walking,
fishing, cycling, horse riding and golf tourism among others have been
targeted for development.

It is also an area of distinctive historical and cultural resources, including the
castles and fortified mansions in an area that was for several hundred years a

153

nglish and Scots. The Borders possess unique
the Common Riding festivals in most of its towns,
notably associated with Sir Walter Scott.

ration of historic houses and castles that play a
e region's tourism. Several of these are residences of
gentry, and have great architectural and historic appeal.
the major houses and castles, with their opening policies in
of these are linked in formal marketing consortia, such as The
es of Scotland, which includes Thirlestane and Traquair.

Scottish Borders' major visitor attractions opening schedules, 1999

tion	Opening period	Time variations	Description
Abbotsford	Mid-March–end October	Daily, whole day Sundays only in summer months	Historic house – Sir Walter Scott
Bowhill	House: July Country Park: mid-April–end August	Afternoons Afternoons, but educational groups all year	Private stately home and country park
Floors Castle	April–October inclusive	Mornings/afternoons daily	Private stately home/ castle
Manderston	Mid-May–end September	2 days a week, afternoons; pre-booked groups throughout the year	Private stately home
Mellerstain	Easter + May– September inclusive	Mon–Sat, afternoons	Charitable trust-run stately home
Paxton	Easter–end October	Daily; garden/park extended hours	House and country park; seasonal activities/events programme
Thirlestane	Easter week + May–October inclusive	6 days a week, 6 hours per day; special opening for pre-booked groups	Castle, charitable trust
Traquair	April– September: daily October: Fri– Sun	Summer months: am/ pm Shoulder months: pm	Private stately home; hosts events and fairs

Sources: publicity materials for each attraction

Apart from the historic houses, a distinctive feature of the region's tourism is the small-scale and independent nature of tourism supply. Corporate-branded hotel groups are almost non-existent, and family-run businesses are especially prevalent throughout the accommodation and activity operations sectors. These are often operated as secondary businesses allied to agriculture/farming/livestock, or run as a part-year 'lifestyle' occupation.

Seasonality in the Scottish Borders

The region exhibits strong seasonal patterns of visitation to attractions, with 82 per cent of visitors arriving between April and September in 2000 – the same percentage as in the previous year (STB, 2001). This is more marked than the pattern for Scotland as a whole, as demonstrated in Table 9.4.

Table 9.4 Quarterly analysis of visits to visitor attractions, 2000

Quarter	Scottish Borders	Scotland
January–March	7%	14%
April–June	37%	31%
July–September	45%	40%
October–December	11%	15%
No. of visits	784 800	36 600 000
Base (attractions)	49	696

Source: STB (2001)

The seasonal operation of Borders visitor attractions is endemic. Those shown in Table 9.3 represent some of the larger attractions in terms of visitor numbers and turnover. Small-scale operations, limited annual visitor numbers and diverse ownership patterns (as illustrated in Table 9.5) pose a great challenge for the region's tourism and local economic development agencies in their quest to achieve consensus among attractions operators to extend their operating season. Meanwhile, six of the region's eight tourist information centres open from April until October.

In recent years, a fall in tourism trade to the Borders during the 'peak' summer months, including spend from local residents and commercial trades, has reduced the income surplus that has traditionally acted as a buffer to

Table 9.5   Seasonal visitor attractions in the Scottish Borders, 2000

Attraction	Ownership type	Visitor numbers (in thousands)
Ayton Castle	Private	1–5
Dryburgh Abbey	Historic Scotland	25–50
Jedforest Deer and Farm Park	Private	10–25
John Buchan Centre	Trust	<1
Manderston (stately home)	Private	5–10
Neidpath Castle	Private	1–5
Robert Clapperton Studio	Private	<1
Smailholm Tower	Historic Scotland	5–10
Halliwell's House Museum, Selkirk	Local authority	5–10
Kittiwake Gallery	Private	10–25
Old Gala House	Local authority	5–10
Sir Walter Scott's Courtroom	Local authority	1–5

Source: STB (2001)

subsidize the quieter off-season periods. A particular concern of many 'micro-business' operators such as tea shops, craft shops and bed and breakfast operators is that the short and irregular seasonal trading patterns of the major attractions acts as a deterrent to their own market development.

A seasonality strategy

In recent years, the Borders tourism authorities have commissioned several research studies on seasonality, designed to 'tackle' what is perceived as a symptom of market failure and to tie in with the Seasonality Strategy for Scottish Tourism (STB, 1999). An outcome of this, in market development terms, has been an attempt to reposition the Borders as a secondary short break destination for 'young urbanites' and 'young activists', high discretionary spend city dwellers, particularly from the north of England and central Scotland. Furthermore, emphasis is being given to the development of golf tourism and business support for the development of activity breaks and low season events, as demonstrated by the embryonic Winter Folk Festival. The development of formalized networking channels for tourism businesses is seen as a priority, and is being spearheaded by the economic development agency and the tourist board.

Ultimately, the long-term success of the Scottish Borders' tourism economy will depend to a significant degree on the seasonal trading policies and market development priorities of its visitor attractions.

Conclusion

A key hypothesis of this chapter is that seasonality in tourism should be treated as a broad and complex phenomenon, rather than seen purely in terms of fluctuations in visitor numbers or spend. As has been demonstrated, it encompasses a variety of perspectives beyond the immediacy of the marketplace. For attractions operators, these perspectives raise many issues in identifying and possibly influencing the wider causes of temporal imbalances; in managing visitor demand and acknowledging the destination-based impacts of seasonality, as well as those specific to the individual attraction. Some causal factors, such as climatic conditions, are clearly beyond the control of tourism attractions and destination management organizations. However, attractions are not powerless to extend their seasonal operations, even if a twelve-month operating season remains an unrealistic target. Urban attractions may be best placed to take advantage of wider markets and the 'honey pot' effect of visitor attraction clusters. Nevertheless all attractions can benefit from reappraising their role in the wider context of destination seasonality and considering their responses tactically or strategically, or indeed by accepting and adapting to the seasonal 'downtime' in a proactive way.

References

Allcock, J. (1995). Seasonality. In *Tourism Marketing and Management Handbook* (S. Witt and L. Moutinho, eds) pp. 92–104, Prentice Hall International.

Bar On, R. (1975). *Seasonality in Tourism: A Guide to the Analysis of Seasonality and Trends for Policy Making*. Economist Intelligence Unit.

Baum, T. and Hagen, L. (1999). Resonses to seasonality: the experiences of peripheral destinations. *International Journal of Tourism Research*, **1**, 299–312.

Blass Nogueira, M., Casamayor Lagarda, J., Diaz Mier, M. and Rivas, P. (1968). *La estacionalidad en el turismo y sus posibles correctivos*. Cuadernos Monograficos No. 11. Instituto de Estudios Turisticos, Madrid.

Britton, S. and Clarke, W. C. (eds) (1987). *Ambiguous Alternative: Tourism in Small Developing Countries*. University of the South Pacific.

Bull, A. (1995). *Economics of Travel and Tourism*. Longman.

Butler, R. W. (2002). Seasonality in tourism: issues and implications. In *Seasonality in Tourism* (T. Baum and S. Lundtorp, eds), pp. 5–21, Pergamon.

Commission of the European Communities (1993). *All Season Tourism: Analysis of Experience, Suitable Products and Clientele*. Commission of the European Communities and Fitzpatrick Associates.

Deery, M. and Jago, L. (2001). Managing human resources. In *Quality Issues in Heritage Visitor Attractions* (S. Drummond and I. Yeoman, eds) pp. 175–193, Butterworth-Heinemann.

ETC (2000). *Action for Attractions*. English Tourism Council.

Flogenfeldt, T. (2002). Long-term positive adjustments to seasonality: consequences of summer tourism in the Jotunheimen area, Norway. In *Seasonality in Tourism* (T. Baum and S. Lundtorp, eds), pp. 109–117, Pergamon.

Fyall, A., Leask, A. and Garrod, B. (2000). Scottish visitor attractions: issues for the new millenium. In *Reflections on International Tourism: Management, Marketing and the Political Economy of Travel and Tourism* (M. Robinson, N. Evans, P. Long, R. Sharpley and J. Swarbrooke, eds) pp. 161–178, The Centre for Travel and Tourism, and Business Education Publishing Ltd.

Fyall, A., Leask, A. and Garrod, B. (2001). Scottish visitor attractions: a collaborative future? *International Journal of Tourism Research*, **3**, 211–228.

Goulding, P. and Hay, B. (2001). Tourism seasonality in Edinburgh and the Scottish Borders: north–south or core–periphery relationship? Proceedings of the 7th ATLAS International Conference, June 2000, Discussion and Working Papers Series No. 3, ATLAS and Finnish University Network for Tourism Studies.

Goulding, P. and Leask, A. (1997). Scottish visitor attractions: revenue versus capacity. In *Yield Management: Strategies for the Service Industries* (I. Yeoman and A. Ingold, eds) pp. 160–182, Cassell.

Grant, M., Human, B. and Le Pelley, B. (1997). Seasonality. *Insights*, **8**, A5–A9.

Hartmann, R. (1986). Tourism, seasonality and social change. *Leisure Studies*, **5**, 25–33.

Holloway, J. C. (1998). *The Business of Tourism*. Addison Wesley Longman.

Jago, L. and Deery, M. (2001). Managing volunteers. In *Quality Issues in Heritage Visitor Attractions* (S. Drummond and I. Yeoman, eds) pp. 194–217, Butterworth-Heinemann.

Laws, E. (2001). The analysis of quality for heritage site visitors. In *Quality Issues in Heritage Visitor Attractions* (S. Drummond and I. Yeoman, eds) pp. 61–77, Butterworth-Heinemann.

Leask, A., Fyall, A. and Goulding, P. (2000). Scottish visitor attractions: revenue, capacity and sustainability. In *Yield Management Strategies for the Service Industries* (A. Ingold, U. McMahon-Beattie and I. Yeoman, eds), 2nd edn, pp. 211–232, Continuum.

SBTB (1999). *Scottish Borders Tourism Strategy*. Scottish Borders Tourist Board.

Smith, R. (1998). Visitor attractions in Scotland. In *Tourism in Scotland* (R. MacLellan and R. Smith, eds) pp. 187–208, International Thomson Business Press.

SoSEP (2000). *South of Scotland Objective 2 Programme, 2000–2006: Consultation Document, February 2000*. South of Scotland European Partnership.

SQW (1997). *Tourism as a Year Round Activity for Business: A Report for Highlands and Islands Enterprise*. Segal Quince Wicksteed Ltd.

STB (1999). *A Seasonality Strategy for Scottish Tourism*. Scottish Tourist Board.

STB (2001) *The Scottish Visitor Attraction Monitor*. Scottish Tourist Board.

STCG (1994). *Scottish Tourism Strategic Plan*. Scottish Tourism Coordinating Group, Scottish Tourist Board.

Wanhill, S. (1998). Attractions. In *Tourism: Principles and Practice* (C. Cooper, J. Fletcher, D. Gilbert, R. Shepherd and S. Wanhill, eds), 2nd edn, pp. 289–312, Addison Wesley Longman.

10

Management challenges for religion-based attractions

Myra Shackley

Introduction

Religion-based visitor attractions form an immensely diverse assemblage, varied in scale, location, visitor motivation and management style. Most are sites that are sacred to one or more religious traditions, including many places of worship or pilgrimage that have been receiving visitors for hundreds (or sometimes thousands) of years. But the category also includes crassly commercial theme parks with some religious motifs, as well as many sites which fall somewhere on the continuum between these two extremes. The author has attempted elsewhere to classify sacred sites (Shackley, 2001) and to provide an overview of one specific category (Shackley, 2002). This chapter focuses especially on two operations management fields especially significant at religious sites that have become visitor attractions, namely, the management of visitor flows and the generation of revenue, and also introduces the recent phenomena of commercially managed visitor attractions based on a religious theme.

Classifying religion-based attractions

The range of religion-based attractions in the world is enormous and the problem of classifying them could be tackled in any number of ways (Vuconic, 1996). They could be divided, for example, by religious tradition, by the level of site utilization or by the balance between the worshipping community and the number of tourist visitors. They could be categorized by management type (sacred or secular, public or private sector, commercial or not for profit) or by size (which can vary from a small isolated shrine to an entire city such as Jerusalem, a small state such as the Vatican or tens of square miles of cultural landscape). They could be divided roughly on the basis of the number of visitors that each receives, on the premise that the difficulty of managing a religious site is in direct proportion to the number of people who visit it, unless that site is a commercially managed venture. A typology of visitors could also be constructed, perhaps on the basis of the distance they have travelled, which could be a pilgrimage of several hundred miles or a journey just round the corner from their homes. The context of the site could be a means of classification whether, for example, it was urban, rural, linear, nodal, and how it was linked to other attractions (Borg, van der Costa and Gotti, 1996). It might form part of a pilgrimage or cultural route, or have been included in a marketing promotion that encourages visitors to sample a number of linked attractions in the course of one tour or visit. An even simpler division of religious sites would split off those sites actively used for worship from those that, while still visited by tourists, are, in religious terms, only of historical or archaeological interest.

Broadly speaking, religion-based visitor attractions can be:

- components of the natural environment (sacred mountains, lakes, groves, islands)
- human-made buildings, structures and sites originally designed for religious purposes but which may now also be attracting tourists
- human-made buildings with a religious theme designed to attract tourists.

Inevitably, some sites combine elements of all three categories. A further category, of special events with religious significance that take place at non-religious sites, could also be added. This typology is unpacked further in Shackley (2001). Although for many people the idea of a religion-based attraction is synonymous with built heritage, this is not globally true. Many cultural landscapes such as that of Uluru in Australia, Sagarmartha in the Himalayas or the Tien Shan mountains in China include sacred sites, elements of built heritage and the component elements of a local religious tourism industry. A nodal site such as St Katherine's Monastery in Mount Sinai (Egypt) may be the focus of an entire sacred landscape, venerated by adherents of different worshipping traditions and also visited by casual tourists (Shackley, 1998). In addition to the single-nodal building (cathedral, shrine, temple or mosque), built religious heritage may also consist of a complex of such features, or entire towns like Jerusalem, Amritsar, Varanasi or Assisi. This category of religion-based attractions could also be extended to include 'New Age' sites such as Glastonbury (although Glastonbury also has an older, Christian religious heritage). There is also a difficult and controversial category of secular sites associated with socially traumatic or politically significant events which have become sacralized, including some battlefield and Holocaust sites, and localities associated with the Slave Route in West Africa.

Trends in today's consumer services marketplace have also created a new category of purpose-built religious tourism attraction that to some extent makes a commodity of the religion which it purports to promote. Instead of being based around a traditional sacred site these new attractions have been devised to create a visitor environment with a religious theme, but without any authentically sacred elements. In some cases the stimuli for such projects are blatantly commercial, but most claim educational motivation. Many substitute a sanitized pilgrimage experience for a travel venture, which is either historically unavailable or geographically or socially undesirable. 'Nazareth Village', a new project in the town of Nazareth in north Israel, is an example of the latter, where a first-century village is being re-created near the supposed location of Jesus' childhood home. The objective is to enable visitors to experience what life would have been like at that time, but the project moves from museum to theme park with items such as the 'Parable Walk', where visitors can speak with costumed volunteers acting in character. Published justification for the scheme has included the observation that contemporary urban Nazareth not only resembles a building site but is also overshadowed by a huge cathedral and its high Arab population, leading to disappointment from overseas visitors who had anticipated simple rural life.

A more extreme example of this genre has now been constructed near Orlando in Florida. The $16 million 'Holy Land Experience' developed by Zion's Hope, a non-profit-making and non-denominational Christian ministry has opened this park on 15 acres near Universal Studios and attempts to re-create Jerusalem, down to the camel prints in the cement, Goliath burgers and strolling Middle Eastern minstrels. The park has encountered much opposition from local Jewish leaders and has also fallen foul of tax inspectors who deemed it to be a theme park (and thus liable for property tax), rather than a religious and educational entity as its developers claim (http://www.itec.com/PR/zion/holyland.htm). There are many other American examples, starting with Heritage Village (O'Guinn and Belk, 1989; Shackley, 2001), and projects in the planning stage include 'The Holy Lands' religious theme park in Mesquite, Nevada, and 'Marianland', a Catholic theme park containing replicas of major Marian sites including Lourdes and Fatima, proposed for south Texas. Such projects are likely to flourish in the future as American tourists become increasingly reluctant to visit the original sites. Major Buddhist projects in construction include the huge Maitreya project near Buddha's birthplace in north India, as well as the largest Buddhist temple outside Asia that recently opened on the outskirts of Denver as a result of fourteen years' work and $2.7 million of voluntary donations.

Many such artificially created religious sites make such travel substitution their major selling point. This is not a new idea; Shoval (2000) pointed out that the St Louis World Fair in 1904 included a 13-acre 1:1 model of Jerusalem. But this kind of substitution is in direct opposition to the pilgrimage ethic that stresses the need to leave normal life (including its constraints and conveniences) behind. There is a marked contrast between the product offered by a religious theme park and the experience of the sacred that might be gained by a visitor to a sacred site. The religious tourism market (Bywater, 1994) is thus divided between religiously motivated visitors seeking an authentic religious experience, and tourists who utilize religious sites as a background for other activities. Religious sites have always been commercial; the selling of souvenirs is an integral part of all major religious traditions. It is only a small step from building entrepreneurial opportunities to take advantage of visitors to religious sites, to building entire environments to attract new categories of visitor. But this is a recent trend; by far the majority of the world's religious tourism attractions are sacred sites (Carmichael, Hubert and Reeves, 1994).

Managing religion-based attractions

What is the core product of a religious site? The main benefit to the consumer/ visitor is intangible and subjective, including atmosphere and spiritual experience (Brown and Loades, 1995). Within the world of secular heritage, visitor attraction managers are generally trying to optimize visitor numbers and revenue, while minimizing adverse impact. Many religious sites generate no revenue from visitors at all, and none generate sufficient to cover operating costs. Religious sites (unless purpose-built for commercial reasons) have limited capacity to generate revenue from visitors, although their existence generates a lot of money for associated private sector operators. Moreover, religious sites are usually encumbered by tiers of public and private sector interests, which can vary from the volunteers directly involved in their day-to-day management, through to the United Nations Educational, Scientific, and Cultural Organization's (UNESCO's) World Heritage Committee if the site has been placed on the World Heritage List. There will be national, regional and local governmental organizations, non-government organizatons (NGOs), charities, pressure groups and other organizations concerned with the site. These represent the interests of local people, the religious establishment, planners at regional and national levels, tourism, resource management and a host of others. Considering sacred heritage as a tourism product generates problems, since by comparison with other elements of the service sector such sites lack integrated management. There is seldom any linear agreement between resource use through production to 'sale' and subsequent 'consumption' by visitors or worshippers.

The effectiveness of the management and marketing of a religious site is related to the type and size of the site and to the religious tradition represented. Many religious sites have rigidly hierarchical, clerically dominated management structures which may have functioned in the same way for thousands of years. Such structures are largely unaffected by modern management trends, with the exception of their peripheral activities (often financial). Some religious sites seem not to be managed at all, and merely exist in a management vacuum where things happen by custom and nobody is too bothered with achieving specific targets. Others (but very few) are competent professional organizations with proper accounting systems and business plans. Unless the site is one of the above mentioned commercially run religious attractions (many might consider this concept a contradiction in terms), its managers might not recognize themselves as such, but might prefer to identify themselves primarily as facilitators of worship and custodians of a site or building. Only built heritage (versus landscapes) is usually managed, and the site manager of a religious site is almost always starved of resources. His (operating religious-based attractions is almost exclusively a

163

male prerogative) operations are usually grossly undercapitalized. Moreover, the manager will probably see dealing with planning or financial issues or other aspects of operational management as something that he neither wishes to get deeply involved with, nor has the ability to cope with at the required level. The managers of religious sites are usually religious leaders, to whom concepts such as product development and strategic planning may be quite foreign. Perhaps, in spiritual terms, this is a good thing. Yet when sites become visitor attractions, which may necessitate coping with thousands, and sometimes millions, of visitors each year, operations management is no longer a luxury, but becomes essential.

Management methods vary and site managers have to perform a delicate balancing act. On the one hand they need to preserve the site, which may be ancient, fragile and weighed down by traditions, which means that the installation of visitor facilities becomes unfeasibly expensive, if not downright impossible. Yet to conserve the site requires money (and sufficient cash will never be forthcoming from worshippers), and money comes, directly or indirectly, from visitors. Visiting a religious site is, or should be, an emotive experience, so site managers are also charged with the task of preserving that elusive spiritual quality referred to as 'spirit of place'. At the same time they must facilitate the religious use of the site (if, indeed, the site is active) and cater for the frequently conflicting demands of worshippers and visitors. Religious sites often rely heavily on volunteers to assist with day-to-day operations, with all the problems that incurs. They are not (primarily) commercial operations yet are functioning in a commercial world where customers have become more discerning and more critical, can choose between competing destinations and have easier access to information.

Access and visitor flows

Very few religious sites take active steps to restrict overall visitor numbers, but many popular sites have problems in controlling visitor arrivals. There are exceptions to this generalization – at the Church of the Holy Sepulchre in Jerusalem the tiny Chapel of the Angel, which contains the stone on which the angel sat to tell of Christ's resurrection (Matthew 28:1) is so small that only four visitors can enter at any one time, placing an obvious limit on numbers. At religious sites where there are very high levels of visitation or marked seasonal variations, it is often necessary to manage visitor flows to, around and within the site in order to optimize multiple use. Sometimes, visitor access to a religious site is controlled by the type of transport required to reach it. The easiest access systems to control are, inevitably, to islands, and the most difficult are at complex urban sites. For example, visitor access to Holy Island (Lindisfarne) off the Northumbrian coast can be gained only when the causeway road is exposed at low tide. Access to the pilgrimage destination island of Iona in Scotland is by ferry, and markedly seasonal. Fifty times more visitors use the ferry in August than in January, yet the ferry size and operating costs remain roughly the same. During July and August large numbers of visitors cause congestion around Iona Abbey and the ferry landing, with the rest of the island largely deserted. One management strategy under consideration is a combination of better signage and better information which might disseminate visitors more widely throughout the island, if the footpath network could be rationalized and stabilized. Almost all access issues are closely connected with ever-present financial constraints. For example, since 1999 visitors to the ancient site of Jericho in Jordan Valley of Israel can now reach the neighbouring Monastery of the Temptation, high on a mountainside above the village, by a new cable railway. Many claim that the railway is a visual pollutant and destroys the 'spirit of place' of the area. However, the reason for its construction was not to assist with visitor flow but to generate revenue in a West Bank area with little access to tourism development funding.

Visitor flows within sites can be controlled in various ways. In the case of a religious attraction where an entrance fee is charged, access to the entire site may be restricted by the utilization of some kind of 'pay perimeter'. This refers to that portion of the site that can only be accessed after payment of a fee. Some sacred sites designate a pay perimeter, spatially located beyond an area where normal worship or prayer takes place. This allows both paying tourists and non-paying visitors access to the facility. But such arrangements are frequently resented. Some sacred sites make the payment voluntary. Lincoln Cathedral (Figure 10.1) has recently instituted a compulsory entrance charge, but adjusted its pay perimeter so that visitors entering the building are able to get an excellent overview and panorama of the nave for free. They are also able to enter a small chapel reserved for prayer and gain access to the cathedral bookshop without charge, but cathedral catering is within the charging zone. Figure 10.1 shows the location of the current pay perimeter and the areas to which visitors have access. Like all sacred sites, some areas are restricted areas reserved for staff, administrative or storage use or for sacramental purposes, where unlimited visitation is not encouraged. Other visitor flow management methods include queue control, often used for special exhibitions such as the Turin Shroud or art exhibitions in religious buildings.

Access to and around religious sites can, therefore, be physically limited and controlled, but it can also be socially limited by policies that include the implementation of booking and queuing systems, which may or may not be associated with various types of charges. Charging for access to sacred sites is a highly emotive issue and one that frequently causes disagreement on the grounds

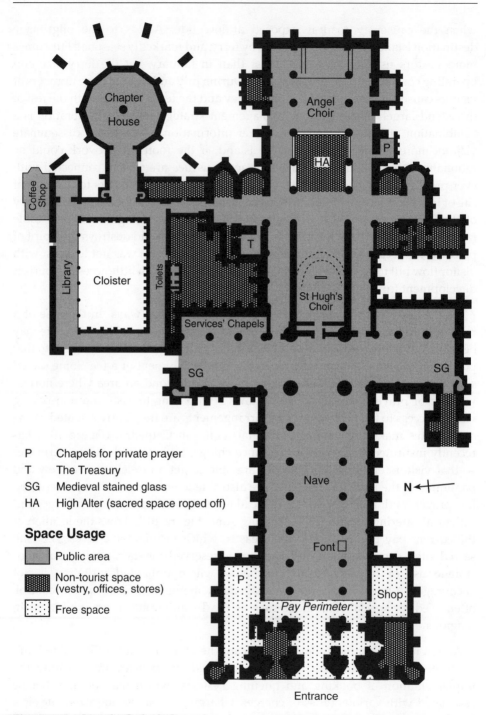

P   Chapels for private prayer
T   The Treasury
SG   Medieval stained glass
HA   High Alter (sacred space roped off)

Space Usage

Public area

Non-tourist space
(vestry, offices, stores)

Free space

Figure 10.1   Lincoln Cathedral

that access should be universal, a human right. The following case study integrates some aspects of charging, visitor management and access, by focusing on visits to English cathedrals.

Case study: charging for entry to English cathedrals

Although the forty-three Anglican Diocesan cathedrals in England attracted 31 million tourist visits per year in 1999 (ICOMOS-UK, 2001), their major function is as places of worship for the Christian community. However, they are also museums, centres for pilgrimage and foci for the performing arts. Cathedrals form a major peg in the urban tourism industry and a most significant element in Britain's cultural heritage (Nolan and Nolan, 1992). They are one of the few categories of visitor attraction to show growth in visitor numbers over the last decade, although growth has not been systematic and in recent years there has been a decline (Hanna, 1992). Table 10.1 shows the most recent list of numbers of visits to cathedrals and greater churches. It is immediately possible to see a correlation between visits to cathedrals and the proximity of the building to major domestic holiday areas (for example, Chester, Truro or Norwich). Running a cathedral is very expensive. Few English cathedrals have an operating budget of less than £500 000 per annum and in many cases this has to fund conservation and management of a complex building, as well as to provide a wide range of services for visitors, pilgrims and worshippers. It is not surprising that cathedrals look to their visitors as sources of extra income.

Tourists visit cathedrals for many reasons (Winter and Gasson, 1996). Some are seeking a life-changing experience, others merely somewhere to while away a wet afternoon. Some wish to worship, others to marvel or just to explore. The size, grandeur and splendour make English cathedrals prominent visitor attractions (Binney and Hanna, 1978) and most, but not all, function as the heart of an urban tourism industry. In some locations, such as York, the existence of a cathedral and associated sites has acted as catalyst for the development of newer, purpose-built visitor attractions which capitalize on the visitors attracted to older historic sites. Although the cathedral constitutes a managed visitor attraction, its core business is to provide a focus and facility for those who wish to worship, pray or meditate. However, in order to do these things it needs to earn some revenue from visitors to help maintain fabric and services (Binney and Hanna, 1978).

Cathedrals are underfunded visitor attractions with enormous annual maintenance bills and few opportunities for generating revenue from visitors. Continuous maintenance is expensive, as cathedrals are less than optimally organized and resourced for the functions they are expected to perform in the

Table 10.1   The ten most-visited cathedrals in 1998

Ranking	Cathedral	Visitors	Charges?
1	Westminster Abbey*	3 000 000	Free*
2	York Minster	2 000 000	Free
3	Canterbury	1 500 000	Charge
4	St Paul's	1 000 900	Charge
5	Chester	1 000 000	Free
6	Salisbury	800 000	Free
7	Norwich	540 000	Free
8	Truro	500 000	Free
9	Durham	466 559	Free
10	Exeter	460 000	Free

Note: * Westminster Abbey is a 'Royal Peculiar' and instituted admissions charges in March 1998.
Source: ETB (1998)

modern world (Winter and Gasson, 1996). Cathedrals provide relatively few paid jobs, and those jobs that do exist are poorly paid, with the majority of employment created in the field of ancillary services. A small cathedral often receives less than 25 per cent of its operating budget from the Church Commissioners and must generate the remainder of its income from its investments or property. There is always a substantial shortfall, which is why cathedrals rely heavily on revenue from visitors, whether direct (by admissions charges) or indirect (for example, from shop franchising).

In order to avoid cuts in the services that the cathedral provides (in both senses) this money has to be generated either from regular worshippers or from visitors. Visitors are not generous with donations; most cathedrals without a fixed charge request a £2.50 donation and receive around 30p to 40p per visitor. It is scarcely surprising that many have resorted to compulsory admissions fees, although these are almost universally resented.

Charging for admission to cathedrals is currently a most contentious issue and some cathedrals have substituted systems of voluntary donations or implement charges only for special exhibitions. Instituting an admissions charge in a cathedral involves calculating what discounts or free access must be given to local people, how access for worshippers is maintained and how to provide visitors, who have now become customers, with value for money. Opponents of compulsory charges argue that visiting a cathedral should be an intense spiritual experience with the cathedral management doing everything in its power to preserve the holiness of these spectacular buildings in an increasingly secular world. This is undoubtedly true, but the difficult financial position of most cathedrals makes it imperative to derive revenue from visitors, just to keep the building open. However, with the exception of Westminster, St Paul's and York Minster, most cathedrals do not derive the majority of their visitors from international tourists, who are more accustomed to paying admissions fees. Smaller cathedrals may be visited mainly by local people, and have few reserve funds or investments to supplement their income. If visitors do not donate more money then the cathedral cannot maintain services and staffing. This will result in a decrease in visitation and considerable anxiety among the worshipping community. Charging for admission would seem to be the answer but local people will resent paying. Moreover expenses associated with the installation of appropriate tills, devising new visitor management techniques and undertaking additional staff training, would need to be recouped from visitor revenue. One cathedral which recently introduced compulsory charges, estimated that it subsequently lost 30 per cent of its visitors, but it cannot reverse the decision since there is no money to recoup the set-up costs.

The sheer volume of visitors to cathedrals indicates sustained demand for their religious product which, from a tourism perspective, is to offer its visitor a glimpse of the numinous. The challenge for cathedral managers is to generate revenue without being overtly commercial, while maintaining the high quality of visitor experience valued by worshippers and tourists alike.

Conclusion

One of the most interesting features of tourism to religion-based attractions is that visitor numbers continue to increase at the same time as the number of people in regular congregations is in decline. However, this observation applies more to Western, Christian sites in the developed world than to, for example, major Hindu, Buddhist or Muslim pilgrimage sites in the developing world that continue to attract huge numbers of seasonal visitors. With the West becoming an increasingly secular society, it will be interesting to see whether this trend continues, and equally interesting to speculate on the reasons for it. Are visitors to religious sites looking at a quick-fix substitute for the commitment required to become a regular worshipper? Has spending a short time in a religious building become a substitute for prayer and worship? Since many (but not all) religious sites are major historical sites of great significance to the cultural tourism sector, it seems likely that continued growth in cultural tourism also plays a part in the phenomenon. It is, of course, very difficult to generalize as the motivations of visitors to a major site (such as St Peter's in Rome) will include the whole spectrum from eagerly anticipated pilgrimage to idle curiosity.

The phenomenon of travel substitution is also likely to become more important, at least in the short term, and it would be surprising if there were not considerable growth in purpose-built managed religion-based attractions offering the experience of pilgrimage with none of the dangers and inconveniences. Religious sites in Europe and the Middle East will certainly receive fewer visitors from America over the next few years, and it is possible that overall visitation to such prominent buildings as cathedrals, mosques and temples could decline if they are perceived as terrorist targets. On the other hand, in the wake of the events of 11 September 2001, visits to almost all religious sites in the Western world increased very sharply, as people turned to religion for comfort, strength and explanation at a time of great uncertainty. It is probable that this phenomenon will be only temporary, and that the preoccupations of site managers will once again turn towards generating visitor revenue, balancing tourists with worshippers and juggling conservation priorities. But it seems likely that religion-based attractions will continue to flourish and diversify during the next decade, providing the visitor with at least a fleeting encounter with the numinous in an increasingly secular world.

References

Binney, M. and Hanna, M. (1978). *Preserving the Past: Tourism and the Economic Benefits of Conserving Historic Buildings*. SAVE Britain's Heritage.

Borg, J. van der, Costa, P. and Gotti, G. (1996). Tourism in European heritage cities. *Annals of Tourism Research*, **23**, 306–321.

Brown, D. and Loades, A. (eds) (1995). *The Sense of the Sacramental*. SPCK.

Bywater, M. (1994). Religious travel in Europe. *Travel and Tourism Analyst*, **2**, 39–52.

Carmichael, D., Hubert, J. and Reeves, B. (1994). *Sacred Sites, Sacred Places*. Routledge.

ETB (1998). *Visits to Tourist Attractions 1998*. English Tourist Board.

Hanna, M. (1992). *Anglican Cathedrals and Tourism: The Way Forward*. Sightseeing Research.

http://www.itec.com/PR/zion/holyland.htm

ICOMOS-UK (2001). *Visitor Management Policies in Cathedrals and Large Churches in the UK*. ICOMOS-UK.

Nolan, M. L. and Nolan, S. (1992). Religious sites as tourism attractions in Europe. *Annals of Tourism Research*, **19**, 68–78.

O'Guinn, T. C. and Belk, R. W. (1989). Heaven on earth: consumption at Heritage Village USA. *Journal of Consumer Research*, **16**, 227–238.

Shackley, M. (1998). A golden calf in sacred space? The future of St Katherine's Monastery, Mount Sinai (Egypt). *International Journal of Heritage Studies*, **4**, 123–134.

Shackley, M. (2001). *Managing Sacred Sites: Service Provision and Visitor Experience*. Continuum.

Shackley, M. (2002). Space, sanctity and service: the English cathedral as managed visitor attraction. *International Journal of Tourism Research* (in press).

Shoval, N. (2000). Commodification and theming of the sacred: changing patterns of tourist consumption in the 'Holy Land'. In *New Forms of Consumption: Consumers, Culture and Commodification* (M. Gottdiner, ed.) pp. 251–265, Rowman and Littlefield.

Vuconic, B. (1996). *Tourism and Religion*. Pergamon Press.

Winter, M. and Gasson, R. (1996). Pilgrimage and tourism: cathedral visiting in contemporary England. *International Journal of Heritage Studies*, **2**, 172–182.

11

Visitor attractions and human resource management

Sandra Watson and Martin McCracken

Aims

The aims of this chapter are to:

- analyse the role of human resource management (HRM) in visitor attractions
- highlight contextual influences which visitor attractions have to address in relation to managing people
- examine the role of HRM in improving competitive advantage
- discuss key issues, including labour intensity, service quality and competitive environments influencing HRM practices
- identify the philosophy and underlying attitudes pertinent to an HRM approach, through analysing Storey's (1995) model of HRM
- examine people-management skills required by visitor attraction managers and look at how these can be implemented by studying a case study of good practice.

Introduction

Delivering tourism products and services to increasingly discerning customers, in highly competitive and dynamic market conditions, presents a range of organizational challenges. Given the increasing dependence on high service quality in the tourism industry, ensuring that there is a systematically selected, properly trained and highly committed workforce in place is now essential for all visitor attractions. The overriding objective of this chapter is to illustrate how the adoption of an HRM approach may represent a valuable means for meeting many of the fundamental challenges, especially those related to service quality where a visitor attraction's people are paramount to ensuring success. However, prior to exploring the nature of HRM in visitor attractions, it is pertinent to discuss briefly some environmental factors, which are influencing how human resources may be managed more generally.

The contextual arena of visitor attractions

This section of the chapter provides a brief overview of the many influences that are forcing visitor attractions to develop new approaches to managing people. In analysing the environment with specific reference to visitor attractions and their operation in the future, Swarbrooke (1999) addresses political, social, economic and technological influences. The impact of these developments is to change the customer profile, as well as to increase the importance of the skills and capabilities of staff needed to deliver services and products in different ways to different people.

In earlier work designed to understand what issues might be important for future success in managing visitor attractions, Swarbrooke (1995) held that such sites would have to consider seriously a number of issues in relation to the management of staff. These issues comprised:

- an increased emphasis on quality
- flatter structures and empowerment of staff
- greater emphasis on effective recruitment, development and appraisal
- a growth in performance-related pay for employees.

The impact of technological advances on attractions offering visitors experience has been highlighted by key experts in Scottish tourism (McCracken and Watson, 2000). The most important influences include distribution and access, as well as virtual reality. Graham (2000) presents direction on potential policies and practices which may allow better management of a key human resource within many attractions, namely, the (normally unpaid) volunteers upon whose goodwill the attraction will often have to rely. Jago and Deery (2001) also develop this issue regarding the most effective way of managing volunteers.

Additionally, in a report commissioned by the Skills Task Force designed to investigate the nature, pattern and extent of skill requirements and shortages in the UK leisure sector, it was found that across the leisure sector as a whole a major skills gap existed among the workforce. The authors emphasized the lack of apparent entrepreneurial and management skills as most worrying. Information technology and customer care skills were sadly lacking, and there also appeared to be little training for volunteers (Keep and Mayhew, 1999).

In their paper presenting evidence based on research carried out with the key industry experts who promote and manage visitor attractions in Scotland, McCracken and Watson (2000) highlighted the impact of key environmental factors. These related to legislative changes (requirements on health, safety and employment issues) and developments in technology, as well as to rapidly evolving socioeconomic trends. The industry experts underlined that increasing globalization, greater competition and demographic changes would raise the need for visitor attractions to be more creative, particularly in relation to managing people.

The contextual issues and resultant pressures discussed above may prove to be catalysts for organizations to adopt a more systematic HRM approach for the management of their people. Fundamentally, this requires an understanding of the importance of effective people management strategies to sustain business performance. Key HRM issues for the visitor attractions sector which need to be addressed include:

- selecting and retaining quality staff
- training and development to meet new and changing demands
- managing the employee–employer relationship to meet organizational objectives.

In the next section the rationale of HRM will be explained, and arguments will be developed relating to why an HRM approach is particularly relevant for visitor attractions.

Human resource management in visitor attractions

While the term human resource management is universally used in organizations, there has been widespread debate as to its meaning and significance (Guest, 1991; Legge, 1995). During the 1970s and early 1980s, such activities as management development (MD), management by objectives (MBO) and organizational development (OD), often involving considerable input from the personnel function, were heralded as the keys to organizational success. Such developments gave some credence and legitimacy to personnel professionals, who up to that point had been much maligned. In practice, however, the personnel function was still often vulnerable and marginalized (Tyson, 1995), and tended to be left to focus on more operational and administrative duties.

Against this background, Armstrong (1988) and Guest (1989) suggest that HRM began to be acknowledged as a more distinct and valuable management function in the 1980s, and was frequently cited as a factor explaining why certain organizations were successful (Peters and Waterman, 1982). Storey (1995: 6) defines HRM as 'a distinctive approach to employment management which seeks to achieve competitive advantage through the strategic deployment of a highly committed and capable workforce, using an integrated array of cultural, structural and personnel techniques'. For those authors who support the assertion that HRM is something more distinct from the personnel function, an essential difference between those organizations that fully embrace HRM and those who do not is their acknowledgement of the vital importance of employees, who are placed at the top of the business agenda. In order to appreciate fully the vital role that HRM can play in the success of visitor attractions, this chapter utilizes Storey's (1995) HRM model, which is based upon four key tenets:

- *beliefs and assumptions* (of HRM): the underlying belief that people are critical to business success
- *strategic qualities* (of HRM): that people management issues are considered at the highest level of the organization
- *the critical role of managers* (in ensuring the successful delivery of HRM strategies): line managers are the key players in managing people
- *key levers* (which also ensure that HRM strategies can be implemented): the culture of the organization and integration of people management procedures enhance effective people management.

Each of these key themes is discussed in some detail in the following paragraphs. Their pertinence to visitor attractions is highlighted by citing examples derived from a recent research study (Watson and McCracken, 2001; 2002) involving the most successful visitor attractions in Scotland.

The study involved a questionnaire survey of the top twenty attractions which charge for admission and the top twenty where admission is free (based on visitor numbers), drawn from the Scottish Tourist Board's monitoring survey of 1998. Additionally, nine new visitor attractions were included in the sample, all of which had opened since the Scottish Tourist Board data had been compiled in

1998 but were felt to be likely to feature in the top twenty paid or free attractions in the next monitoring survey.

Respondents were asked to rate forty-five managerial skill statements in relation to current and future importance of the skill on a five-point Likert scale. The questionnaire also included seven factual biographical questions and four open-ended questions where the manager could describe organizational, training and development issues in the visitor attraction. In addition, five in-depth case studies were undertaken in an attempt to understand the complexities of running a visitor attraction.

Beliefs and assumptions of HRM

Storey (1995) asserts that if an HRM perspective is central to an organization's activity there will be underlying beliefs that stress the importance of staff. Based on these assumptions, the professional management of staff will enhance competitive advantage. In the final analysis, it is considered that human capability and commitment distinguishes successful companies from others. A cornerstone of HRM theory is that employees should be carefully selected and developed to their full potential. Therefore, it is such beliefs and assumptions that inform the approach to managing people within the organization.

When considered in relation to visitor attractions, certain factors may undermine an organization's ability to adopt such beliefs and assumptions. One of the most fundamental relates to the diverse nature of the workforce, which can make it difficult for managers to engender full commitment in such organizations. In attractions, particular staff may hold conflicting values that are not fully aligned with the goals of the organization. Cossons (1994) argues, for example, that museum professionals (curators, archaeologists and conservationists) often demonstrate more commitment to scholarly functions associated with their area of interest than to the needs of visitors. Also Ames (1994) contends that cultural heritage managers have difficulty coming to terms with meshing the organization's mission with the reality of the marketplace. Lennon and Graham (2002) consider that staff involved with commercial business activities (ticketing and merchandising) will sometimes be more receptive to HRM than professional attraction staff, who may consider the time spent on managerial tasks (staff and resourcing issues, for example) more as a distraction from their intellectual interests than a key part of their jobs. This conflict may be more profound in small, isolated visitor attractions where the professional (general manager) is often the individual who is expected to manage the commercial realities of the attraction. For example, at one of the attractions considered by the authors (Culloden Moor Visitor Centre), the visitor attraction manager (a trained historian), communicated the dilemma he faced in promoting the historical relevance of the site while ensuring its commercial viability. This can lead to potential conflict in skills development and resourcing decisions. However, there was also evidence from the research that through dialogue and collaboration, a mutual understanding and appreciation of how both the more traditional activities of an attraction manager in such a site (for example, promotion through giving lectures or holding seminars) and the more commercial activities can be reconciled, thereby contributing to the overall goals of the attraction.

Nevertheless, in the research conducted by the authors examples were found of visitor attraction managers who demonstrated the beliefs and assumptions of HRM. This is exemplified by the following quote from the manager of Holyrood Palace: 'If staff do not trust your ethos then you will not succeed – nothing is more important than keeping staff on board.'

Strategic qualities

A key cornerstone emerging from Storey's HRM model relates to the location and nature of decisions being made within organizations. In essence, Storey asserts that to be implementing a true HRM approach, human resource decisions should be seen as being of strategic importance, on a par with other organizational decisions, and hence fully involving top management. With this in mind, there is an argument that HRM should have board-level representation. However, Storey's thesis proposes that as long as the chief executive and senior management are addressing HRM issues, the actual composition of the board is of secondary concern. The full integration of human resource policies and business strategy is posted as another distinguishing feature of true HRM integration into any business (Storey, 1995).

A problem emerges when applying such a strategy to the visitor attractions sector, which has a tradition of weak functional management, with many organizations being operated through inadequate systems of administration led by people with little or no managerial skills. Aligned with this there is scant evidence of a strategic approach being taken to HRM (Lennon and Graham, 2002).

The Skills Forecasting research (CHNTO, 1999), a labour market analysis of the Scottish Cultural Heritage sector, also confirmed that there was a distinct lack of the skills needed to develop management strategies in visitor attractions. In fact, even though attempts have been made by advisory agencies and academics to encourage the industry to be more proactive in ensuring that attraction managers develop strategies to achieve quality business objectives, to date a lack of effective managerial direction has led to an inconsistent take-up of HRM (Graham, 2000). However, what is obvious, even from the brief analysis included in this chapter, is that developments in the competitive environment require a more business-orientated approach to be taken when one considers the ever-increasing competition to secure funding and adequate visitor numbers, as well as appropriately competent staff. There is also evidence emerging from a range of sources which indicates that high commitment management practices are associated with better economic performance, enhanced workplace well-being and an improved employment climate (Cully et al., 1999).

In case study research carried out by the authors, evidence was found of executive and senior management addressing HRM issues. These organizations were in the profit-making, private sector of the attractions sector. In interviews with the general manager at Baxters Highland Village (an industrial visitor attraction) and chief executive of Our Dynamic Earth (see the case study below), human resource issues were clearly considered at a strategic level. Additionally, both of these attractions had been awarded the Investors in People (IiP) accreditation (a national-level award, which illustrates that HR initiatives were considered central to the organization's operations). Such initiatives as IiP and Best Value Management are beginning to be used to raise the profile of HRM and its strategic importance to organizations.

Critical role of line managers

The involvement of line managers in both delivering and driving human resource policies is cited as being fundamental to an HRM approach to people management, because human resource practice is seen as being critical to the core activities of any business. Line managers are crucial to the effective delivery of human resource policies, and are ultimately charged with taking responsibility for conducting staff appraisal interviews and team building, as well as coaching and training. When one considers the central role of line managers in delivery of human resource, it is also important that they play a key role in driving through changes in human resource policies. This can be seen in areas such as quality management, change management and knowledge management.

Again, as with many of the human resource issues discussed here, although heritage and voluntary sector agencies have been promoting management techniques for over twenty years to attractions, research has shown that managers have rigidly resisted to embrace wholeheartedly or to display commitment to such management tasks (Graham, 2000). Such assertions are further supported by the results of the Skills Forecasting survey (which took place in 1999) of 178 cultural heritage organizations, in which 79 per cent of operators reported an important to very important need for management skills, with the remainder reporting little (8 per cent) or no need (13 per cent).

There is also evidence about the existence of such an HRM skills deficit within the sector. The Skills Forecasting survey (CHNTO, 1999) also found that 66 per cent of these operators reported an important to very important need for HRM skills. The remainder reported little (11 per cent) or no need (20 per cent). Levels of actual skills shortages varied, with 61 per cent of operators confirming an important to acute shortage, whilst 15 per cent reported little skills shortage. Watson and McCracken (2001) also found that HRM skills were viewed as essential, both now and in the future, by managers of the top visitor attractions in Scotland, for example, in training and developing, attracting and recruiting, and motivating staff. However, they also reported that people management skills, including team thinking, communication, self-empowerment, leadership and motivational skills, were lacking among managers.

Key levers

Storey describes the fourth distinguishing feature of HRM as relating to the 'key levers', which need to be present to ensure that there is effective implementation of HRM. One of the most important of these relates to organizational culture and how it is managed. Basically, an organization's culture defines the amount of consensus, flexibility and commitment there is among its workforce. Consensus implies that a common set of beliefs and values can be achieved, which will reduce conflict. Flexibility can be achieved when the culture is changed to remove restrictions, and can result in greater productivity. Commitment would result in greater perform-ance of employees who are willing to go beyond what is expected (Meyer and Allen, 1997). Other key levers cited by Storey include integration of selection, communication, training, reward and development activities, and enabling em-powerment and devolved responsibility through restructuring and job redesign.

Watson and McCracken (2001) found that many of these key levers were viewed as important. For example, the attraction managers who completed the questionnaire asserted that vital skills included leading staff, establishing trust and effective communication, encouraging staff involvement and creating and maintaining shared values in the organization. Indeed, in the follow-up case study stage of this research, the general manager of Baxters Highland Village articulated the importance of creating and maintaining shared values amongst his staff when he indicated that 'a member of staff is an ambassador for the company . . . so that member of staff has to have the same knowledge, skills and passion for the business as I do'. This manager clearly understood that a vital role for him was to motivate staff to be enthusiastic, partly through implementing a range of integrated personnel practices, but fundamentally by ensuring that he was open and communicative towards their needs. This manager also felt that the task of motivating staff was easier if the organization possessed effective selection, training and management of staff, as well as an awareness of the need to socialize them into the attraction's culture.

One of the difficulties in addressing key levers in this sector surrounds effectively managing a diverse workforce. For example, staff may be employed on flexible contracts, be part time or be volunteers. However, there is an explicit assumption among both volunteers and their supervisors that the same managing mechanisms may not be applicable to them, compared with paid staff (Lennon and Graham, 2002). Indeed, 'volunteers do not expect to be managed and are less likely to be interested in training and development than paid staff' (Lennon and Graham, 2002). However, volunteers clearly have a vital role in helping the organization to achieve its strategic objectives. It is interesting to note that Watson and McCracken (2002) found that 'the ability to effectively manage diverse employee groups, including volunteers and seasonal workers' was perceived to be essential, by managers.

Therefore, it can be seen that HRM can be presented as an approach to managing people which can address many of the unique issues inherent in managing the staff of a visitor attraction. This is not intended to be a prescriptive approach, rather it is offered as a philosophy which can be translated into operational practice depending on specific organizational contexts. As this chapter endeavours to illustrate, there are particular dilemmas and potential conflicts which make visitor attractions more complex to manage. However, if the sector is going to continue to play a major role in the UK economy, there is an urgent need for visitor attractions to address the philosophies underlying such an HRM approach to managing people.

Case study

Our Dynamic Earth was one of the first millennium projects to be opened in the UK.[1] Situated in Edinburgh, at the base of a volcano that last erupted 350 million years ago, Our Dynamic Earth is essentially an interpretation and visitor centre devoted to displaying as well as educating the public about issues relating to geology and the environment. Since opening, Our Dynamic Earth has been one of the few success stories of the millennium project. In an interview with the chief executive, held at the end of April 2000,[2] it was reported that the attraction in the first ten months has welcomed 460 000 visitors including 17 000 season ticket holders (30 per cent ahead of forecasts in terms of visitor numbers and revenue). This has been further underlined by the fact that within its relatively short life, already it has been rated as the fifth most popular Scottish attraction in terms of visitor numbers (STB, 2000).

Our Dynamic Earth considers people to be critical to its business success, as exemplified by the following quote from the chief executive where she asserted that 'we're in a business where the people are actually making the business happen, therefore it is imperative that we understand this and manage the attraction with staff being seen as central to its success'. This consideration of staff appeared to permeate throughout the organization, from a strategic perspective to the day-to-day operation of the site.

As a self-funding charitable trust, Our Dynamic Earth has several operational dimensions structured around four key areas. The first is operations, which cover everything from visitor services to maintenance. Second, there is the retail function, which is responsible for the merchandising element in the attraction. Third, because banqueting and conferences are so vital for the attraction, there is a separate food and beverages function. Finally, there is the education product, which is characterized by its non-profit-making role in the business. Overall the attraction employs eighty-six full-time employees across these functions.

There is evidence of a wide diversity of staff employed, with many highly educated, international staff working for a few months in visitor services and merchandising. There is a core team of food and beverage workers who deliver banquet and conference services, and a team of scientists and educators who are responsible for delivering the educational product. Maintenance workers have a key role in ensuring efficient and effective facilities for the whole of the attraction. This results in a range of potentially different perspectives on the values and goals of the attraction being present.

Again, the chief executive summed up the benefits that she believes such a rich diversity of employees gave in terms of gaining a wide view of issues surrounding staff and customer experiences: 'They [the staff] have come up with many really useful suggestions and proposals and ideas.' However, it was also noted that 'they don't always sense the bigger picture in terms of the commercial issues'. The dilemma of ensuring that staff members understand both the commercial and operational aspects of the business is clearly of utmost importance to management. Hence communication is part of the central ethos of the attraction, where a range of vehicles including consultative committees and staff suggestion schemes are used to emphasize a strong focus on open and informal communications, often through employees' line managers.

The organization is managed in an open way, with all staff having access to business performance information. This is presented in a fairly basic format (presentations are given to staff on the results of visitor surveys) in order that staff can be made aware of the commercial implications of decisions made at the highest levels. The staff consultative committees meet on a regular basis and look at different aspects of the business. Staff members are encouraged to suggest ways of improving the business, and are listened to so that much of the attraction's actual operation is a direct result of feedback from staff. Such communication and suggestion schemes are recognized as a strength by the chief executive, as the following quotation indicates: 'I think that probably is one of the strengths that we have . . . we have given staff a sense of ownership, make them feel that they are masters of their own destiny to the extent that they have a job to do.'

The selection of staff centres on attracting individuals who will ultimately align with the organizational culture. Before Our Dynamic Earth opened there was a major publicity drive designed to attract suitable staff for the site. In the recruitment advertisements, visual scenes illustrating the diversity of the Earth's environment, such as bubbling lava, tropical rain storms, polar ice caps, were used under the caption 'the perfect working environment'. The whole idea behind such advertising was to communicate to potential employees exactly the kind of culture that Our Dynamic Earth was based upon (young, vibrant, creative and fun). In addition to asking for specific skills for the jobs, generic skills were required. These were geared towards ensuring that employees possessed good communication and customer service skills. A key part of the selection process was profiling individuals on the basis of how well they could work together in teams. Hence group interviews were used as well as situational exercises to determine individuals' personal styles of communication. Underlining the whole recruitment and selection process was the overriding objective of ensuring that employees could fit into Our Dynamic Earth's warm, caring, open and friendly culture.

Another implicit understanding which the chief executive had about staff, was that ultimately the majority did not have long-term career aspirations within the attraction. The focus was therefore to be on ensuring that they do a good job while they are employed, with training, development and facilities to encourage commitment. Hence there were many examples of initiatives designed to instil commitment to the attraction among such staff; for example, the coffee and drink machines were on free dispense, subsidized meals were available, staff events and parties were held regularly. In addition, the organization ran a staff profit day, when all revenues generated on that day were distributed among non-salaried staff.

In terms of training and development in the site, detailed training programmes were designed to give staff the skills required to meet organizational goals. The chief executive believed that 'everyone has responsibility for training' but clearly understood that effectively it started with her, through encouragement, support and allocation of resources. There is a personnel manager who works closely with all the managers to identify training needs and organize the appropriate delivery of training. There is also an intensive induction process, which concentrates on ensuring staff understood the values and goals of the organization. In addition, there is a formal performance review system in place, which incorporates everyone, including staff who might only be employed for a summer season. An assessment review occurred after six weeks of employment because it was conceivable that within ten weeks staff may return to university or move elsewhere.

As well as engineering commitment and enthusiasm amongst the staff in the attraction, the chief executive also underlined the importance of motivating and stimulating the top management team. To that end the most senior managers undertook 'busman's holidays' to other successful attractions to gain ideas to motivate constantly and to build up their professional knowledge of how to manage their employees effectively. The chief executive expressed her strong commitment to continuous professional development, as illustrated by her pledge of gaining IiP accreditation a full eighteen months before opening. It was considered that going through this accreditation process would help with devising business processes. Our Dynamic Earth was awarded the full IiP accreditation seven months after opening.

The chief executive took the lead in encouraging a culture where staff and their contributions are valued. She reiterated the importance of the culture by noting that 'managing the culture is everything we do, even the staff uniforms are a reflection of what this culture is all about, open, friendly, young, contemporary'. The focus is on comfort with a 'kind of a street quality'. The uniform is cargo trousers, combo jacket and a choice of six colours of T-shirts, polo necks and fleeces. Staff members are encouraged to wear what they want from within this selection.

Another indication of the open culture was the fact that there was also no segregation of staff levels and, although everyone was required to wear a name badge, supervisors were not marked apart from other staff. This is seen as appropriate to the kind of product being offered and the culture at Our Dynamic Earth.

As can been seen, the importance of and focus on staff issues is paramount to the successful operation of Our Dynamic Earth. As a way of summing up this case study, a final view expressed by the chief executive, which exemplifies their approach to managing people was 'we do feel it is important that irrespective of the length of time the staff are with us, whether it is short or long, they will still take something of value away with them'.

Conclusion

The authors would contend that adopting an HRM approach, as illustrated in the paragraphs above, is vital to ensure the future success of many visitor attractions. It is argued that in understanding the major tenets of the HRM approach (Storey, 1995), some of the dilemmas faced by visitor attraction managers (such as managing diverse sets of employees, reconciling commercial with other goals, and so on) can be better appreciated and managed. The HRM approach is portrayed not as a prescriptive one but one that allows managers to understand the types of thought process they need to engage in and to begin to enhance their people management strategies. This requires ensuring that there is an underlying belief that people are the key to competitive advantage and that human resource decisions are made and supported by top management, engaging line management commitment to human resource policies and developing a culture which embraces the key levers. This chapter provides real-life examples from research to support this position, while raising awareness of the complexities associated with managing people in this sector.

This chapter advocates the need for a new direction to be embraced by visitor attractions, to ensure that there is an increased focus on securing employee commitment to improve business performance. It is argued that such an HRM approach allows a greater appreciation of the diverse needs of existing and potential employees when devising strategies to select, develop and reward, as well as to engender greater trust. It is recognized that such skills may not currently be present among the majority of visitor attraction managers, but as has been shown through research carried out previously by the authors (Watson and McCracken, 2001) and others (CHNTO, 1999), many managers recognize the importance of such skills and have articulated a willingness to develop in these areas. In itself, such a development is worthy of note in a sector much maligned for its lack of managerial skills or coherent professional approach (Lennon and Graham, 2002). However, as a further illustration of how such an HRM approach can help to improve the competitive position of visitor attractions, the preceding section has sought to demonstrate how one very successful visitor attraction has embraced, and sought to implement, an HRM approach to managing people.

Notes

1 Our Dynamic Earth was opened on the 2 July 1999.
2 Much of the information contained in this case study is based on this interview as well as other survey responses from staff at the attraction.

References

Ames, P. J. (1994). A challenge to modern museum management. In *Museum Management* (K. Moore, ed.) pp. 15–21, Routledge.

Armstrong, M. (1988). *A Handbook of Personnel Management Practice*. Kogan Page.

CHNTO (1999). *Skills Forecasting Scotland: A Labour Market Analysis of the Scottish Cultural Heritage Sector*. Cultural Heritage National Training Organization.

Cossons, N. (1994). Scholarship or self-indulgence? In *Museum Provision and Professionalism* (G. Cavanagh, ed.) pp. 237–246, Routledge.

Cully, M., Woodland, S., O'Reilly, A. and Dix, G. (1999). *Britain at Work*. Routledge.

Graham, M. (2000). The impact of social change on the roles and management of volunteers in Glasgow museums. PhD thesis, Glasgow Caledonian University.

Guest, D. (1989). Personnel or human resource management: can you tell the difference? *Personnel Management*, **21**, 48–51.

Guest, D. (1991). Personnel management: the end of orthodoxy? *British Journal of Industrial Relations*, **29**, 149–175.

Jago, L. K. and Deery, M. (2001). Managing volunteers. In *Quality Issues in Heritage Visitor Attractions* (S. Drummond and I. Yeoman, eds) pp. 194–217, Butterworth-Heinemann,

Keep, E. and Mayhew, K. (1999). *The Leisure Sector*. Skills Task Force Research Paper No. 6, DFEE Publications.

Legge, K. (1995). *Human Resource Management: Rhetorics and Realities*. Macmillan.

Lennon, J. and Graham, M. (2002). The dilemma and limitations of operating a strategic approach to human resource management in the Scottish visitor attraction sector. *International Journal of Contemporary Hospitality Management*, **14** (in press).

McCracken, M. and Watson, S. (2000). Impact of environmental trends for managers in Scottish visitor attactions. Paper presented at CHRIE Conference, New Orleans.

Meyer, J. P. and Allen, N. J. (1997). *Commitment in the Workplace, Theory Research and Application*. Sage.

Peters, T. and Waterman, R. (1982). *In Search of Excellence: Lessons from America's Best Run Companies*. Harper and Row.

Storey, J. (1995). *Human Resource Management: A Critical Text*. Routledge.

STB (2001). *The Scottish visitor attraction monitor*. Scottish Tourist Board.

Swarbrooke, J. (1995). *The Development and Management of Visitor Attractions*. Butterworth-Heinemann.

Swarbrooke, J. (1999). *The Development and Management of Visitor Attractions*. 2nd edn. Butterworth-Heinemann.

Tyson, S. (1995). *Human Resource Strategy*. Pitman.

Watson, S. and McCracken, M. (2001). Managerial skill requirement: evidence from the Scottish visitor attraction industry. Academy of Human Resource Development Conference Proceedings, Tulsa, USA.

Watson, S. and McCracken, M. (2002). No attraction in strategic thinking! *International Journal of Tourism Research* (in press).

Part Four

Marketing visitor attractions

Part Four of this book focuses on a theme of considerable importance to all visitor attractions, that of marketing. While there has been considerable growth in the literature on the marketing of visitor attractions in recent years, arguably much of what is said about visitor attraction marketing is premature. First, little is known about the fundamental nature of the visitor attraction product by those marketing them, particularly those sites of a heritage nature. Second, there is frequently a lack of suitable marketing information available upon which to make sound judgements about marketing strategy. The marketing research base of many attractions is extremely limited, and where research has been undertaken it is arguably still relatively unsophisticated. This has implications for the management and marketing of visitor attractions, severely limiting the scope for effective marketing. Third, whereas branding is a major marketing issue in most other parts of the tourism industry, to date it has played a relatively limited role in the visitor attraction sector. As with marketing research, where branding does exist it has tended to deliver limited benefits. Finally, there is also a tendency in the literature to discuss the marketing of individual visitor attractions in isolation from one another. Pressures in the funding and visitor marketplaces are serving as catalysts for a more collaborative response from many visitor attractions, especially the smaller, resource-poor attractions that often constitute the majority in visitor attraction sectors around the world.

In Chapter 12, Stephen Boyd begins to address some of the above issues with particular reference to heritage visitor attractions. In view of the complex nature of the heritage product, Boyd provides some new insights by taking the discussion beyond the conventional marketing mix and examining new areas where opportunities exist to market heritage tourism. Boyd highlights the importance of the need to move towards a position of sustainability of the heritage product, and places particular emphasis on the role partnerships can play in the marketing of the heritage tourism experience. This theme is expanded with two case studies looking at the role played by product development clubs and partnerships in the marketing of heritage attractions.

The heritage theme continues in Chapter 13, where Michael Hall and Rachel Piggin explore the branding potential of heritage with specific reference to existing practices surrounding visitor attractions with World Heritage status. Hall and Piggin begin by indicating the important role of World Heritage sites as visitor attractions and illustrate the role of institutional procedures and processes in developing the values underlying the World Heritage brand. Although the authors question the extent to which lessons learned elsewhere in the tourism industry can be applied in the World Heritage context, the authors identify specific problems in the management of the World Heritage values that underlie the brand, and outline some impediments to the branding of visitor attractions. Hall and Piggin then illustrate the importance of recognizing the manner in which the brand values of a visitor attraction may be differentially understood or interpreted. The chapter closes with a look at how the World Heritage brand is understood and used in New Zealand. The authors conclude that there is limited consensus of understanding and usage of the World Heritage brand. This can partly be attributed to the failure of tourism businesses to create and maintain customer and visitor records, as well as to the absence of broader macro-level research on reasons for travel to World Heritage sites.

Chapter 14 analyses another important aspect of marketing: that of pricing. With a detailed case study investigation of the competitive marketing and pricing practices of theme parks in Central Florida, Bradley Braun and Mark Soskin spell out a number of lessons for managers of large-scale, predominantly themed, visitor attractions. The large-scale and highly commercial nature of such attractions offers challenges and opportunities quite different to many of the examples outlined in the preceding two chapters. With considerable financial sums required for investment and reinvestment in ride technology, detailed research, as a foundation for sound management decision-making, is a necessity rather than a luxury. This is particularly the case in mature market conditions, where industry structures are still emerging and where there are evident changes in global tourism markets. Braun and Soskin use a demand estimation model to illustrate the nature of the pricing relationships and strategic interdependencies in the sector, a demand model being made possible by the richness of data available in this part of the wider visitor attraction sector.

Given the increasingly difficult competitive environment in which many visitor attractions now find themselves, Part Four concludes with an exploration of the extent to which collaborative marketing strategies offer a potential solution to problems and challenges too large or complex for individual attractions to address in isolation. In Chapter 15, Alan Fyall outlines the conditions in the visitor attraction sector that encourage a collaborative approach to marketing and identifies some of the benefits and drawbacks of collaboration. More specifically, Fyall explores the situations where collaborative strategies are most appropriate and desirable, and introduces a set of guiding principles for effective collaboration. With reference to a 'true-to-life' case study, the feasibility of collaboration is examined, with the author concluding that competing attractions are no longer the competitive threat they once were; they should now be viewed as the source of future strength and collaborative survival.

12

Marketing challenges and opportunities for heritage tourism

Stephen W. Boyd

Aims

The aims of this chapter are to:

- show that the term 'heritage' is complex, and that heritage tourism overlaps with other tourism types
- identify the components that constitute the marketing mix, in particular new thinking on this concept
- examine new areas where opportunities exist to market heritage tourism
- highlight the importance of moving towards the position of sustainability of the product, particularly the role partnerships can play towards the marketing of the heritage tourism experience.

Introduction

Heritage tourism is not a new type of tourism. While it may be promoted as part of special interest tourism, it is a form of tourism that has been visible for as long as the concept of tourism has received academic attention. The Grand Tour, often regarded as the precursor to modern mass tourism, was essentially heritage tourism, as the elite of Western society travelled to places to be educated on that area's past, culture and physical make-up. Since those days, what has changed with heritage tourism is its overall share of travel activity. At the advent of the boom in mass tourism in the 1960s and 1970s, and the desire for places offering a hedonistic experience, interest in things heritage within destinations was low. Places promoted themselves on the basis they could offer a five Ss experience of 'sand, sun, sea, surf and sex'. Things cultural and heritage were viewed as key attractions for places that could not market themselves as sun-kissed destinations. At present, heritage has shifted to having greater importance both as a focus of attraction as well as a theme against which places can be marketed. The WTO states that almost 40 per cent of all travel has a heritage component involved. A major reason for this is the emergence of significant 'grey' (fifties plus) markets within the major tourism sending regions. What has started to emerge over the past decade has been an interest in promoting the past (in its many guises) as a tourist product and understanding and reliving the past as a key tourist experience (Wall and Nuryanti, 1996).

In marketing heritage there is the need to understand that it is a complex commodity. Heritage may be viewed as taking on the identity of an interest in the past, an interest in cultures, buildings, artefacts and landscapes of both the past and present. However, it is more than simply tourism based on the past. It is an interest that has more often than not been determined by the sets of values and criteria imposed on it, values that differ over time, space and across society. As such, heritage becomes that which society deems it to be, removing or obscuring those elements they consider not suitable for the tourist gaze, or which present a less than favourable impression to visitors (Ashworth and Tunbridge, 1996). Heritage is also part of a region's resource base, but only exists as such when it has been determined to have some utility function (Hall and McArthur, 1998). Furthermore, heritage exists at different scales, ranging from the international to the local, and is also shaped by the context within which it exists.

An early argument to make in this chapter is that any future marketing of heritage must embrace the holistic nature of the term to involve its natural, cultural, historical, built, industrial and personal components, and to present each as they exist within destinations. Furthermore, heritage should be viewed as a type of tourism that traverses a mix of landscapes and settings, where overlap

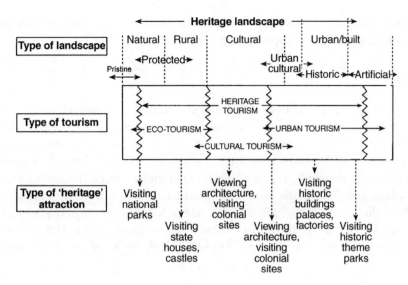

Figure 12.1 Heritage tourism: an overlapping concept
Source: Timothy and Boyd (2002)

occurs with other types of tourism (see Figure 12.1). Failure to adopt such a holistic and inclusive understanding of heritage will perpetuate a myopic perspective that limits what elements of heritage within settings are presented to visitors.

In building on the understanding of what constitutes heritage, this chapter also presents new thinking associated with the marketing mix concept and its association with heritage. It also explores areas of heritage that have not been as effectively marketed for tourism as others. The chapter then addresses the challenge of creating sustainable heritage tourism development, in which one particular principle, that of partnership development, is expanded on through case studies.

Going beyond the conventional marketing mix

A conventional definition of marketing is the production of goods and services to suit the needs and wants of an end-user or consumer. This has involved elements such as price, product, promotion and place – well known as those elements that make up the marketing mix of a product (Kotler, Haider and Rein, 1993). Recent thinking has witnessed expansion from these four Ps to include elements such as people, programming and partnership (Goeldner, Ritchie and McIntosh, 2000). The marketing mix has been adopted and used in tourism to illustrate how places

191

market themselves. This section develops thinking on how the new elements of the marketing mix have applicability within a heritage tourism context.

People

From a marketing perspective, the focus is often on the product itself, with less attention to the experiences on offer. The heritage industry has emerged from how a region's past has been commodified and sold to the visitor, where emphasis has been on the tangible products of the industry. The 'people' element suggests that equal attention should be focused on the experiences behind the heritage settings themselves and that, while tourism is product driven, ultimately tourists are in search of the intangible within settings where focus is on the actual experiences they seek to take away from visits (Timothy and Boyd, 2002). This experiential dimension to heritage is often tied to the learning aspect of heritage tourism.

Programming

Under this heading, the focus is on how the products and experiences can be better packaged for the customer. In tourism, this is often in the form of running special events, and in the case of heritage tourism much attention has focused on festivals and how they can be representative of places themselves (Getz, 1991). In addition, packaging can involve putting together a mix of product and experience by linking a number of attractions together. Recognized as cluster development, or attraction clusters, this type of programming is often only accomplished through the presence of partnerships between tourist operators.

Partnerships

This element is linked to wider ideas of collaboration and network development. Defined by Bramwell and Lane (1999: 179) as 'regular, cross-sectoral interactions between parties, based on at least some agreed rules or norms, intended to address a common issue or to achieve a specific policy goal or goals', it is emerging as almost standard practice within tourism management to involve some sort of partnership agreement or dialogue between different parties. It is not a new concept, but one that has been around for several decades particularly within management and corporate sectors (Gray, 1989). It is relatively new within tourism research circles, where the focus has been descriptive and centred on presenting case studies. There has emerged some work that has developed a conceptual dimension to this area of inquiry that is focused on heritage tourism. Working in the context of World Heritage sites, Boyd and Timothy (2001) stressed the importance of three key elements within any partnership: type (informal to formalized), the approach taken (grass roots to agency led) and the extent of co-operation between partners (full to limited).

New and existing opportunities

Linear heritage features

The tourist's gaze over the heritage landscape has been a rather selective one. Attention has focused on the impressive, such as natural and cultural features that have been given World Heritage status, or has been directed to those attractions that exist as point or nodal sources (old buildings, mills, factories, monuments) or as areas (historic cities, commemorative sites and national parks). Scope exists to market heritage attractions that are linear in their configuration, like designated coastlines, trails and rivers. Some examples follow to suggest that market attention be broadened to include such linear elements within the heritage landscape.

With respect to heritage coasts, few countries have labelled parts of their coastline with a heritage designation. One exception is the UK where forty-five stretches of coastline around England and Wales have been designated as heritage coasts. While some are clearly associated with resort regions such as the Torbay area in the south-west of England, most are not marketed as tourist attractions. Instead, they often exist as part of local and regional leisure and recreational spaces, with others linked to long-distance walking trails with emphasis on the natural heritage of the regions they pass through. Scope therefore exists to market the heritage dimension of such landscapes as part of the larger heritage attraction base present across the UK.

Trails offer potential as a base against which heritage can be represented. Ranging in scale from international to local, trails have been developed within resource-based, intermediate and user-orientated environments. Resource-based environments, which often include remote areas, national parks and long-distance walking routes through rural regions, provide the means to represent the natural heritage of places. The extent to which this has been capitalized upon varies between countries. The national scenic and historical trails system in the USA is underutilized (Zinser, 1995), whereas many of the trails within New Zealand's national parks are overused, particularly those known as the Great Walks, where crowding and displacement are becoming the norm (Kearsley, 1997). User-orientated environments focus on urban places or areas within close proximity to densely populated regions. Urban places are important for tourism, containing historic cores, interesting street patterns, cultural and heritage features. Within this attraction mix, urban heritage trails have received limited attention, both from an academic and research perspective, as well as by local authorities in how they promote their urban attractions. In many cases, heritage trails often exist as part of the attraction base of historic city cores (Ashworth and Tunbridge, 2000) but assume secondary importance over specific attractions within these areas. Potential exists to market urban heritage trails as one means of linking attractions within historic cores and offering diversity to the tourist experience.

Rivers are elements within the landscape that have seldom been associated with heritage. Potential exists to identify those stretches or complete watercourses that may be set aside for their natural, cultural and recreational value. This has been undertaken in Canada where over 7000 kilometres have been given heritage designation within a system of twenty-nine rivers (Parks Canada, 1997). The potential, however, to market them for tourism is rather limited as most stretches are in isolated regions where the lack of access is difficult to overcome. Where access is not a problem, the heritage features of rivers and their catchment areas can become tourist attractions, as has been the case with the Grand River in south-west Ontario.

Cultural heritage of indigenous peoples

This cultural resource has taken on increased significance as indigenous groups have opened themselves up to tourism (Butler and Hinch, 1996; Mercer, 1994). While the growth in interest towards visiting these cultures may be tied in with a more discerning market that seeks different experiences within wanderlust destinations, the attraction for indigenous people is both economic, in that tourism brings benefits to their communities, and educational, in that it satisfies their desire to inform visitors about their way of life (Hall, 2000). The extent to which such culture is marketed in the future will depend upon the degree to which these groups choose to remain in tourism, as well as the control they have over how their way of life is promoted and sold to visitors. One issue here is how authentic should the experience be. In order to preserve this type of cultural heritage attraction, perhaps it is necessary to protect the real culture and offer a staged one to visitors. This in turn may have implications on these cultures remaining attractive to the heritage tourist.

Building on existing attraction bases

Marketing should continue to focus on existing opportunities, especially where no real alternative beyond heritage exists and where heritage is the *raison d'être* for what attracts people to certain places. In the first case, what often emerges is that tourism in a local area or region is based around the heritage theme. Tourism in Northern Ireland, for example, fits this description well, where heritage characterizes the majority of attractions and encapsulates the experiences tourists take away from a visit (Boyd, 2000a). One area that offers an opportunity to build on such an attraction base, and this has generic application beyond the Northern Ireland setting, is to integrate more effectively cultural tourism and the arts with heritage. As for the second case, where heritage is the reason for the attractiveness of the location, the historic cores of mono-functional and multi-functional urban places (Ashworth and Tunbridge, 2000) are apt examples. Here Ashworth and Tunbridge classify them as resource based and demand based. Perhaps the greater opportunity to develop heritage further exists for demand-based locations, whereas the greater challenges remain to safeguard resource-based locations from being altered in ways that reflect on their heritage appeal.

The challenge to ensure sustainability of the product

Ensuring the sustainability of the product is a key challenge that cannot be ignored, as marketing arguably should focus on attractions and opportunities that have long-term viability. Heritage tourism differs from other types of tourism, and sustainability principles must reflect this. Research by the author would suggest that appropriate principles on which heritage tourism ought to be planned and managed are as follows (Boyd, 2001):

- ensuring authenticity of product and experience
- the provision of a learning environment through interaction and involvement
- conserving and protecting resources
- building partnerships between visitors, managers and stakeholders.

Authenticity

Authenticity is central to heritage tourism as the product(s) on display are often re-creations of a region's past built and cultural landscape. Given that places and objects are subject to change and decay, how much of what is regarded as the cultural and heritage landscape is truly authentic? In such circumstances, authenticity in the built environment may be limited to few places, which have been termed 'heritage gem cities' by Ashworth and Tunbridge (2000: 13), where the 'historic resource is so dramatic, extensive, and complete and where the past has survived intact with little to no change'. In contrast to the heritage setting itself, tourists' experiences can be often subject to a staged product (MacCannell, 1973), but then do visitors really care about adaptations made to the experiences

195

they are offered? While there is justification to ensure that authenticity is not staged – that it remains real with the realization that this may vary given the culture involved – it should also be acknowledged that authenticity can be reaffirmed in how visitors consume the experience (McIntosh and Prentice, 1999).

Learning

A key distinction between heritage tourism and other types is the learning dimension present and the perception of a greater willingness to learn on the part of the tourist (Light, 1995; Prentice, 1995). Much of the overall tourist experience here is comprised of learning about a region's past, and this is often best provided through interpretation in the form of detailed on-site literature, displays, visitor centres, re-enactments and guided tours (Hall and McArthur, 1998). While multiple methods exist by which learning may be communicated, caution needs to be exercised to avoid the danger of elevating educating the visitor above what they are willing and open to accept.

Conserving and protecting resources

Heritage tourists are one set of users of the resources within destination regions, and as such it is important to recognize other users, both tourists and non-tourists, that are present. This often requires that an integrative approach be adopted to planning, where heritage tourism is viewed as being compatible with other tourism use of the region, thereby providing diversity of type of attractions available for the visitor (Hall and McArthur, 1998). It is often against this background that the third principle of conserving and protecting resources emerges to ensure compatible use.

Conservation and protection can often be viewed as meaning different things in different settings. Within a natural heritage context such as a national park, a conservation focus requires that the ecological integrity of the attraction itself be promoted against abuse and overuse, but at the same time allowing for participation and enjoyment (Boyd, 2000b). Linked to this is the need to control access to sites to ensure the safety of tourists. Where cultural heritage tourism is concerned, the emphasis must be placed on protecting and respecting the rights of different ethnic groups, ensuring that benefits feed back (Butler and Hinch, 1996), and that the rights of the host culture are also respected (Hall, 2000; Mercer, 1994). If respect is present, conserving cultural heritage attractions requires that a community-based perspective be taken, where the community that 'owns' the cultural attraction collectively decides the extent to which it is open to visitors

(Prentice, 1993). A 'conservation-focus', particularly for built heritage attractions, often takes on a different emphasis of either safeguarding (protecting) selective elements of the past (Larkham, 1995) or conserving past inherited characteristics using traditional construction techniques but which allow for conversion to modern use, where appropriate.

Building partnerships

Discussion has taken place on partnerships earlier in this chapter, and the focus here is to link this principle to the acceptance of adopting a long-term focus. This, however, first requires that consideration be given to whether or not a long-term market actually exists, and if certain attractions have a long-term product and experience to offer the visitor. Here the nature of ownership of attractions must also be taken into account, given that most public sector bodies and agencies are often constrained by the short-term mandates of their political masters. The author of this chapter would argue that if partnerships are developed that they be broad-based, encouraging empowerment between members, and ranging from large corporate arrangements to private and community-led initiatives. Partnerships should, however, not just exist at the planning and management level, but should translate down to the users themselves and be reflected in how they respect the sites and attractions (Boyd and Timothy, 2001). That the heritage tourist is more likely to be willing to be educated on site, where learning is a principal element to the overall visit, makes this all the more feasible. The current sociodemographic profile of heritage tourists would suggest this level of respect to be present. The challenge will come when heritage tourism is marketed across society as a whole, where the same level of respect may not be so evident.

Case studies: product development clubs and partnerships

Of the four key principles addressed in this chapter, building partnerships is perhaps the one that may influence the direction of heritage tourism in the future as private sector enterprises join with the public sector to offer heritage opportunities. This section describes two examples of the role that partnership can play here. Both case studies are taken from Canada. The first looks at product development clubs, particularly focusing on one within south-west Ontario. The second looks at the heritage tourism strategy in Banff National Park in Alberta, and examines the role that partnerships can play in assisting with how the experience is conveyed to visitors as well as how this heritage resource base is managed.

Product development clubs

The Canadian Tourism Commission (CTC, 1998) described these as a consortia of small and medium-sized businesses that agree to work together in order to develop new tourism products or enhance existing products. Through pooling knowledge, efforts and resources, key objectives of the product club are to:

- increase the range and quality of tourism products in Canada
- build business networks to increase the exchange of information
- encourage co-operative ventures and partnerships.

There are currently twelve such clubs in operation across Canada. With respect to heritage, these range from the independent innkeepers' cultural and ecotourism club, that develops new packages to complement stays at high-quality heritage inns in Ontario, to a festivals network product club that brings together organizers of festivals in association with the tourism industry for the National Capital Region. One of the most successful is the Conservation Lands Product Club in south-western Ontario. The Conservation Lands of Ontario is an alliance of the Grand River, Halton Region, Hamilton Region, Long Point Region and Niagara Peninsula Conservation authorities in south-western Ontario, designed to market natural heritage tourism (ecotourism along with soft adventure) within their watersheds (Bruno, personal communication, 1998). Over fifty private sector partners have joined the Conservation Lands, ranging from outfitters (for example Grand Experiences), to specific attractions (for instance Wellington County Museum). Combined, they offer visitors and tour operators the opportunity to enjoy the near urban experience of the outdoors/heritage across thirty-nine Conservation Areas west of Toronto and Niagara Falls. With respect to specific heritage attractions, the visitor can view within the Conservation Lands of Ontario the following sites: Dundas valley, a spectacular Carolinian habitat (Hamilton Region); Ball's Falls, a nineteenth-century industrial village (Niagara Peninsula); Crawford Lake, a reconstructed Iroquois village (Halton Region); and Backus Heritage, Backus Woods pioneer village (Bruno, personal communication, 1998). Given that the Conservation Lands of Ontario is a relatively new initiative, it is too early to measure the success of this partnership. What is probably going to emerge over the long term is the attraction of a few key places above the rest, but key attractions that cater to either adventure or heritage visitor experiences. In terms of marketing, this example illustrates the importance of developing networks that focus on niche areas, where a range of attractions, operators and accommodation providers exist in clusters that can easily be accessed by visitors. Furthermore, while the product club involves a mix of partners, it is essential that an overall project manager oversees the partnership. The success of product development clubs across Canada will be linked to how well project managers can integrate individual partners with the overall visitor experience provided in those regions where the clubs exist.

Selling heritage through an orientation programme

In this case study the providers of heritage to the end-user, namely, the visitor, use partnership to communicate the heritage product. A secondary focus is that partnership can also be used in how the heritage base is managed. The heritage orientation programme in Banff National Park, Alberta, developed from a sense within the community of Banff that they needed to market their attraction base better. The programme evolved as one outcome of a larger study that addressed concerns within the Banff-Bow Valley region. With Banff receiving over 4 million visitors per year and being the most visited national park in Canada, there was concern regarding impacts and inappropriate uses being promoted (Banff-Bow Valley Study, 1996). One outcome of the study undertaken on the Banff-Bow Valley, was the development of a heritage tourism strategy on the basis that promoting heritage tourism was regarded as an example of an appropriate use. The goals of the heritage tourism strategy were to (Parks Canada, 1998):

- create visitor awareness of being in a national park through fostering visitor appreciation and understanding of nature, culture and history of the park itself
- encourage and develop opportunities, products and services that were consistent with heritage values
- encourage environmental stewardship initiatives upon which sustainable heritage tourism could be based
- set up a heritage orientation programme with the express purpose of giving residents the knowledge base upon which they could share their understanding of heritage of the park, both natural and human, with visitors.

In implementing the last goal, the local community is charged with the responsibility of making sure visitors understand and appreciate the unique opportunity they have in visiting this national park and World Heritage site. Indirectly, the community becomes involved in how the park is managed. The type of partnership that exists between community members and Parks

Canada, the public sector agency responsible for managing national parks in Canada, is one that is formalized and where equality exists between partners. The approach taken is community led, with a strong grass-roots movement that has been given the support of Parks Canada. This equality between partners is demonstrated by the fact that Parks Canada played a role in developing the heritage tourism strategy in association with the community of Banff. A high level of co-operation exists between partners, and the orientation strategy has the potential to develop new thinking in how the park should be managed. Management needs to move away from being the sole responsibility of public sector agencies, to embrace the views of those affected by activities undertaken within the region, and to shift thinking towards promoting appropriate activities (Boyd and Timothy, 2001).

The orientation programme educates residents about the park, its history, the role tourism has played throughout the years, the diversity of attractions present, and the changes in how the park has been managed, to name but a few. Since being offered to residents in 1998, over 1000 people have taken the orientation programme. By creating a knowledgeable resident population, visitors are being informed about heritage through the eyes of those whose lives are inextricably linked to the success of this activity. Potential exists to expand this type of community partnership far beyond the boundaries of Banff National Park by utilizing it as a tourism model for 'educating' visitors as to the purpose, heritage or otherwise, of national parks and historic sites across Canada and, indeed, more widely.

Conclusion

This chapter has presented several strands of thinking about marketing heritage tourism. Today's student of heritage needs to accept that as a concept it should be marketed to include its varied elements, and that a holistic approach to heritage is beneficial. This way, all the heritage attributes of a region are considered. There exists the opportunity to elaborate on the traditional approach to marketing, to include new dimensions like people, programming and partnership. While marketing as a product still relies on the traditions of product formulation, price, place and promotion, opportunities to expand beyond these should not be ignored. Part of this new thinking also relates to marketing new opportunities within any heritage landscape. As discussed in this chapter, the potential within linear heritage environments has remained relatively unexplored by marketers and researchers alike. While new opportunities should be explored, it is also essential that well-established markets and attractions not be ignored. In both the new and the established attraction base, a key challenge will be to ensure the sustainability of the heritage products and experiences on offer. An important principle of ensuring sustainability is the development of partnerships. The case studies presented here illustrate the benefits that partnerships offer in how heritage is presented and marketed. As heritage tourism gains in recognition and importance, new opportunities need to be explored and different approaches need to be considered to how heritage should be marketed. The discussion in this chapter offers some thinking along these lines.

References

Ashworth, G. J. and Tunbridge, J. E. (1996). *Dissonant Heritage: The Management of the Past as a Resource in Conflict*. Wiley.

Ashworth, G. J. and Tunbridge, J. E. (2000). *The Tourist-Historic City: Retrospect and Prospect of Managing the Heritage City*. Pergamon.

Banff-Bow Valley Study (1996). *Banff-Bow Valley: At the Crossroads*. Summary report, Ministry of Supply and Services Canada.

Boyd, S. W. (2000a). Heritage tourism in Northern Ireland: opportunity under peace. *Current Issues in Tourism*, 3, 150–174.

Boyd, S. W. (2000b). Tourism, national parks and sustainability. In *Tourism and National Parks: Issues and Implications* (R. W. Butler and S. W. Boyd, eds) pp. 161–186, Wiley.

Boyd, S. W. (2001). Cultural and heritage tourism in Canada: opportunities, principles and challenges. *International Journal of Tourism and Hospitality Research*, 3, 211–233.

Boyd, S. W. and Timothy, D. J. (2001). Developing partnerships: tools for interpretation and management of World Heritage Sites. *Tourism Recreation Research*, 26, 47–53.

Bramwell, B. and Lane, B. (1999). Collaboration and partnerships for sustainable tourism. *Journal of Sustainable Tourism*, 7, 179–181.

Butler, R. W. and Hinch, T. (eds) (1996). *Tourism and Indigenous Peoples*. International Thomson Business Press.

CTC (1998). *Information Brochure on the Development of Product Clubs*. Canadian Tourism Commission.

Getz, D. (1991). *Festivals, Special Events and Tourism*. Van Nostrand Reinhold.

Goeldner, C. R., Ritchie, J. R. B. and McIntosh, R. W. (2000). *Tourism: Principles, Practices, Philosophies*. Wiley.

Gray, B. (1989). *Collaborating*. Jossey-Bass.

Hall, C. M. (2000). Tourism, national parks and aboriginal peoples. In *Tourism and National Parks: Issues and Implications* (R. W. Butler and S. W. Boyd, eds) pp. 57–71, Wiley.

Hall, C. M. and McArthur, S. (1998). *Integrated Heritage Management: Principles and Practice*. The Stationery Office.

Kearsley, G. (1997). Managing the consequences of over-use by tourists of New Zealand's conservation estate. In *Tourism Planning and Policy in Australia and New Zealand: Cases, Issues and Practice* (C. M. Hall, J. Jenkins and G. Kearsley, eds) pp. 87–98, Irwin.

Kotler, P., Haider, D. H. and Rein, I. (1993). *Marketing Places: Attracting Investment, Industry, and Tourism to Cities, States and Nations*. Free Press.

Larkham, P. J. (1995). Heritage as planned and conserved. In *Heritage, Tourism and Society* (D. T. Herbert, ed.) pp. 85–116, Mansell.

Light, D. (1995). Heritage as informal education. In *Heritage, Tourism and Society* (D. T. Herbert, ed.) pp. 117–145, Mansell.

MacCannell, D. (1973). Staged authenticity: arrangements of social space in tourist settings. *American Sociological Review*, **79**, 589–603.

Mercer, D. (1994). Native peoples and tourism: conflict and compromise. In *Global Tourism: The Next Decade* (W. F. Theobald, ed.) pp. 124–145, Butterworth-Heinemann.

McIntosh, A. J. and Prentice, R. C. (1999). Affirming authenticity: consuming cultural heritage. *Annals of Tourism Research*, **26**, 589–612.

Parks Canada (1997). *The Canadian Heritage Rivers System*. Annual report, 1996–7. Ministry of Supply and Services Canada.

Parks Canada (1998). *Banff-Bow Valley Heritage Orientation Strategy*. Canadian Heritage, Parks Canada.

Prentice, R. (1993). *Tourism and Heritage Attractions*. Routledge.

Prentice, R. C. (1995). Heritage as formal education. In *Heritage, Tourism and Society* (D. T. Herbert, ed.) pp. 146–169, Mansell.

Timothy, D. J. and Boyd, S. W. (2002). *Heritage Tourism*. Prentice-Hall.

Wall, G. and Nuryanti. W. (1996). Guest editors: heritage and tourism. Special issue of *Annals of Tourism Research*, **23**, 2.

Zinser, C. (1995). *Outdoor Recreation: US National Parks, Forest and Public Lands*. Wiley.

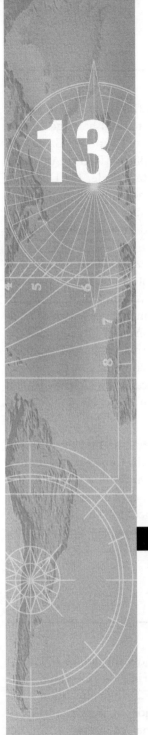

World Heritage sites: managing the brand

C. Michael Hall and Rachel Piggin

Aims

The aims of this chapter are to:

- indicate the important role of World Heritage sites as visitor attractions
- illustrate the role of institutional procedures and processes in developing the values underlying the World Heritage brand
- identify specific problems in the management of the values which underlie the brand
- illustrate the importance of understanding the manner in which the brand values of a visitor attraction may be differentially understood or interpreted.

Introduction

World Heritage status represents the pinnacle of international efforts to identify and conserve some of the most significant cultural and natural heritage sites in the world, including examples as diverse as the Pyramids of Egypt, the Great Wall of China, the Grand Canyon in the USA, and the Great Barrier Reef in Australia. World Heritage sites are recognized as such by their listing under the UNESCO World Heritage Convention. To talk of World Heritage and branding in the same title may seem anathema to some but in tourism and heritage conservation terms, World Heritage represents an extremely strong brand that is based on the outstanding heritage values of World Heritage sites as well as their potential attractiveness to visitors. Indeed, the rigour that is applied to reviews of nominations of potential World Heritage sites and the protocol that surrounds use of the term 'World Heritage' also indicates that the relevant authorities are seeking to reinforce brand identity and protect it from misuse, even if such authorities would probably define such actions more in terms of protection of the integrity of the World Heritage idea than in marketing terms. Nevertheless, given that in marketing terms a brand represents a unique combination of product characteristics and functional and non-functional added values, which have taken on a relevant meaning which is linked to that brand, then World Heritage clearly exhibits brand characteristics.

The chapter is divided into three main sections. The first section conducts an overview of the nature of World Heritage sites and the broad management framework which surrounds them, and considers the contribution this makes to brand values. The second section discusses the tourism and visitor significance of World Heritage and the role of such sites as visitor attractions. The third section makes an account of some of the management and marketing issues which arise at World Heritage sites. This will include a New Zealand case study of the management of the World Heritage brand.

World Heritage values

The Convention Concerning the Protection of the World Cultural and Natural Heritage, to give the World Heritage Convention (WHC) its full name, was adopted by a UNESCO conference on 16 November 1972. The convention is an innovative, international legal instrument which provides a permanent legal, administrative and financial framework for international co-operation for the protection of cultural and natural heritage sites of outstanding value to humanity.

The Convention came into force in December 1975, when twenty nations had ratified it. As of the end of 2001 there were 721 sites inscribed on the World Heritage List consisting of 554 cultural (places of historical significance, monuments, groups of buildings or sites), 144 natural (natural features, geological and physiographical features, and natural sites) and twenty-three mixed properties in the 124 different countries that are party to the Convention. Countries that are signatories to the Convention commit themselves to assist in the identification, protection, conservation and preservation of World Heritage properties. They also undertake to refrain from deliberate measures which might damage cultural or natural heritage, and to take appropriate legal, scientific, technical, administrative and financial measures necessary for heritage identification, protection, conservation, presentation and rehabilitation. All signatories to the Convention are invited to identify and submit nominations of outstanding universal value to the World Cultural and Natural Heritage List. This is a select list of the most internationally outstanding cultural and natural properties. By inclusion on the list, a location becomes officially recognized as being a World Heritage site.

The international nature of the Convention is reflected in its administration through the Intergovernmental Committee for the Protection of the World Cultural and Natural Heritage (the World Heritage Committee), which is composed of twenty-one states elected at a general assembly of state parties to the Convention every two years. The Committee is the key policy and decision-making body and is responsible for all decisions pertaining to nominations to the World Heritage List and to requests for financial assistance under the World Heritage Fund. The Committee elects a bureau which is responsible for detailed examination of new nominations and requests for funding. The bureau consists of a chairperson, a rapporteur and five vice-chairpersons elected from World Heritage Committee membership. The Committee and the Bureau receive technical advice for 'cultural' sites from the International Council for Monuments and Sites (ICOMOS) and the International Center for Conservation in Rome (ICCROM), while for 'natural' properties the advisory body is the International Union for Conservation of Nature and Natural Resources (IUCN). UNESCO provides a secretariat to help implement the decisions of the committee. A World Heritage Fund has also been established to provide financial and technical assistance to those nations which otherwise would not be in a position to fulfil their obligations under the Convention. Although such a framework may sound overly bureaucratic, it must be noted that the listing process is lengthy due to the amount of information that must be gathered before a heritage site can become recognized as a World Heritage site, while governments which nominate sites must also be able to ensure that such places have appropriate long-term

Table 13.1   Criteria for World Heritage listing

Cultural properties
(i)   represent a masterpiece of human creative genius; or

(ii) exhibit an important interchange of human values, over a span of time or within a cultural area of the world, on developments in architecture or technology, monumental arts, town-planning or landscape design; or

(iii) bear a unique or at least exceptional testimony to a cultural tradition or to a civilization which is living or which has disappeared; or

(iv) be an outstanding example of a type of building or architectural or technological ensemble or landscape which illustrates significant stage(s) in human history; or

(v)   be an outstanding example of a traditional human settlement or land-use which is representative of a culture (or cultures), especially when it has become vulnerable under the impact of irreversible change; or

(vi) be directly or tangibly associated with events or living traditions, with ideas, or with beliefs, with artistic and literary works of outstanding universal significance (the Committee considers that this criterion should justify inclusion in the List only in exceptional circumstances and in conjunction with other criteria cultural or natural).

Natural properties
(i)   be outstanding examples representing major stages of Earth's history, including the record of life, significant ongoing geological processes in the development of land forms, or significant geomorphic or physiographic features; or

(ii) be outstanding examples representing significant ongoing ecological and biological processes in the evolution and development of terrestrial, fresh water, coastal and marine ecosystems and communities of plants and animals; or

(iii) contain superlative natural phenomena or areas of exceptional natural beauty and aesthetic importance; or

(iv) contain the most important and significant natural habitats for in situ conservation of biological diversity, including those containing threatened species of outstanding universal value from the point of view of science or conservation.

Source: UNESCO (1999: s.24, 44)

conservation management strategies. Acceptance of a nomination of a site to the World Heritage List is regarded as extremely prestigious because it is seen as having a 'universal value' to humankind. The criteria for listing cultural and/or natural World Heritage properties are provided in Table 13.1. Cultural sites also have to meet a test of authenticity in design, material, workmanship or setting (or, in the case of cultural landscapes, their distinctive character and components) and have adequate legal and/or contractual and/or traditional protection and management mechanisms to ensure the conservation of the nominated cultural properties or cultural landscapes.

In addition, World Heritage sites should also fulfil a number of conditions regarding their integrity, including containing all or most of the key interrelated and interdependent elements in their natural relationships. Thus, World Heritage sites should:

- have sufficient size and contain the necessary elements to demonstrate the key aspects of processes that are essential for the long-term conservation of the ecosystems and the biological diversity they contain
- be of outstanding aesthetic value and include areas that are essential for maintaining the beauty of the site
- contain habitats for maintaining the most diverse fauna and flora characteristic of the biographic province and ecosystems under consideration
- have a management plan, with adequate long-term legislative, regulatory, institutional or traditional protection
- be the most important sites for the conservation of biological diversity (UNESCO, 1999).

The brand values of World Heritage

The brand values of World Heritage are derived from both the profile of the brand in certain countries and communities, such as the international heritage community, and from the rigorous process by which a site comes to be listed as World Heritage. In countries such as Australia and New Zealand, for example, where the World Heritage listing processes have been controversial and received a high media profile, World Heritage is of substantial importance. This has led to the development of domestic legislation to help ensure that heritage sites are protected and that other economic, social and scientific heritage values are recognized (Hall and McArthur, 1996). The substantial conflicts which occurred over the protection of World Heritage sites in Australia and New Zealand have, however, only served to reinforce the brand values of World Heritage. The efforts of conservationists in both countries to stop degradation of World Heritage values in high-profile sites in Tasmania, Queensland, Australia's Northern Territory and the South Island of New Zealand through logging activities, road building, mining or dam building, have helped create an emotional basis of support for conservation on a site-by-site basis, which has been transferred to the value of World Heritage overall (Hall, 1992). For example, according to Environment Australia (2001: 1):

Inscription of a property on the World Heritage List can produce many benefits for Australia, and in particular, for local communities. Australia's World Heritage properties are a clearly identifiable part of our heritage. In the case of properties such as the Tasmanian Wilderness, Kakadu and Uluru-Kata Tjuta National Parks and the Great Barrier Reef, World Heritage listing has featured in promotions which have resulted in greatly increased tourist visitation from overseas and within Australia. In addition to possible increases in employment opportunities and income, local communities could also expect benefits from improved planning and management of the region. A major focus for Commonwealth Government assistance for World Heritage properties has been the provision of resources for strengthening management and improving interpretation and visitor facilities. World Heritage listing also cultivates local and national pride in the property and develops feelings of national responsibility to protect the area.

The benefits of listing as a site are also argued for in the UNESCO Press Kit regarding World Heritage. Under the heading of public awareness, UNESCO notes:

> The prestige that comes from being a State Party to the Convention and having sites inscribed on the World Heritage List often serves as a catalyst to raising awareness for heritage preservation on the part of governments and citizens alike. Heightened awareness, in turn, leads to greater consideration and a general rise in the level of protection and conservation afforded to heritage properties. A State Party may receive both financial assistance and expert advice from the World Heritage Committee as support for promotional activities for the preservation of its sites as well as for developing educational materials. (UNESCO World Heritage Center, 2000: 1)

Yet for many people, the value of World Heritage does not lie in any direct, tangible benefits; the simple fact that it exists is often enough for them to support the World Heritage ideal. Indeed, association with some of the high-profile heritage sites around the world can be enough to demonstrate value to the conservation-minded. The brand values of World Heritage therefore rely substantially on an emotional appeal, based on regard for heritage, but increasingly spilling over into other areas including the tourism industry. Significantly, World Heritage listing can also serve to reinforce the value of place brands through association and identification (Morgan, Pritchard and Pride, 2002). Yet while the value of World Heritage relies on universal significance, it must be noted that recognition of such values is not always universal at the level of the tourism consumer.

In many less developed countries, World Heritage has been recognized as a source of local pride as well as potential economic development through tourism and/or overseas aid projects. Nevertheless, in some countries, such as the USA, World Heritage is not well known even at some of the sites that are on the list such as the Grand Canyon or the White Cliffs in Mesa Verde National Park. Nevertheless, World Heritage provides a focal point for much education about nationally and internationally significant heritage, with campaigns regarding World Heritage values active at internal and national levels. For example, UNESCO initiated a 'World Heritage in Young Hands' campaign in 1994, while the Australian government sees one of the objectives of implementing the Convention as being 'to strengthen appreciation and respect of the property's World Heritage values, particularly through educational and information programs' (Environment Australia, 2001: 1). However, education and public awareness regarding World Heritage may not only lead to interest in conserving World Heritage sites and their heritage values, it may also lead to furthering the desire to visit such locations. Therefore, the next part of the chapter turns to the tourism significance of World Heritage.

Tourism and World Heritage

Given the criteria for World Heritage listing and their clear potential to act as heritage attractions, it is perhaps not surprising that World Heritage sites are regarded by many academic commentators, as well as those in government and industry, as being of great importance for tourism. For example, Shackley describes them as 'magnets for visitors' with World Heritage designation 'virtually a guarantee that visitor numbers will increase' (Shackley 1998, preface). Indeed, several commentators have suggested that World Heritage status increases the popularity of a destination with visitors (see, for example, Hall, 1992; Shackley, 1998; Thorsell and Sigaty, 2001; UNESCO, 1995). Undoubtedly, there is substantial evidence for the attractiveness of World Heritage sites for tourism. For example, a survey of 118 natural World Heritage sites by Thorsell and Sigaty (2001) reported a total annual visitation of nearly 63 million people. Fifteen of the sites surveyed recorded over 1 million visitors a year with the Great Smoky Mountains in the USA having the highest number (9 265 667). The thirty-two sites in the USA, Canada, Australia and New Zealand accommodated over 84 per cent of all visitors, while the average visitation for the thirty sites in Africa was only 22 705 per year, compared with 2.6 million visitors per year in the sixteen sites in the USA and Canada.

Further evidence of the significance of tourism for World Heritage is illustrated in Table 13.2, which indicates some of the key factors relating to World Heritage

Table 13.2 World Heritage sites in OECD countries and key factors related to World Heritage status and tourism

Site name	State party	Criteria	Date of inscription	No of visitors at last count	Change in visitors since WH	% change in visitors since WH	Formal records kept	WH used to attract international visitors	WH used to attract domestic visitors	Area explaining WH Convention	Area explaining WH Status of site	Overall effect on tourism
Great Barrier Reef	Australia	N	1981	2 200 000	↑	6–10	✓	✓	✓	X	✓	∅
Kakadu National Park	Australia	N/C	1981	212 038	↑	?	✓	X	X	X	✓	∅
Lord Howe Island Group	Australia	N	1982	10 000	?↑	?	✓	✓	✓	✓	✓	++
Central Eastern Australian Rainforest Reserves	Australia	N	1986	2 000 000	↑	>30	X	✓	✓	X	✓	+
Wet Tropics of Queensland	Australia	N	1988	4 775 485	↑	?	X	✓	✓	✓	✓	++
Australian Fossil Mammal Sites (Naracoorte)	Australia	N	1994	500 000	↑	1–5	✓	✓	✓	✓	✓	+
The Historic Centre of the City of Salzburg	Austria	C	1996	6 500 000	#	?	✓	✓	✓	X	X	∅
Gros Morne National Park	Canada	N	1987	130 000	↑	26–30	✓	✓	✓	X	✓	++
Nahanni National Park	Canada	N	1978	700	↑	6–10	✓	X	X	X	X	+
Dinosaur Provincial Park	Canada	N	1979	79 000	↑	6–10	✓	✓	✓	X	✓	++
Canadian Rocky Mountain Parks	Canada	N	1984	4 000 000	↑	11–15	✓	✓	X	✓	✓	+
Tatshenshini-Alsek/Kluane/Glacier Bay National Park	Canada	N	1979	2 500	→	1–5	✓	X	X	X	?	+
Waterton Glacier International Peace Park	Canada	N	1995	350 000	#	?	✓	✓	✓	X	X	+
Historic Centre of Prague	Czech Republic	C	1992	2 830 000	↑	61–70	X	✓	X	X	X	+
Old Rauma	Finland	C	1991	20 000	↑	1–5	✓	✓	✓	✓	X	++
Palaces and Parks of Potsdam and Berlin	Germany	C	1990	2 052 653	#	?	✓	✓	✓	✓	✓	++
Collegiate Church, Castle, and Old Town of Quedlinburg	Germany	C	1994	600 000	↑	6–10	?	✓	✓	✓	✓	+
Yakushima	Japan	N	1993	250 000	↑	1–5	X	X	✓	X	✓	∅
Historic Centre of Puebla	Mexico	C	1987	3 000 000	#↑	?	X	X	X	X	?	∅
Sian Ka'an	Mexico	N	1987	20 500	↑	6–10	✓	✓	?	✓	✓	+

Site	Country	Category	Year	Number	Trend	% intl						Attitude
Te Wahipounamu – South West New Zealand	New Zealand	N	1990	450 000*	↑	?	√	√	√	√	√	++
Tongariro National Park	New Zealand	N/C	1990	500 000	#	X	√	√	X	√	√	∅
Bryggen	Norway	C	1979	250 000	↑	1–5	√	√	X	X	X	?
Beloveshskaya Pushcha/ Bialowieza Forest	Poland	N	1979	102 000	↑	1–5	X	X	X	√	X	∅
Cultural Landscape of Sintra	Portugal	C	1995	324 128	↑	16–20	X	√	√	X	X	+
Historic Centre of Evora	Portugal	C	1986	350 000	↑	1–5	√	√	√	X	X	++
The Historic Walled Town of Cuenca	Spain	C	1996	100 000	↑	16–20	√	√	√	X	X	?
Doñana National Park	Spain	N	1994	250 000	#	?	X	X	?	?	X	++
Santiago de Compostela (Old Town)	Spain	C	1985	3 000 000	↑	1–5	X	√	√	X	X	+
Hanseatic Town of Visby	Sweden	C	1995	800 000	#	?	√	√	√	√	X	∅
Göreme National Park and the Rock Sites of Cappadocia	Turkey	N/C	1985	5 477 000	#	?	√	√	√	√	X	∅
Hierapolis – Pamukkale	Turkey	N/C	1988	1 110 000	#	?	X	√	√	√	√	∅
Gough Island Wildlife Reserve	United Kingdom	N	1995	50	#	?	X	X	X	?	?	?
Giant's Causeway and Causeway Coast	United Kingdom	N	1986	430 000	#	?	X	√	√	√	√	++
St Kilda Island	United Kingdom	N	1986	1 800	↑	1–5	X	X	X	X	X	∅
City of Bath	United Kingdom	C	1987	2 800 000	↑	1–5	√	√	√	√	X	∅
Everglades National Park	USA	N	1979	1 087 790	↑	1–5	√	√	√	√	√	+
Yellowstone	USA	N	1978	2 889 513	↑	1–5	X	√	X	X	X	∅
Grand Canyon National Park	USA	N	1979	500 000	↑	71–80	X	√	X	√	√	∅
Redwood National Park	USA	N	1980	369 987	↑	31–40	X	√	X	X	X	∅
Mammoth Cave National Park	USA	N	1981	2 000 000	↑	?	X	√	X	X	X	∅
Olympic National Park	USA	N	1981	4 621 829	↑	1–5	X	√	√	X	X	+
Great Smokey Mountains National Park	USA	N	1983	9 000 000	↑	1–5	X	√	√	√	X	+
Yosemite National Park	USA	N	1984	5 000 000	↑	11–15	X	√	√	√	√	—
Hawaii Volcanoes National Park	USA	N	1987	1 800 000	↑	1–5	X	√	√	√	√	∅
Carlsbad Caverns National Park	USA	N	1995	522 174	→	1–5	X	X	X	X	X	∅

Note: * No figure stated in questionnaire. Figure calculated from percentage of international visitors who go to Milford Sound and Fox and Franz Josef Glaciers. Does not include allocation for domestic visitors.

Key: ↑ Increase; ↓ Decrease; # No change; ? Don't know; √ Yes; X No; > Greater; < Smaller; ∅ Neutral; — Extremely negative; + Positive; ++ Extremely positive status and tourism in a survey of management bodies of World Heritage sites in Organization for Economic Cooperation and Development (OECD) countries conducted in 1999. However, as Hall and Piggin (2001) indicate in a survey of tourism at World Heritage sites in OECD countries, a causal link between World Heritage listing and increased visitation over and above existing tourism trends may be regarded as somewhat tenuous, particularly where the sites were major attractions prior to heritage listing. Indeed, the actual rate of increase in visitation is often similar to that of tourism overall in the countries concerned. Such a situation also reflects the fact that, currently, little is really known about the fundamental nature of the visitor attraction product of World Heritage by those marketing the site. Although, as Chapter 8 has noted, such increases may still have substantial impacts on the environmental quality of sites, Chapter 12 highlights the substantial challenges to the marketing of heritage in terms of retaining the very qualities which lead to World Heritage recognition in the first place. Nevertheless, in spite of such concerns, World Heritage listing is clearly a significant factor for tourism management on the basis of the inherent qualities of the site, let alone the potential to attract tourists (Hall, 1992; Shackley, 1998).

Arguably, from an attraction branding perspective, the realities of the relationship between World Heritage listing and tourism growth may not be hugely important. Instead, the belief that such a relationship exists and that for many people an emotional link exists between individual international heritage attractions and the World Heritage concept is enough to establish a unique association for the consumer. This can then go on to strengthen the World Heritage brand through the creation of a very significant point of difference in the heritage attraction marketplace. However, if such unique associations are created then, clearly, this places substantial pressures on the capacity to manage the values on which the emotional appeal of World Heritage is based.

Managing the brand

Several issues arise in managing the physical and educative dimensions of World Heritage which provide the supply-side foundations for the brand. First, there is the ability to manage the impacts of tourism and other human activities on the heritage values of the World Heritage sites on which the brand is based. This is not the focus of this chapter, although issues associated with the management of heritage attractions are found throughout the book and a prerequisite for World Heritage listing is that a management plan must be developed so as to maintain the integrity of the sites concerned. Second, there is a requirement to conduct ongoing reviews of the qualities of World Heritage sites so as to ensure that they retain the values that allowed them to be listed in the first place. This is undertaken through a regular formal review process, as well as through the development of the World Heritage in Danger List. This list is used to publicize sites which are under threat and may be a precursor to removal from the World Heritage List altogether. As at the end of 2000, some thirty-one properties were listed as being under threat including not only sites threatened by war such as the Okapi Wildlife Reserve in the Democratic Republic of the Congo and Angkor in Cambodia, but also the Everglades and Yellowstone National Parks in the USA. The latter have come under increased human pressure in recent years, including that of visitor impacts. The significance of a site being placed on the list is witnessed in that the US government has spent considerable sums of money in an attempt to alleviate threats to heritage values in both the parks. The third issue related to brand management is the management of the use of the World Heritage name by tourism operators and other agencies. Given the substantial educative and scientific role of World Heritage, misuse of the World Heritage name might not only lead to misunderstandings regarding the meaning and value of World Heritage, but could also lead to the devaluing of the public good function of World Heritage. Under the operational guidelines for World Heritage the use of the World Heritage emblem and name is restricted in order to prevent 'improper uses' (UNESCO, 1999: para.128), while Annex 3 of the guidelines states the responsibilities of state parties with respect to the use of the emblem: 'State Parties to the Convention should take all possible measures to prevent the use of the Emblem in their respective countries by any group or for any purpose not explicitly recognized by the Committee. State Parties are encouraged to make full use of national legislation including Trade Mark Laws.'

Case study: understanding and use of the World Heritage brand in New Zealand

Despite the stated desire of UNESCO to protect the World Heritage name and emblem, few studies have investigated the use of the World Heritage brand as a promotional tool. In the (antipodean) summer of 1998–9, a survey regarding the tourism industry's understanding and use of World Heritage was conducted of businesses operating in or near two of New Zealand's World Heritage sites. The first, Southwest New Zealand – Te Wahi Pounamu (SWNZ), is an area in the south-west of the South Island comprising four national parks (Fiordland, Mount Aspiring, Mount Cook and Westland) and various other reserves and protected areas. The second, Tongariro National Park (TNP), is situated in the central North Island volcanic plateau. A sample population of 372 tourism businesses was developed from field visits to visitor centres, industry listings and memberships, and listings in relevant directories. A total of 142 businesses responded to the survey (a response rate of 37.2 per cent), of which 131 responses were usable (a usable response rate of 35.2 per cent). Such research was focused on tourism businesses as it was believed that they are important intermediaries between the brand of the visitor attraction and the visitor. Tourism businesses are therefore likely to influence not only the visitors' understanding of the brand, but also the nature of the visitor experience.

Half the operators surveyed believed that World Heritage had been a positive or extremely positive effect for their business, while 70 per cent of the businesses thought World Heritage listing had a positive or extremely positive effect on the region. Overall 48.4 per cent of respondents believed that World Heritage status attracted visitors to their region, while just over 20 per cent believed it did not. Significantly, the remainder replied that they did not know, which was a direct reflection of the failure of businesses to create and maintain customer and visitor records, as well as the absence of broader macro-level research on reasons for travel to the World Heritage sites.

The division in belief as to the benefits of World Heritage listing was also reflected in the extent to which World Heritage was mentioned in the promotional materials of tourism businesses, including brochures, media advertising and videos. Almost 42 per cent of respondents use the term 'World Heritage' in their promotional materials while the remainder did not. The most widely stated reason of why World Heritage status was mentioned in promotions was that it is seen as a way to attract visitors (n = 38). It was also seen as a positive aspect in that the area has international significance (n = 34) and that World Heritage is seen as something important (n = 33) and relevant to certain businesses (n = 33) (ecotourism and educationally-oriented businesses in particular). World Heritage status was also viewed as an advantage over other regions in the country (n = 23). Three businesses stated that the site manager had encouraged them to mention their World Heritage status. However, this was a surprisingly low number of operators considering that the site managers for each area had indicated to the authors that they encourage operators to use World Heritage to market their businesses. A fraction of the businesses used World Heritage because other businesses do so (n = 2).

The most frequently stated reason for not using World Heritage in business promotion was that it did not occur to the respondent to use it (n = 35). It was also considered that World Heritage was not relevant to the business (n = 18), or would not influence someone's decision to visit it (n = 18). Limited space on promotional material was also noted (n = 15). Eleven respondents indicated

Table 13.3   Statements on information regarding World Heritage

I didn't know we had World Heritage status. (SWNZ)

No guest has ever asked what it is all about and we would be hard put to explain. (SWNZ)

World Heritage Status has never been adequately explained or promoted to tourist operators or visitors. (SWNZ)

I was/am ignorant until now as to what effect World Heritage status would/means to our area. (TNP)

I don't really know much about it myself. Maybe some promotional brochures would help us be more informed. (TNP)

I do not know myself. Not had any information myself, so how can I tell people something I know nothing about? (TNP)

We are relatively uninformed about World Heritage, so don't tell our clients much if anything. (SWNZ)

that World Heritage was not important and a small number said they were unaware of the status of the area (n = 5) and of what World Heritage means (n = 5). Another reason stated by the business operators was that the national parks were attractions enough in themselves. Some mentioned (incorrectly) that the sites concerned had only just received World Heritage status.

Even though they were all operating on or near to a World Heritage site, the type of business operation also influenced whether World Heritage is used in promotion. Three-quarters of the ecotourism and wildlife businesses in the study areas use World Heritage, while most restaurants, bars and museums and galleries did not use it at all. All boating and educational businesses promoted World Heritage. Around two-thirds of the scenic flight operators used World Heritage, although less than half the accommodation operators did so. Perhaps surprisingly, a low proportion of tour operators that responded (28 per cent) used World Heritage to promote themselves.

A total of seventy-four business operators explained what World Heritage status meant to them and what they told their clients about the World Heritage status of the area. Some general themes emerged and indicated that the operators were not always sure of the meaning of World Heritage or that the area had been granted World Heritage status. The statements in Table 13.3 indicate that World Heritage is not always a widely or, indeed, adequately understood concept, and illustrate a failure of brand management in terms of educating business operators with respect to the significance of the brand and

Table 13.4   Perceived relevance of World Heritage attributes in relation to Southwest New Zealand

Criteria	Extremely relevant 1	Moderately relevant 2	Relevant 3	Not very relevant 4	Irrelevant 5	Mean
N (i)	30	11	14	4	3	2.02
N (ii)	32	8	8	4	8	2.13
N (iii)	50	6	4	1	1	1.34
N (iv)	33	12	7	5	5	1.98
C (i)	3	1	3	11	42	4.47
C (ii)	4	1	7	13	34	4.22
C (iii)	8	3	11	17	22	3.69
C (iv)	4	0	3	7	45	4.51
C (v)	5	1	8	10	35	4.17
C (vi)	4	0	3	7	45	4.20

Note: N = natural; C = cultural

the values which underlie it. Indeed, questioning by the authors indicated substantial differences between the perceived and official attributes of the World Heritage sites in the study. Tables 13.4 and 13.5 illustrate how the relevant business operators in each area thought of the attributes that make

Table 13.5   Perceived relevance of World Heritage attributes in relation to Tongariro National Park

Criteria	Extremely relevant 1	Moderately relevant 2	Relevant 3	Not very relevant 4	Irrelevant 5	Mean
N (i)	31	8	5	1	2	1.62
N(ii)	31	6	5	4	2	1.75
N(iii)	35	8	2	0	2	1.34
N (iv)	20	11	9	4	3	2.13
C (i)	1	2	5	9	26	4.33
C (ii)	5	8	7	12	14	3.48
C (iii)	21	8	7	4	6	2.26
C (iv)	5	7	7	10	18	3.62
C (v)	6	10	5	13	13	3.36

Note: N = natural; C = cultural

up the criteria for inclusion in the World Heritage List (the actual criteria are listed in Table 13.1).

Southwest New Zealand – Te Wahipounamu obtained its World Heritage status by meeting the four natural criteria, although it is interesting that the third cultural criteria C (iii), representing a testimony to cultural tradition or civilization, shows more relevance than any of the other cultural criteria. Tongariro National Park gained its World Heritage status by meeting natural criteria N (ii) and N (iii), and also meeting cultural criteria C (vi). The fact that N (iii), which relates to the beauty of the area, is seen as the most relevant to the operators mirrors some of the perceptions of operators that World Heritage is predominantly defined by natural beauty rather than by scientific significance. It is interesting to note that although TNP is listed under C (vi), the majority of operators considered C (iii) to be more relevant to the area. This criterion relates to the area being testimony to a cultural tradition or civilization, rather than what the park was accepted onto the list for, which was for being associated with events or traditions or beliefs. This indicates that there are substantial differences between the perceived and defined attributes of the site.

The study also found substantial evidence of failure to manage the World Heritage brand in line with the operational guidelines, in that 62.5 per cent of respondents who answered a question as to whether or not use of the term 'World Heritage' could be restricted did not believe this to be the case, while almost 30 per cent of the businesses did not know if they were restricted or not. Similarly, almost 25 per cent of respondents utilized the World Heritage emblem in their promotion but, again, few realized that it was copyright and one operator who used it did not even realize it was the symbol for World Heritage.

This case study highlights the substantial gaps that can occur between the heritage values associated with a site at an international level and those recognized at the local level. Such gaps represent significant problems for heritage managers, for if they continue to exist they can serve to lead to poor or misleading information being provided to tourists. This may then result in a loss of confidence by the consumer. In addition, the case study illustrates the importance for heritage managers to educate not only the visitor about the values attached to sites, but also those businesses that are part of the local industry. Tourism operators, no matter what sector of the industry they are in, not only serve to distribute or accommodate tourists, but also act as conduits of information which affect consumers' relationships to destinations and attractions, and therefore influence their loyalty.

217

Conclusions

This chapter has described a number of key issues relating to understanding the marketing and management of heritage attractions. First, it has indicated some of the reasons as to how an attraction can develop the values which underlie the brand. In the case of World Heritage, the role of institutional processes and procedures, which at first glance may seem cumbersome or slow, have in fact made the claims of the brand 'believable'. Second, it has indicated that relatively little is known, even in the case of such high-profile heritage attractions as World Heritage sites, about the fundamental nature of the visitor attraction product by those marketing and managing such sites. For example, in the case of World Heritage, while visitor numbers are substantial and have grown over time there is no conclusive evidence that such growth has been directly due to listing. Indeed, many sites were clearly visitor attractions prior to listing. Yet the belief that such relationships exist continues to add value to the World Heritage brand. Third, it has highlighted the different perceptions of intermediaries, in the form of various tourism businesses, of the nature and values of a heritage visitor attraction, which may then substantially influence the construction of the visitor experience. Fourth, the chapter has indicated some of the problems of brand management and the need to realize that while guidelines for the use of brands may exist in regulations, conditions on the ground with respect to interpretation and use may be substantially different to what was intended. Finally, this chapter has highlighted the value of research on the production and consumption of visitor attractions and the realization that, even in the case of World Heritage which comprises some of the most high-profile visitor attractions in the world, what is regarded as an attraction by one tourism business is not by another.

The key issues identified in this chapter also serve to highlight some of the concerns surrounding the future of World Heritage attractions. Most important is the need to find appropriate management mechanisms to ensure that core heritage values are not undermined by inappropriate visitor activities and behaviour. Although direct experience of World Heritage through visits is important for the creation of relationships between consumers and the World Heritage brand, wider emotional relationships and therefore support for the World Heritage concept have arisen through vicarious appreciation and association. Any physical threats to World Heritage sites would undoubtedly serve to endanger such brand loyalty.

Although this chapter has provided a case study of sites which are primarily valued because of their natural heritage, it needs to be recognized that the majority of World Heritage sites are cultural properties. The issues identified in the New Zealand case study are generic to many properties, but a broader issue lies in ensuring that there is more balanced representation between cultural and natural heritage sites on the World Heritage List. Moreover, it highlights the need to develop selection and management criteria that ensure that any World Heritage site is, and continues to be, of universal significance. As this chapter has highlighted, such a goal can only be successful if attention is given to the perceptions and understandings of all stakeholders in the production and consumption of heritage attractions.

References

Environment Australia (2001). *Implications of World Heritage Listing*, Canberra: Environment Australia. http://www.ea.gov.au/heritage/awh/worldheritage/implications.html

Hall, C. M. (1992). *Wasteland to World Heritage: Preserving Australia's Wilderness*. Melbourne University Press.

Hall, C. M. and McArthur, S. (eds) (1996). *Heritage Management in Australia and New Zealand*. Oxford University Press.

Hall, C. M. and Piggin, R. (2001). Tourism and World Heritage in OECD countries. *Tourism Recreation Research*, **26**, 103–105.

Morgan, N., Pritchard, A. and Pride, R. (2002). *Destination Branding: Creating the Unique Destination Proposition*. Butterworth-Heinemann.

Shackley, M. (ed.) (1998). *Visitor Management: Case Studies from World Heritage Sites*. Butterworth-Heinemann.

Thorsell, J. and Sigaty, T. (2001). Human use in World Heritage natural sites: a global inventory. *Tourism Recreation Research*, **26**, 85–101.

UNESCO (1995). Tourism and World Heritage. United Nations Educational, Scientific and Cultural Organization. *The World Heritage Newsletter*. http://www.unesco.orgLwhc/news/8newseng.htm

UNESCO (1999). *Operational Guidelines for the Implementation of the World Heritage Convention*. United Nations Educational, Scientific and Cultural Organization Inter-governmental Committee for the Protection of the World's Cultural and Natural Heritage. UNESCO. http://www.unesco.org/whc/toc/mainf8.htm

UNESCO World Heritage Center (2000). *World Heritage Information Kit: Benefits of Ratification*. http://www.unesco.org/whc/nwhc/pages/doc/main.htm

Competitive theme park strategies: lessons from Central Florida

Bradley M. Braun and Mark Soskin

Introduction

As major theme park players continue to expand internationally (Milman, 2001), the lessons learned from the living laboratory in Orlando Florida are invaluable to park managers. In the early days of the Central Florida industry of Orlando, the dominant firm, Walt Disney World (WDW), had its way with a competitive fringe of price followers. The competing parks required price discounting to compensate for Disney's financial and name brand advantages. The hypothesis of a dominant firm and an industry without price competition was supported by results of a regression model on prices for WDW and its primary rivals (Braun, Soskin and Cernicky, 1992).

A subsequent paper (Braun and Soskin, 1999), however, revealed that significant transformations in the early 1990s had radically altered the Central Florida theme park industry. Florida tourism was thrown into stagnation from a series of shocks, including interruptions of international tourism due to the Gulf War, a worldwide recession and adverse global media coverage of violent crimes against tourists. After these shocks diminished, it was clear that the days of rapid growth in park attendance were over, as the industry entered a mature industry stage characterized by level attendance, a higher proportion of return visitors and new competition from outside markets. Furthermore, as happens in all mature markets, consolidation of the industry occurred as three competing parks were combined under one management, while at the same time a major Disney rival from the Pacific coast, Universal Studios, established a substantial foothold in Central Florida.

In the spirit of the previous work cited, this chapter investigates two issues. The first deals with how market shocks and structural shifts have affected the long-term strategic pricing behaviour in the last half of the 1990s and into the new millennium. The analysis here is based on quarterly averages to monthly changes in theme park prices, trends in price stability, collusive price co-ordination, and price differentials. The results of the investigation indicate that pricing behaviour has evolved rapidly to a highly disciplined four-firm oligopoly characterized by conscious parallelism and pricing parity across the industry. This behaviour is found to be consistent with the new industry structure and market changes in global tourism.

The second issue concerns the inter-industry relationships in a geographical area as revealed by a demand estimation model. The most important perspective on the positioning of a theme park is on the competitive structure of its marketplace (Fodness and Milner, 1992). Fodness and Milner correctly assert that understanding the nature of the competitive environment enables managers to formulate more effectively both offensive and defensive competitive strategies. A demand analysis reveals the relationships between parks. If competing theme parks offer different experiences and complement one another, joint product promotion may be effective. On the other hand, if parks offer similar experiences, and are therefore substitutes, it is important for managers to understand guest perceptions and to differentiate their products.

Evolution of the industry

Changes in industry structure

The first lesson that can be learned from the Orlando experience is that managers can expect expansion and consolidation in their regional market. Since 1990, major structural changes have occurred in the theme park market. First, Anheuser

Busch carried out a series of acquisitions to complete a successful horizontal merger of WDW's three largest rivals (Busch Gardens, SeaWorld and Cypress Gardens). Busch then mobilized its financial resources, management experience and park development expertise to match Disney's US$10 billion investment in Central Florida.

The second change in market structure resulted from the entry of Universal Studios, the first major entrant since SeaWorld, ten years earlier. Universal entered with a replicated set of market-proven attractions from its thriving southern California parent site. Universal also drew upon scale economies to diversify its product mix into high-tech rides. When technical delays threatened its reputation for quality, Universal redoubled investment. The high sunk costs demonstrated its commitment to the Central Florida theme park market. In addition, Universal exploited economies of scope derived from complementarities in movie and television production. The entry of Universal Studios had an immediate effect on local labour markets and theme park prices.

Universal attacked two previously unexploited vulnerabilities of WDW. First, WDW had always enjoyed its strongest appeal among families with younger children. Thus, the under thirty-five-year-old crowd presented a large market niche attracted by high-tech thrill rides and more sophisticated attractions. Second, WDW's portfolio had expanded into a wide range of themes, including amusements and rides, water parks, a World's Fair, nightclubs and nature settings. Although this traditional brand proliferation strategy was effective in limiting the market shares of its existing Florida rivals, WDW was late to recognize the dangers from a potential entrant with deep pockets, Universal. From a game theory perspective, if a market niche is large enough for only one firm to enjoy economic profits, a pre-emptive strategy of committing large investments irrevocably in that niche provides a credible signal to deter other firms from entry (Dixit, 1980). Disney exploited its regional presence to be the first to open a Central Florida movie themed attraction, Disney-MGM Studios. However, it was too late to forestall Universal's entry. Because of the enormous capital commitments already made, Universal was locked into the Florida market.

Rival entry had occurred before when WDW underestimated the size of the profitable water parks and nightclubs market niches. But with Universal's entry, WDW was forced, for the first time, to play a technological catch-up game against a financially rich rival. As a result, Universal became the only Florida theme park to consistently match WDW's premium pricing strategy, even in the soft market of the early 1990s. Disney's price leader position was clearly being challenged.

Beyond these structural changes, broader market factors may also have affected the Central Florida theme park industry. The industry appeared to be entering the mature phase of its product life cycle, and a consequent levelling of its customer base (Scherer and Ross, 1989). A maturing tourism industry, like its durable goods counterpart, must obtain an increasing share of business from repeat customers (Braun and Milman, 1994). Attracting repeat business requires potential guests to be convinced that previous visits are inferior substitutes for vacation experiences at the new and improved parks. For this strategy to be effective, new and more exciting rides, attractions and entire parks must be designed and constructed. For example, Disney opened its Animal Kingdom in 1998, which was closely followed by the opening of Universal's Islands of Adventure. This form of non-price competition involves high sunk costs as parks race to bring state-of-the-art designs on line. Without a proven market demand, this investment commitment raises the stakes by increasing the chance for a runaway product proliferation race and the possibility of a game-of-ruin, single-victor scenario. It also has the side effect of cannibalizing the customer base. The first lesson, then, is that the expansion and consolidation of a regional market presents both opportunities and pitfalls.

Changes in market conditions

The second lesson that can be learned from the Orlando experience is that managers in a concentrated market will have less power to use pricing strategies. For example, in a study of local visitors to Central Florida theme parks, Milman (2001) could find no relationship between admission price consciousness and the frequency of visits. Throughout the 1980s and 1990s, Central Florida boomed as the world leader in numbers of visitors and hotel rooms. As domestic highway visits peaked, WDW maintained market growth by successfully tapping into an expanding international market. By early 1990, both road and air arrivals to Florida stagnated as a result of the Gulf War and worldwide recession. At the same time, competition for tourist dollars was expanding into cruises and all-inclusive resorts, in both of which Disney later became a major player. Also, competition intensified for WDW's brand of wholesome, 'family-style' vacation. Massive investment by hotels in Las Vegas successfully merged casino operations with a new version of the theme park model.

With changes to industry structure and the weaker market of the 1990s, the pressure on pricing discipline intensified. The pressure was sufficient to elicit more aggressive and independent pricing conduct, thus weakening the leadership–followership behaviour observed in the 1980s.

Central Florida theme park pricing behaviour during the 1980s

The 1980s were a period of steady growth in attendance, and theme park prices increased faster than consumer inflation. In the 1980s, WDW's entrance price rose at a compound annual rate of 12.1 per cent. WDW's pricing strategy provided an umbrella for similar price hikes at rival parks. Cypress Gardens and SeaWorld each raised prices at an annual average rate of more than 11 per cent. Busch Gardens, hampered by its distance from WDW, was only able to raise prices at an annual rate of 9.5 per cent.

In fact, WDW succeeded in widening the price margin over its rivals throughout the 1980s (see Figure 14.1). Busch Gardens saw its relative price erode the most, from a 10 per cent price gap in 1983 to 30 per cent in 1990. SeaWorld and Cypress Gardens also saw their prices lose ground to WDW. Because this widening price margin occurred even before the external market shocks, the difficulty of matching costly expansions and diversifications by the industry leader must have been the primary cause. Viewed as inferior substitutes for WDW, competing parks tempered price increases. In addition, corporate cash flow problems necessitated an aggressive price strategy to restore market share.

Because of its unique market advantages, WDW was able to retain industry dominance while continuing to command a premium price. The land holdings Disney acquired in the 1960s spatially insulated WDW from subsequent entrants.

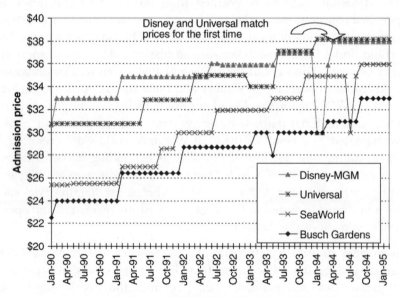

Figure 14.1 Little price co-ordination among theme parks

Its rivals did not match a relentless wave of expansion and diversification by WDW. Disney invested heavily in new attractions, transportation, shops, hotels, restaurants, clubs and water parks. Multi-day discount pricing helped keep visitors at WDW, limiting the residual market available to rivals.

During the 1980s, WDW was able to ignore the individual actions of its rivals. The only way the competitive fringe could attract customers away from WDW was by charging lower prices. WDW was free to fine-tune its prices to maintain optimal profits, consistent with its position as the dominant price leader. From 1982.1 to 1990.1, Disney raised prices in twenty of the thirty-two quarters. Rival parks had equally frequent price changes, but followed WDW's price increases with a significant lag (Braun, Soskin and Cernicky, 1992).

By the early 1990s, however, changes in industry structure and market conditions began to exert dramatic effects on pricing behaviour. The lagged response of followership behaviour finally broke down, replaced by pricing strategies resembling parallel behaviour once prevalent in the cigarette, steel and car industries.

Changes in pricing behaviour in the 1990s

Three developments in pricing patterns provide evidence that strategic behaviour in the Central Florida theme park industry has changed substantially. The growth rate of park admission prices slowed substantially, prices converged and the frequency of price changes has fallen. Despite costly upgrades and expansions, the growth in prices slowed dramatically. From 1990 through 1995, the annual average rate of price escalation was less than 7 per cent at each of the major theme parks. At WDW, prices rose only 3 per cent, barely one-quarter that of the previous decade. The result was a steady narrowing of the price gap between Disney and the other parks.

As described by Braun and Soskin (1999), prices were observed to have nearly converged by 1993. Universal reached price parity with WDW, and SeaWorld narrowed its price margin to within 5 per cent of WDW. Although Disney responded briefly with an aggressive price cut, it quickly resumed matching Universal's price. It was also noted in the 1999 study that the Central Florida theme park industry experienced a statistically significant increase in price stability following the 1990 opening of Universal Studios Florida. Braun and Soskin concluded that WDW and Universal had begun to act as co-market leaders that contemporaneously matched increasingly infrequent price changes. The dominant-firm price leadership behaviour of the 1980s had been permanently replaced by a classic case of collusive oligopoly pricing.

Table 14.1 Park prices stable, changing on average every nine or ten months

Major Central Florida theme park	Percentage of months they changed prices	
	Jan 1990–Feb 1995	Mar 1995–Feb 2001
Disney	13	10
Universal Studios	8	10
SeaWorld	15	13
Busch Gardens	10	8
Average for the four major parks	11	10

Upon revisiting the industry five years later, the authors confirmed that the co-ordinated pricing behaviour was clearly continuing into the twenty-first century. Moreover, the newer evidence strongly indicates that the Central Florida theme park industry had moved towards an even greater degree of co-operation and inclusiveness among the major parks. Table 14.1 supports the authors' previous research contention that price changes remained at least as rare during the succeeding six years as they had become since the entry of Universal at the beginning of the 1990s. Price adjustments (nearly all of them increases) continued to average only about one every ten months. This reticence to alter prices is consistent with recognized interdependence, while operating under oligopolistic uncertainties (Cecchetti, 1986). While dominant price leaders freely respond to changes in costs or demand, fear of misinterpreted market signals may deter oligopolists from initiating most price changes.

Moreover, price co-ordination became substantially more successful. Table 14.2 shows that nearly four-fifths of the months from March 1995 through February

Table 14.2 Major theme parks more successful recently in co-ordinating price changes

Number of parks changing price	Percentage of months	
	Jan 1990–Feb 1995	Mar 1995–Feb 2001
No parks changed price	66	79
One or two parks changed price	32	12
Three or all four parks changed price	2	8

2001 witnessed no price changes by any of the four major parks. This represents a sizeable increase over the two-thirds of months experiencing no price changes during the first half of the 1990s. By contrast, industry disharmony or independent behaviour would manifest itself in price changes by some parks and not others. Table 14.2 also reports a dramatic decline in this type of industry pricing behaviour. The incidence of only one or two parks changing prices fell from about one-third to one-eighth of the months. Finally, nearly two-thirds of price changes in the later 1990s occurred in concert with price changes by at least two other parks in the same months. As a result, only 8 per cent of the months contained the bulk of all price changes.

As industries move towards stronger collusive behaviour, variable pricing mechanisms often emerge to orchestrate co-operative actions. As already mentioned, one such mechanism is infrequent price changes. However, market pressures and inflation eventually make price modifications necessary. The question is how to alert rival parks of a price change so as not to cause misunderstandings that could trigger a mutually destructive price war. One common device is to reserve price changes for specific times of the year. The car industry, for example, raises prices each autumn when it launches new models. During the 1990–5 period (see Figure 14.1) price changes occurred at least once in every month except October. But by the second half of the 1990s, the Central Florida theme park industry appears to have settled on a handful of months to alter its prices. While price changes were completely absent in five of the months (February, July to September, and November), January and March became the favorite months for orchestrating broad industry prices hikes.

Price co-ordination also broadened and became firmly entrenched during the later 1990s. With the exception of the first quarter of 1994, Disney and Universal prices were within 25 cents of each other from June 1993 to February 1995. However, their prices were never identical until they both raised admission prices to US$39.22 in March 1995. From that month on, the two parks mimicked one another's prices through five subsequent price hikes (see Figure 14.2). Price increases were duplicated the following two months of March to US$40.81 in 1996 and US$42.14 in 1997. Thirteen months later, in April 1998, Disney and Universal raised prices to US$44.52, and thirteen months thereafter their prices went up to US$46.64. At the time of writing, the two most recent price increases were made in January of 2000 and 2001 (to US$48.76 and US$50.88 respectively). This ratcheting-up of prices recalls the heyday of cigarette pricing during the 1930s.

Some of this price regimentation was extended to include the other two theme park giants in Central Florida (see Figure 14.3). SeaWorld had poured enormous amounts of capital and advertising in an attempt to attain price parity. It

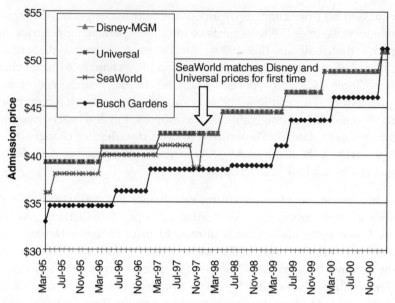

Figure 14.2 Progressively more theme park price co-ordination

narrowed its price to slightly more than US$2.00 below Disney and Universal in September 1994. In May 1995, it shaved the price gap to only about US$1.25. This gap was maintained for the next eighteen months, but with a submissive overture to the pricing regime created by Disney and Universal. SeaWorld chose to raise

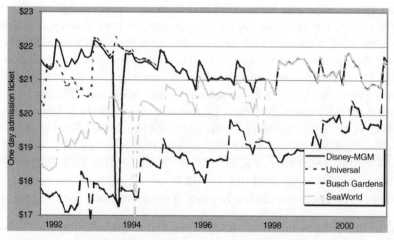

Figure 14.3 In constant 1982–4 admission dollars, Disney Florida park prices since 1992 while other Central Florida parks raised prices to match Disney

prices in 1996 and 1997 in the same month that Disney and Universal did. Previous price moves by SeaWorld had all occurred at different times to those of its two biggest rivals. Having matched the timing of their price changes, SeaWorld made its final move by replicating the industry leaders in price in December 1997, and again the following April when all three proceeded with a matching price hike. It was clear that a collusive triopoly had been established in Central Florida. February 2001 marked the thirty-ninth consecutive month of identical pricing by these three theme parks.

Up until then, Busch Gardens seemed to be the odd park out, despite owning two other parks in the market. Pricing independence could be anticipated by its relatively remote location from tourists arriving by air into Orlando, combined with access to Florida's distinctive West Coast tourism market. Yet Busch was heavily promoting its Tampa park in the Orlando media and bundling their parks with extended and discounted admission prices. As the convergence and co-ordination of pricing firmed up among the other three major parks, it was predictable that Busch would not be willing to remain aloof. But Busch Gardens had a larger price gap than SeaWorld to make up. As recently as February 2000, Busch Gardens was still charging US$5.00 less than its three main rivals. The following month, a price increase cut this margin to under US$3.00. Busch Gardens, which had never timed its price hikes to coincide with the other parks, made sure that its next one did – virtually duplicating the new price of Disney, Universal and SeaWorld. Although it is premature to conclude that a four-firm, collusive oligopoly is now in force, the Central Florida theme park industry definitely operates in a much more orchestrated environment than in the days when Disney did what it pleased, and left its competitors to scramble for the crumbs.

Over the combined eleven-year period under study, Busch Gardens raised its prices US$8.00 more than did Disney in order to reach pricing parity, an annual increase of 7.4 per cent. SeaWorld increased prices 6.3 per cent per year on average to make up its US$5.00 initial deficiency from the beginning of the 1990s. By comparison, Universal and Disney each averaged a smaller, but still respectable 4.6 per cent annual price increase over that same period. It remains to be seen whether the two Busch-owned parks can generate sufficient visitation rates without discounting. The competitive structure determines whether such a strategy can succeed. A further constraint is the depth of Busch's pockets; the question is whether its pockets are deep enough to maintain investments in attractions and promotions to fend off pressures to cut prices.

The smaller parks still hold on to a modest share of the theme park market in Central Florida. The largest of these are Cypress Gardens and the Wet'N'Wild water park. Cypress Gardens has been unable to keep up with the billion dollar investment budgets of the four majors. Thus, they must content themselves with drawing away tourists from those attractions for day trips at a lower admission price. In the 1990s, Cypress Gardens charged about 70–75 per cent of Disney's admission price. There are even signs that their price is losing ground to the big four parks, slipping to barely 65 per cent by 2001. Wet'N'Wild prices are even lower, averaging 60 per cent of Disney's. Both of these second-tier parks relied on whole-dollar price hikes, with prices ending in US$0.95. As a result of this pricing device, Cypress Gardens and Wet'N'Wild have needed to change prices only about once a year, as infrequently as their bigger rivals. Stable pricing thus extends across the industry. Because they must compete against other water parks, including several at Disney, Wet'N'Wild can no more risk starting a price war than Disney or Universal. Similarly, Cypress Gardens is dissuaded from short-term market advantage of cutting prices, for they must be concerned about their smaller rivals such as Gatorland, Silver Springs in Ocala and Disney's own animal nature theme park, Animal Kingdom.

The second lesson, that of managers in a concentrated market having less power to use pricing, means that other strategies must be employed. The appropriate strategy is dictated by the competitive structure.

Demand analysis

Besides the two lessons of consolidation and decreased power to use a pricing strategy as indicted by the statistical price analysis, additional insights may be gleaned from demand analysis that reveals the competitive structure of the market. The most important lessons from the demand analysis are how consumers view theme parks both individually and as a part of a vacation package.

The demand analysis was conducted for data over the nine-year period, 1992–2000. All variables (see Table 14.3 for description and sources) are deflated by the overall consumer price index (CPI) to constant dollar terms, and then expressed in natural logarithms so that estimated coefficients represent elasticities. The log-linear model contains all requisite components of a demand function, such as income, market population and prices of major substitutes and complements confronting each potential theme park visitor. Specifically, combined attendance at Disney's Central Florida theme parks is regressed on the prices charged by the three theme park competitors, personal disposable incomes, population, and prices of related goods and services such as lodging, air travel and petrol. The fitted regression equation is the following:

Table 14.3 Variable definitions and sources for demand analysis regression

Variable	Description and source
Disney attendance	Disney Florida combined attendance (scotware.com.au/theme)
Disney price	1-day park admission at Disney Florida (monthly average)
Busch price	1-day park admission at Busch Gardens (monthly average)
Universal price	1-day park admission at Universal Studio (monthly average)
SeaWorld	1-day park admission at SeaWorld (monthly average)
Per capita disposable income	Real per capita disposable personal income (BEA, quarterly)
Population	US population (quarterly, mid-period)
Unleaded petrol price	Unleaded petrol prices (BLS, monthly)
Air fares	Air fare price index (BLS, monthly)
Lodging prices	US lodging away-from-home price index (BLS, monthly)

$$\begin{aligned}
\text{Disney attendance} = {} & -22.0 - 0.03 \text{ Disney price} + 0.44 \text{ Busch price} - \\
& 0.68 \text{ Universal price} + 0.10 \text{ SeaWorld price} + \\
& 1.00 \text{ per capita disposable income} + \\
& 2.89 \text{ population} - 0.14 \text{ unleaded petrol price} - \\
& 0.38 \text{ air fares} + 0.42 \text{ lodging prices}
\end{aligned}$$

All variables tested significant at the two-tailed, one-per cent level except for Disney's price itself and SeaWorld prices (see Table 14.4). The overall fit, adjusted for degrees of freedom, was 96 per cent.

Coefficient signs and magnitudes for the statistically significant variables in the demand model are extremely revealing. The elasticities for the prices charged by Disney's competitors reveal the relationships between theme parks in the Central Florida area. Busch Gardens, which is located in Tampa, Florida, a ninety-minute drive west from WDW, is clearly a substitute. Its positive elasticity (0.44) indicates that a 10 per cent real price increase by Busch Gardens results in Disney attendance rising 4–5 per cent, other things being equal. In fact, Busch Gardens did increase its prices from 18 per cent below Disney in 1992, to match Disney prices by early 2001 (see Figure 14.1). The lesson for park managers is that the more distant a regional attraction is to the centre of tourist activity, the more it must depend on lower prices (Fodness and Milner, 1992).

On the other hand, Universal Studios was the first theme park with deep enough pockets and a strong brand name to challenge Disney's dominance in Florida (Braun and Soskin, 1999). Disney was therefore forced to accommodate Universal's market entry in 1990 by allowing the latter to share price leadership.

Table 14.4 Regression results of logarithmic model

Predictor	Elasticity coefficient	Standard error	t-ratio	p-value
Constant	−22.0	2.53	−8.73	0.000
Disney price	−0.03	0.11	0.27	0.780
Busch price	0.44**	0.16	2.81	0.006
Universal price	−0.68**	0.18	−3.86	0.000
SeaWorld	0.10	0.13	0.75	0.460
Per capita disposable income	1.00**	0.33	3.06	0.003
Population	2.89**	0.68	4.25	0.000
Unleaded gas price	−0.14**	0.04	−3.48	0.001
Air fares	−0.38**	0.08	−4.82	0.000
Lodging prices	0.42**	0.08	5.03	0.000

Source	Analysis of variance			
	Degrees of freedom	SS	MS	F
Regression	9	2.58	0.287	286
Residual error	98	0.0984	0.00100	
Total	107	2.68		

Note: SEE = 0.03148; Adj – R^2 = 0.96; *significant at 0.05 level; **significant at 0.01 level.

By the mid-1990s, both Universal and Disney were routinely charging identical admission rates and making price changes in unison.

As a consequence, Universal prices have acted as a surrogate for Disney prices, accounting for the lack of significance by Disney prices in the model. Moreover, Universal adds extra predictive information because of its complementary relationship to Disney. Universal appeals much more to teenagers and Generation Y (young unmarrieds), while Disney owns the pre-teen and older crowd. Because the two theme park operators target different demographics, tourists and convention visitors tend to visit both portfolios of park offerings during their stay. The result is that Universal, unlike Busch Gardens, acts as a complementary good that visitors consume along with Disney parks during their Florida visits. The relatively large (–0.68) cross-price elasticity indicates that a 10 per cent real price hike by Universal will reduce Disney attendance by 6 or 7 per cent. The lesson here for park managers is that pricing may not be a viable strategy. Rather, managers must understand their target customers and focus on product differentiation, demonstrating a differential advantage in their experience (Fodness and Milner, 1992). Unfortunately, distinctive and complementary attractions can adversely affect attendance. By contrast, there appears to be no relationship between SeaWorld and Disney. In this case, the ability of Busch to bundle their parks shows that distinctive and complementary attractions can boost attendance when parks are viewed as inferior alternatives.

The impact of demographic factors on theme park demand is especially strong. If the family market remains the core of the market (Milman, 2001), population growth will continue to drive a park's growth and success. Population elasticity has the largest elasticity (2.9), attributable to the traditional family attraction of Disney theme parks. Their stroller-friendly environs and youth-targeted marketing campaign still make Disney the most popular destination for families with young children. For each 10 per cent population increase, Disney attendance rises by nearly 30 per cent.

The income elasticity, by contrast, is unitary (1.0). Disney theme parks now lie on the borderline separating luxury goods from normal goods. As real per capita incomes rise, the appeal to middle-income families for week-long trips to Disney parks goes up by the same amount. The lesson here is that major theme parks will thrive as long as there is healthy growth in both the population and income of the target market. In the near future the developing world will provide the industry many more opportunities to expand (Milman, 2001).

Florida theme parks are both road and air destinations, so factors that raise travel costs will adversely impact Disney's attendance. The negative and significant coefficients on air fare and petrol prices (that is, cross-elasticities of −0.38 and −0.14, respectively) support this contention. Specifically, a 10 per cent rise in air fares will translate to a nearly 4 per cent attendance decline at Disney parks. However, it would require a 25–30 per cent increase in petrol prices to achieve the same attendance declines. The smaller sensitivity of car visitors to petrol price fluctuations is due to the fact that petrol purchases constitute a small portion of highway vacation travel costs. Vehicle depreciation dominates sport utility vehicles, recreational vehicles and luxury touring cars, which is a major fixed cost of this travel market. The lesson here is that theme parks must strive for a diverse transportation mix that is not too dependent on any single mode of arrival. Recent shocks to the petrol and air travel markets support the position that parks need to attract a balanced portfolio of travel modes.

The final component of the model is national lodging prices. The cost of accommodation constitutes a sizeable share of family vacation and convention visitor spending. When hotel and motel prices are relatively high, Disney parks have an additional appeal. The cost of lodging in Orlando is among the lowest of any major metropolitan area, so budget-conscious travellers will tend to look more favourably toward visiting WDW. Furthermore, travel surveys consistently report that a large portion of Florida visitors stay with friends and relatives rather than pay for their accommodation. Central Florida's population has passed 3 million and grows even larger during peak tourist months when seasonal 'snowbirds' come to Florida. The seasonal and permanent residents provide a ready supply of alternative free lodging to Disney's theme park visitors. The model lends strong support to the substitute relationship that national lodging price plays. The relatively large positive cross-price elasticity (0.42) implies that a 10 per cent real price increase in average US lodging prices translates into a 4 per cent increase in Disney attendance.

Conclusion

The living laboratory of Central Florida's theme parks provides a number of lessons to managers. Substantial changes in both industry structure and the overall market environment have led to a dramatic alteration in pricing strategies of the Central Florida theme park industry. In the 1980s, WDW operated like a dominant firm with a competitive fringe that matched WDW price changes with a lag. At the dawn of the twenty-first century, parallel pricing patterns are the predictable result of a tight four-firm oligopoly. By the middle of the 1990s, Disney and Universal Studios were matching price hikes in an identical manner. A couple of years later, SeaWorld had converted to the pricing regimen. Most recently, Busch Gardens had added its weight as the final park to co-ordinate prices perfectly. Meanwhile, the second-tier parks like Cypress Gardens and Wet'N'Wild, which lack the investment and promotional budgets, must content themselves with whatever they can draw away from the major attractions by price discounting. The true test for the industry and its collusive pricing regimen is whether undisciplined price cutting can be avoided if an overvalued dollar and economic recession causes tourism demand to decline.

The case of the Central Florida theme park industry shows managers the importance of understanding their target customers. A focus on product differentiation can adversely affect attendance if attractions are complements. On the other hand, attendance at inferior alternatives can be enhanced through product differentiation and bundling strategies.

If Orlando's experience is any guide, managers of theme parks can expect a natural product life cycle to occur in their regional market. They can expect an expansion and consolidation of operations. The expansion will be in part driven by a natural agglomeration of activity, as well as from rising population and per capita income. However, recession nationally or globally will produce predictable slumps in park attendance. Theme park managers may anticipate further consolidation pressures that could affect the relationships between competitors and the competitive strategies available. Managers should build a strong regional customer base that is not reliant on visitors who travel by any single mode of transport because attendance is sensitive to both petrol and air fare price changes. Managers should be supportive of policies that encourage hotel and convention centre development, keeping the price of lodging and bed taxes at a competitive level overall.

References

Braun, B. M. and Milman, A. (1994). Demand relations in the Central Florida theme park industry. *Annals of Tourism Research*, **21**, 150–153.

Bruan, B. M. and Soskin, M. (1999). Competitive strategies in the Central Florida theme park industry. *Annals of Tourism Research*, **26**, 438–442.

Braun, B. M., Soskin, M. and Cernicky, M. (1992). Central Florida theme park pricing: following the mouse. *Annals of Tourism Research*, **19**, 131–136.

Cecchetti, S. (1986). The frequency of price adjustments: a study of the newsstand prices of magazines. *Journal of Econometrics*, **31**, 255–274.

Dixit, A. (1980). The role of investment in entry deterrence. *Economic Journal*, **90**, 95–106.

Fodness, D. D. and Milner, L. M. (1992). A perceptual mapping approach to theme park visitor segmentation. *Tourism Management*, **13**, 95–101.

Milman, A. (2001). The future of the theme park and attraction industry: a management perspective. *Journal of Travel Research*, **40**, 139–147.

Scherer, F. M. and Ross, D. (1989). *Industrial Market Structure and Economic Performance*. Houghton Mifflin.

15

Marketing visitor attractions: a collaborative approach

Alan Fyall

Aims

This chapter outlines a variety of approaches to the collaborative management and marketing of visitor attractions. Given the increasingly difficult competitive environment in which many visitor attractions now find themselves, effective collaboration may make the difference between success and failure. In particular, collaborative strategies offer a potential solution to problems and challenges too large or complex for individual attractions to conduct in isolation.

The specific aims of this chapter are to:

- outline the conditions in the visitor attractions sector which encourage a collaborative approach to management and marketing
- discuss the advantages and disadvantages of collaboration
- identify those situations where collaborative strategies are appropriate and desirable
- introduce a set of guiding principles for effective collaboration
- discuss the feasibility and constraints of collaboration with reference to a specific case example.

Introduction

With a projected slowdown in visitor demand and an acknowledged oversupply of attractions, visitor attractions across the UK are set to face a challenging future. Further, with the transformation in the geography and typology of visitor attractions more generally (Stevens, 2000), the visitor attractions sector arguably needs to adopt a more strategic approach to managing its activities if it is to have a lasting future. The challenges are considerable. For example:

- although the overall number of visits to attractions in England has grown by 14 per cent over the last decade, the average number of visits per attraction is declining
- competition from both within and outside the visitor attractions sector is intense, with considerable additional pressure on people's leisure time
- consumer expectations continue to rise
- the number of European Union (EU) visitors to attractions is in decline in the UK
- National Lottery and EU funding continues to stimulate the development of new attractions, while existing, predominantly private sector attractions struggle to raise funds
- privately-owned attractions continue to experience the displacement effects of the 'free admissions' policy to the national museums and galleries.

Not only are these challenges likely to impact on the quality of the visitor experience, they also determine the very long-run survival of existing and new attractions, most evidently those in the private sector. The challenges identified here are discussed in much greater depth in the ETC's recent report, *Action for Attractions*, which provides an extensive overview of the sector (ETC, 2000). The report outlines a framework for action, which provides a comprehensive set of strategic objectives and recommendations for the visitor attractions sector in England. Ten key areas are identified for attention. These include market measurement, increasing visitor satisfaction, improving attraction management skills, benchmarking, quality, funding and investment, taxation, development and planning. While these are all highly pertinent issues to the future development of the visitor attractions sector, this chapter focuses on the final 'strategic' area deemed to be of future importance, that of improving co-operation and co-ordination between attractions (see Table 15.1).

While designed specifically for visitor attractions in England, the objectives and recommendations set out by the ETC are equally valid for attractions across the UK, and indeed throughout the world. A recent study conducted in Scotland

Table 15.1 Improving co-operation and co-ordination between attractions

Strategic objectives:
The main objective is the creation of a cross-sectoral attractions advisory group to improve co-operation and co-ordination, while recognizing the separate special interests of each type of attraction and the existence of the individual organizations.

Once formed, such an entity should be able to play a central role in:

■ reviewing and revising the Visitors' Charter/Code of Practice;
■ guiding improvements in research analysis and dissemination;
■ developing the most appropriate benchmarking processes;
■ guiding the quality assurance service;
■ guiding and promoting industry-wide IT [information technology] and booking systems;
■ encouraging co-ordination, co-operation and information sharing between attractions and sectoral organizations;
■ helping to revise and monitor the attractions strategy.

Recommendations:
■ The formation by the industry of a cross-sectoral attractions advisory group. The ETC will consult with sectoral organizations and the RTBs [regional tourist boards] with a view to setting up such a group.
■ The ETC will encourage and assist liaison between the new advisory group and the DCMS [Department of Culture, Media and Sport], RTBs and other interested bodies.

Source: ETC (2000)

outlined a number of recommendations for Scottish visitor attractions which are consistent with the above (Fyall, Leask and Garrod, 2001). These included the need to:

■ consider the adoption of collaborative marketing strategies with a view to the collective creation, branding and theming of local, regional and national attractions to make best use of limited resources and limited markets, especially in the peripheral areas of the country
■ investigate the potential for collaborative marketing relationships with other tourism sectors to facilitate the collective creation and development of destinations
■ work in collaboration with the other sectors of the tourism industry in an attempt to co-ordinate all-year-round interest in the wider Scottish tourism product to address the problem of 'seasonality'
■ investigate the viability of joint-ticketing initiatives and marketing consortia membership.

The need to move forward and begin to adopt some of the above recommendations was given early momentum in 1999, when it was suggested that, if current levels of profitability were to be sustained in the new millennium, then visitor attractions would have no choice but to adopt collaborative strategies (Whitehead, 1999). With so many visitor attractions competing for an ever-smaller pool of tourists, it is hard to envisage a more palatable alternative. This chapter will now explore the benefits and drawbacks to visitor attractions of collaboration.

Advantages and disadvantages of attraction collaboration

Collaboration among visitor attractions can potentially take a number of different forms. For example, attractions can share resources, identify areas of mutual benefit, achieve economies of scale or collectively promote the generic appeal of a 'day out' to visitor attractions. The question underpinning all forms of collaboration, however, is the extent to which attractions can best achieve the potential advantages of collaboration, given the severe reservations that pervade the visitor attractions sector when it comes to undertaking collaborative actions. Within this context, the benefits available to attractions from collaborating with one another include:

- the opportunity for attractions to collectively brand, theme and/or package the visitor attraction product within a geographic area
- benefits to be derived from the pooling of resources (time, finance, expertise, human resource and training)
- scope to reduce individual risk and uncertainty through the sharing of market information
- an opportunity to enhance the promotion of attractions and distribute the message through ever more complex channels of distribution
- a chance for attractions to raise their individual profile, launch joint marketing campaigns, conduct and share joint research and partake in attraction-specific forums
- the occasion to develop more effective 'collective' representation with industry and political bodies
- the opportunity to work towards harmonizing the objectives of small-, medium- and large-sized visitor attractions.

Furthermore, both intra- and inter-sectoral collaboration are likely to bring further benefits, including:

- the creation of a 'vehicle' for the natural congruence of tourism objectives between interdependent partners within tourism destinations
- an alternative to uneconomic and inefficient 'free market' solutions whereby decisions are made that are likely to benefit the wider destination rather than individual attractions in isolation.

Despite the many benefits to be derived from collaboration, however, visitor attractions need to be aware of the drawbacks that can potentially arise from such action. Collaboration between attractions can lead to:

- mutual distrust and bad feeling among attractions with contrasting visitor numbers
- possible apathy, due to the potential tension between competitive and collaborative forces in the marketplace
- inertia, owing to the failure or inability of attractions to advance at the same pace
- unhealthy competition from non-participating 'honey-pot' attractions
- conflict between attractions with various ownership backgrounds and objectives.

Likewise, further disadvantages that can be derived from both intra- and inter-sectoral collaboration include:

- broad unease over an apparent loss of control over decision-making, with some partners sensing a greater loss of control than others
- non-achievement as a consequence of limited time, finance and expertise
- general scepticism of too many attractions being involved to achieve an adequate outcome
- widespread unfamiliarity among attractions, which can involve the switching of resources to more familiar, 'safe' strategies.

In view of the current market environment, the author believes that the advantages of collaboration currently outweigh the disadvantages. However, progress will only be made if strategies are seen to be appropriate and desirable. The following section outlines a variety of strategies with existing examples of collaboration 'good practice', first, with regard to the development of attractions and, second, with respect to the management and marketing of visitor attractions.

Collaborative management and marketing of visitor attractions

The visitor attraction product and visitor management strategies

When considering the adoption of collaborative management and marketing strategies, it is imperative to balance collaboration with actions and strategies likely to be conducted in competitive isolation. The first area where collaborative strategies can be adopted is with the visitor attraction product itself and corresponding visitor management strategies. It is unlikely that attractions will collaborate in the search for a differential competitive advantage with regard to their core product offering. In other words, each attraction will display a degree of uniqueness which distinguishes it from competing attractions, locally, regionally, nationally and sometimes even internationally. For example, Vinopolis – City of Wine, on the South Bank of the Thames, is distinct in that rather than being purely a museum of wine, it offers 'all the pleasures of wine under one roof' (Hodges, 2000: 36). Part food store, part wine and merchandise retailer, part corporate hospitality and event organizer, Vinopolis is a unique and multifaceted attraction. However, in raising the profile of the South Bank as an alternative destination to the more traditional tourist sites north of the Thames, it could be argued that a collaborative 'domain destination' strategy would be advisable. Whether through formal or informal collaborative networks, attractions in the vicinity of Vinopolis, such as Shakespeare's Globe, the South Bank Centre and the Tate Modern Gallery, could develop 'destination' visitor management strategies and 'cannibalization avoidance' strategies. This would help to strengthen the collective appeal of the area, while allowing individual attractions to retain responsibility for their own uniqueness, overall quality and core appeal. In order to establish a critical mass of provision, it is advisable for attractions to work in close collaboration with one another.

Further to the above, the search for standards of quality and attainment of quality assurance marks, most probably from the local tourist board, could also be considered to be an individually competitive target for visitor attractions. However, the Hampshire and Dorset Benchmarking Project, which has the collaborative support of Hampshire County Council, the Southern Tourist Board, the South Eastern Museums Service and the Dorset and New Forest Area Tourism Partnership now has over thirty attractions working towards a recognized standard of 'good practice' (LDR, 2000). Of particular interest is the fact that participating visitor attractions are encouraged to seek help from each other, visit one another's facilities and exchange information face to face; in other words, to pursue informal collaboration irrespective of their size, location, ownership or volume of visitors.

One further collaborative strategy is that of 'exhibit leasing'. Although this tends to occur between attractions outside of the local area, it can help to address problems of seasonality and/or contribute to the organization of *ad hoc* special events or exhibitions. Although this approach is only just beginning to be adopted among historic houses and castles in an attempt to 'rejuvenate' and 're-energize' their permanent displays, it is a strategy which has been used for many years among operators of museums and galleries (MGC, 1998).

Price setting and revenue generation

The need to strike a balance between collaborative and competitive behaviour is particularly evident when it comes to price setting and the generation of revenue by attractions. Whereas initial price-setting decisions and the setting of revenue targets are most often the individual attraction's decisions, numerous opportunities exist for collaborative price-banding and joint-ticketing initiatives. These opportunities are, however, highly dependent on the demographic profile of visitors at attractions, visitor dwell time and the complementary nature of attractions. For example, very popular attractions such as Edinburgh Castle are often reluctant to participate in collaborative campaigns unless they are very carefully researched. Joint-ticketing can lead to reduced time spent by visitors at individual attractions, impair visitor satisfaction and reduce the potential for attractions to earn much needed secondary spend. One area that presents considerable scope for collaboration is in the formation of retail collectives and buying groups. Large numbers of attractions source supplies from the same caterers, printing companies and merchandise producers as their competitors, and they frequently promote themselves via the same media. Hence, the enhancement of buying power and the benefits to be derived from economies of scale are a real possibility through collective bargaining and collaborative buying.

Marketing communications, advertising and promotion

Perhaps the area where collaboration can bring the most visible benefits to individual visitor attractions is that of marketing communications, advertising and promotion. Collaborative 'generic' promotional activity, which can encourage people to visit attractions in general, is not only a relatively simple task but also one which is likely to generate a relatively quick and positive response. For example, the outbreak of Foot and Mouth Disease in many rural parts of the UK in 2001, especially in Cumbria and Devon, has seriously impacted on visitor numbers to attractions in general. Rather than to confront the challenge in isolation, collaborative marketing campaigns offer participant attractions a bigger campaign budget with the potential to reach a wider audience than could possibly have been achieved in isolation. This could then lead to the collective theming, branding and packaging of groups of attractions with possible additional benefits such as opportunities to develop corporate hospitality and collaborative web campaigns. Both the Whisky Trail and the Castle Trail in Scotland are testimony to the success of this approach. They also represent good examples of developing an enhanced identity for attractions in peripheral locations, an issue of particular relevance to those attractions suffering from the Foot and Mouth outbreak.

With many attractions drawing visitors from both domestic and overseas markets, a dilemma exists as to how the different campaigns are to be balanced between individual competitive and collective collaborative communication. In many cases, it may be that domestic promotional campaigns are handled on an individual basis, whereas more expensive and high-risk marketing campaigns overseas benefit from collaborative strategies. This would certainly be the case for attraction attendance at overseas trade fairs and exhibitions where a number of attractions can be represented under an umbrella or themed brand. The cost of developing educational packs, a very important segment for a large number of visitor attractions, would also be spread across many attractions with limited competitive damage to individual attractions. Explore Edinburgh in Scotland is a collaborative marketing campaign designed to draw attention to Edinburgh's scientific-based attractions. With a heavy promotional remit, the development of a dedicated Internet site and educational material are key objectives of the collaborative strategy.

Distribution and booking channels

When it comes to the management of distribution and booking channels, visitor attractions can choose to conduct individual peak-season strategies when there are higher levels of demand, and adopt collaborative off-season strategies when visitor numbers are likely to be lower. A collaborative approach on this occasion can broaden awareness of the wider attraction's destination and encourage visitors to visit attractions rather than alternative commercial attractions such as shopping or going to the cinema. Perhaps the greatest benefit here lies with the potential increase in bargaining power and scope of influence of attractions with area and national tourist boards, associated bodies (such as the Association of Leading Visitor Attractions, the British Association of Leisure Parks, Piers and Attractions, and the Association of Scottish Visitor Attractions) and tour operators, than if they were to act alone. With so many individual attractions, over 4500 in England alone, the balance of power is clearly not with visitor attractions. The collaborative approach recommended by the ETC, as shown in Table 15.1, does therefore offer considerable advantages. It can offer the potential for higher margins, serve as the vehicle to engender sectoral harmony, direction and influence, and help to reduce both fixed and variable operating costs. Leaflet distribution networks are just one area where cost savings can probably be made. Furthermore, collaborative booking systems, such as OSSIAN in Scotland (http://www.visitscotland.com), can serve as engines of change and bring 'virtual' collaboration into being.

Research and human resource management

Finally, the benefits and opportunities of collaborative marketing and management can be applied to the undertaking of research and the management of human resources. For example, although attractions can individually monitor aspects of quality control and conduct customer tracking studies, more in-depth research programmes are normally either too expensive to undertake or too time-consuming for staff to conduct. There is also the issue as to whether day-to-day staff have the necessary skills and expertise to conduct such specialized research. For many visitor attractions, the human resource is a fundamental component of the success of the visitor experience. Hence, although individual attractions are likely to retain control over recruitment and attraction-specific training, the acquisition of skills of benefit to the entire sector such as languages, customer care and visitor reception skills, may best be delivered on a more economic and quality footing if delivered collaboratively. While this may prove difficult in peripheral locations, there are considerable advantages for attractions in close proximity to each other, particularly in urban locations. With staff difficult to recruit and train, cost-effective collaborative approaches, which can bring benefits to the entire sector, are to be encouraged. With so many attractions relying on volunteer staff, particularly those of a heritage genre, there are also benefits to be derived from an agency approach to recruitment. Not only does this keep fixed recruitment and employment costs down for attractions, it also guarantees a flexible labour supply of suitably skilled individuals for the destination domain. Through informal discussion forums, there are considerable advantages to be gained from the dissemination of good practice and the bringing together of like-minded commercial and business development orientated individuals, which may be to the benefit of the entire visitor attractions sector.

Collaboration dynamics and effectiveness

Collaboration dynamics

Before adopting any of the collaborative approaches to attraction development, management and marketing proposed in the previous section, it is recommended that operators of visitor attractions consider the likely dynamics of collaboration and the potential effectiveness of collaborative strategies. In evaluating the dynamics of collaboration, it is suggested that operators of visitor attractions consider the motives, membership, mission, structure and desired outcomes of collaboration.

Motives

An understanding of the underlying motives among prospective participants for the adoption of a collaborative approach is important in that motives frequently:

- highlight past or potential problems
- give an indication to collaborative organizational forms
- can identify key individuals and/or a collaboration convenor
- expose outside or internal vested interests
- clarify likely stakeholder groups in the collaboration.

A thorough understanding of the reasons behind the adoption of collaborative strategies is also important in that it identifies whether the strategy has arisen in response to a general trend, to an impetus generated from the public sector, or whether it has been activated by private-sector need.

Membership

The nature, scope, and spread of participants are important in that they are likely to determine the 'domain culture' of the collaborative form. For example, how representative is the collaboration with regard to public and private attractions, those drawing large or small numbers of visitors and/or those that charge for admission? Likewise, are natural attractions, attractions built specifically for tourism (such as museums, galleries and visitor centres) or those built for other purposes (such as castles and historic houses) represented fairly? In short, are sufficient key attractions included to give the collaboration credibility or the scope to achieve desired outcomes? It is frequently the case that the larger the visitor attraction, the less likely they are to participate in collaborative strategies. This was certainly the case in 1994, when Alton Towers, the number one theme park in the UK in terms of visitor numbers, decided against participating in the Year of the Rollercoaster campaign, a collaborative promotion between seventeen theme and amusement parks across the UK (Gilling, 1994). Reasons given for non-participation included the feeling that the promotion was inappropriate, that Alton Towers have a policy of non-participation in discount schemes with other attractions and, as the market leader, collaboration was deemed unnecessary.

Mission

It is also desirable to identify the strategic direction, mission or sense of purpose of the collaborative form, often via the interpretation of the overall objectives. It is essential to clarify:

- the agreed coverage of the collaboration with respect to its span of influence, functional competencies (such as marketing, training and research) and its geographic coverage (whether it is local, regional, national or even international in its remit)
- that participating members share a collective vision for the future
- the extent to which broader benefits, other than purely commercial objectives, exist.

The latter point is a highly topical issue for many museums, galleries and historic houses in their attempt to administer effective social-inclusion strategies to meet the aspirations of central government. More generally, it is necessary to agree the time frame for the collaboration as some participants may view it as a short-term quick fix, while others may view it as something with more substance and for the longer term.

Structure and outcomes

It is always necessary to identify the desired or likely structure and the planned or desired outcomes of collaboration. When considering the constitutional structure, the balance of power (be it political or financial) also needs to be taken into consideration. This leads on to the issue of financial and strategic decision-making independence within the confines of collaboration and raises the dynamic of interorganizational behaviour. For example, is there likely to be a conflict for attractions wishing to preserve their autonomy of decision-making while at the same time participating in collective actions? Although perhaps wanting to minimize collaborative dependencies and preserve autonomy, many visitor attractions will become part of collaborative relationships as a necessity to acquire the relevant skills and financial and/or human resources to effectively achieve their individual goals. In addition, is collaboration membership driven by networking opportunities rather than the need to achieve strategic goals? Whatever the structure, it is necessary to minimize self-interest and free-riding tendencies if the wider visitor attractions sector is to benefit to any great degree from collaboration.

There is also the question of the desirability of having a degree of flexibility in the structure, or the extent to which a rigid organizing committee structure is necessary to achieve the desired outputs. Related to this is the need to consider

Table 15.2   Factors contributing to collaboration effectiveness

The involvement of key stakeholders	An equity share arrangement
A chemistry of good interpersonal relations and the development of trust among participants	The balance of management resources and power
A suitable inclusive management style and organizational culture	A well-planned project, carefully chosen partners, balanced structure and subsequent high payout in relation to cost
Domain similarity and goal compatibility among participants	Decisive leadership
Duration and nature of previous relationships among collaborating partners	Sound administrative support
	A tight focus
Effective contractual conditions and exit barriers	The transparent implementation of policy

the intrinsic nature of the relationship among collaboration partners. This will encompass participants' degree of commitment, extent of participation and general interest. Attendance and contributions at meetings, and involvement by key personalities can all evidence this. The cost of membership, the opportunity cost of non-membership, the desire to avoid duplication and overlap, and the donation of subsidies or grants may impact on structure, as might the timescale given to achieve the desired collaborative outcomes.

In all of the above, the ultimate goal is the achievement of collaborative compatibility. It is now, therefore, necessary to outline those factors which contribute most to long-term, mutually beneficial relationships.

Collaboration effectiveness

It is in the individual attractions' and collective attractions' interest that whatever form of collaboration is adopted, desired outcomes are achieved and maximum effectiveness is reached. A variety of factors are suggested as integral for the achievement of effective collaborative relationships, as seen in Table 15.2.

In addition to the above, a recent study conducted by the Museums and Galleries Commission (MGC, 1998) identified a number of factors which contribute to collaborative failure, as evidenced in Table 15.3.

In reviewing the appropriateness of these factors, it is understandable that different factors will carry more weight in different forms of collaboration. The following section will now discuss many of the issues discussed above and

Table 15.3 **Reasons for collaborative failure**

Lack of clear objectives
Lack of staff time
Slow decision-making process
Changes in personnel
Lack of new ideas/new initiatives
Lack of adequate negotiation
Responsibilities not sufficiently established at the outset
Lack of capital
Lack of communication and vacuum of objectives

Source: MGC (1998)

throughout this chapter in the form of a case study, and will attempt to shed light on the collaborative dynamics and effectiveness of interorganizational collaboration.

Case study: Scotch Whisky Heritage Centre, Edinburgh[1]

With just under 190 000 visitors per annum and a '5 Star' Visitor Attraction Rating, the Scotch Whisky Heritage Centre is one of Edinburgh's largest and most popular visitor attractions. It is thus surprising then that an attraction which welcomes such large numbers of visitors each year, and is located in a central tourist area (its neighbour being Edinburgh Castle which attracts more than 1.22 million annual visitors), actually needs to collaborate in the first place. However, with its variety of active collaborating partners, the SWHC is an excellent example of what may eventually become normal practice across the visitor attractions sector.

At the very outset, the SWHC involved considerable collaborative activity. With nineteen Scotch whisky companies heavily involved in the initial funding of the attraction through a shareholding, the generic promotion of whisky was the catalyst that served as the genesis for the entire attraction concept. With allocated shelf space for their products in secondary spend areas and a high-quality venue for city centre hospitality, the collaborating founders of the SWHC continue to show interest in the attraction.

In its pursuit of collaboration with a variety of partners, the SWHC believes that the benefits of collaboration clearly outweigh the drawbacks. For example, with regard to strategies to increase turnover, opportunities to improve benchmarking, staff networking and joint-marketing campaigns, collaboration is considered to be highly beneficial. However, the SWHC accepts that on occasion there still exist elements of reluctance on the part of competing attractions to participate with competitive suspicion and mistrust pervading some areas of the sector. For the SWHC, however, its increase from two to nine income streams since its launch can clearly be attributed to its collaboration with a variety of partners. With new income streams contributing approximately 30 per cent of total income, the Scotch Whisky Training School, the Scotch Whisky Bar, the restaurant, tutored whisky tastings (both on and off site) and its emergent mail order business, all benefit from collaborative action. Other more specific examples include:

- a reciprocal joint-ticketing initiative with the Royal Yacht *Britannia* whereby, on the exchange of the respective admission ticket, visitors receive a complimentary whisky miniature at the SWHC and a Britannia chocolate bar on entering the Royal Yacht. Although of deliberately limited duration, this exploratory initiative generated a response from over 1000 visitors at each site.
- a collaborative research relationship with Napier University. This entails annual research projects conducted by students and has included marketing initiatives for the education market and extensive visitor surveys. The long-term nature of this relationship is testament to its success.
- a major forthcoming collaborative initiative, 'Scotland the Dram', which will involve extensive collaboration between public and private sector organizations across Scotland. With its long-term aim to exploit whisky synergy in Scottish tourism, this initiative, which is still in its developmental phase, will hopefully demonstrate the power of collaboration to the benefit of both the whisky and tourism industries in Scotland.
- the recent launch of the Scotch Whisky Training School driven by the lack of awareness among barmen of the whisky product. In partnership with numerous hotels and restaurants, the Scotch Whisky Association, shareholders, Keepers of the Quaich (an industry body for those involved in the promotion of whisky internationally) and Scottish Enterprise Edinburgh and Lothians (the regional development agency), the SWHC initiative has so far proved successful. For example, successes to date include an increase in revenue generation, industry-wide networking, enhanced staff motivation, and greater awareness of the SWHC visitor attraction product across Scotland.

With regard to the perceived effectiveness of its collaborative relationships, the SWHC considers collaboration to be highly beneficial not only financially, but also for staff motivation, industry goodwill and the genesis of new projects. The SWHC:

- only collaborates with partners perceived to be of the same high quality, especially attractions, and whereby the convergence of individual competitive goals does not interfere with the pursuit of broader, collaborative initiatives.
- clearly works in collaboration with partners whose size and market power are either relatively similar, or are modest compared with sector or industry leaders. It is interesting that limited collaboration is undertaken with Edinburgh Castle, Scotland's largest attraction in terms of visitor numbers, and neighbour to the SWHC.
- appears to be able to engender a spirit of 'learning' among its collaborating partners, most notably with the Scotch Whisky Training School initiative, at the same time limiting access to proprietary skills.
- benefits from long-term relationships and the establishment of trust with selected partners rather than short-term exchanges with a multitude of suppliers, Walker's Shortbread being one supplier in particular who has benefited from such an arrangement. This having been said, the duration of collaborative initiatives is finite, with the SWHC preferring to avoid open-ended agreements and reserving the right to withdraw if the collaboration is failing.
- is able to share a collective mission with all collaborating partners interested in the long-term future of the whisky and tourism industries in Scotland.

Although many of the SWHC's collaborative relationships are relatively informal, sometimes short to medium term, and frequently of a marketing bias, there can be no doubt as to the commitment given to collaboration by the chief executive of the SWHC. For example, he is currently chairman of the Edinburgh Tourism Action Group (ETAG), which is a collaborative initiative between the public and private sectors to ensure that Edinburgh is perceived as a 'must visit' destination in a 'world-class' category. Along with over 1000 tourism businesses across the Edinburgh and Lothian region, ETAG has been instrumental in helping to counter the damaging effects of the recent Foot and Mouth outbreak.

In addition to the above, the SWHC is also a member of the Edinburgh and Lothians Tourist Board, Visitscotland, the ASVA, both the Edinburgh

Conventions Bureau and the Scottish Conventions Bureau and the local Chambers of Commerce. In addition, it is also part of the Capital Group, which represents a number of visitor attractions working together in Edinburgh to promote and develop the wider destination. On a more informal basis, the SWHC collaborates to varying degrees with other attractions, hotels and bed and breakfast establishments in the vicinity of the Royal Mile to further develop visitor numbers. By offering free entry to the staff of collaborating partners, the SWHC hopes to broaden its profile locally and stimulate positive word-of-mouth. In a similar manner, the SWHC operates an incentive scheme for local taxi drivers whereby drivers can obtain discount vouchers and free whisky if pre-agreed numbers of visitors are brought to the attraction.

It is quite clear that for the SWHC, rather than being a token strategy for short-term gain, involvement in collaborative initiatives is central to its long-term development. This is true both for the wider development of the whisky and tourism industries in Scotland, as well as pivotal to its own future as a proactive private, high-quality and high-profile visitor attraction with a reputation for innovation and creativity.

Conclusion

Current visitor trends across the UK suggest that visitor attractions need to be far more sensitive to the future needs of the marketplace if they are going to survive in the longer term. Considerable competition from within and outside the visitor attractions sector is sufficient to threaten visitor displacement at ever increasing levels. In the UK, with the additional burden of government financial support for free admission policies and generous awards of National Lottery funding to many national museums and galleries, the visitor attractions environment is particularly hostile for smaller attractions which constitute the vast majority of the visitor attractions landscape.

This chapter has outlined a number of collaborative management and marketing strategies which, it is hoped, will encourage attractions to play a much more proactive and participative collaborative role in the creation, development and sustainability of the wider tourist destination, as well as to preserve their individual status. Although endorsing the very positive steps taken by the ETC in the UK in promoting the launch of a cross-sectoral attractions advisory group, the success of any collaborative strategy is ultimately dependent on attractions collaborating with each other. What is required is a far less proprietary, more holistic approach to the management of individual, and potentially collaborative, attractions by managers and owners for the benefit of the entire visitor attractions sector. Competing attractions are no longer the threat they once were; they are now the source of future strength and 'collaborative' survival.

Note

1 This case study originally featured in the article by Fyall, Dunkley and Leask (2002).

References

ETC (2000). *Action for Attractions*. English Tourism Council.

Fyall, A., Dunkley, C. and Leask, A. (2002). Managing visitor attractions: effective collaboration in practice. *Insights* (in press).

Fyall, A., Leask, A. and Garrod, B. (2001). Scottish visitor attractions: a collaborative approach. *International Journal of Tourism Research*, **3**, 211–228.

Gilling, J. (1994). Ticket to ride. *Leisure Management*, **14**, 32–34.

Hodges, T. (2000). Thinking outside the box. *Locum Destination Review*, **1**, 35–37, Locum Destination Consulting.

http://www.visitscotland.com

LDR (2000). Benchmarking attractions. *Locum Destination Review*, **1**, Locum Destination Consulting.

MGC (1998). *Collaboration between Museums*. Museums and Galleries Commission.

Stevens, T. (2000). The future of visitor attractions. *Travel and Tourism Analyst*, **1**, 61–85.

Whitehead, T. (1999). Visitor attractions in the new millennium from a local government perspective. *Tourism*, **102**, 4–5.

Part Five

Future trends

Part Five looks to the future of visitor attractions, the future of the visitor attraction sector more generally and the future visitation patterns of visitors in particular. Visitor attractions have sometimes been viewed as followers rather than innovators within the tourism industry. However, visitor attractions can no longer rely on relatively stable market conditions and reliable sources of funding. In the context of a more dynamic, perhaps more fickle market environment, as well as a rapidly changing funding environment, many visitor attractions are presently facing a 'sink or swim' scenario. Notwithstanding this, a number of themes could be considered to be important for this section. These include the extent to which visitor attractions should respond to the progress of technology and the degree to which technology represents an opportunity or threat for the visitor attraction sector. Also, the decline in the contribution of the public sector and the growth of private sector and 'voluntary' provision is a noticeable trend. The question of funding has major implications, particularly for the perceived need to generate income from visitors and other potential user groups. The increasing need to source additional funding and revenue streams is one factor that has contributed to the gradual migration of professional expertise from the wider 'commercial' leisure industries into the visitor attraction sector. Although it is still a little too early to say what they will be, there are inevitably going to be implications of this trend, in particular for the broadly 'curatorial' culture of the visitor attraction sector. Likewise, the verdict is still out as to how the potential 'McDisneyization' of visitor attractions will carry with it positive or negative implications.

These issues aside, the three themes identified as most appropriate for inclusion in Part Five at the time of writing this book include an overview of future patterns of visitor behaviour, the need to consider the future strategic direction of the sector, and the likely future role and focus of visitor attractions. In Chapter 16, Richard Voase examines how visitor expectations have changed over time and how the expectations of 'old' and 'new' visitors are different. In offering a revised interpretation of what constitutes a 'new' visitor, Voase introduces the concept of the new 'thoughtful' and new 'smart' visitor and explains how 'active' and 'passive' modes of visitor experience require redefinition. In a political context, where 'dumbing down' continues to be an issue across many domains, Voase discounts the applicability notion in the context of visitor attractions and recommends a strategy that engenders a 'popular' threshold of engagement. By providing a real-life example of how one museum, the Royal Armouries Museum in Leeds, UK, is taking account of these new visitor types in its marketing strategies, Voase demonstrates the benefits to be gained by managers of visitor attractions from re-evaluating their understanding of their visitors' expectations.

The visitor attraction sector has in the past been characterized by a lack of strategic direction at the national level. In part, this can be attributed to the lack of representative bodies acting on behalf of the visitor attraction sector. This theme is adopted in Chapter 17 where Victor Middleton outlines the broad context within which any strategy is likely to emerge, and summarizes the circumstances that warrant a strategic approach to attractions and who is likely to be responsible for its development. Middleton questions the extent to which a single body can hope to represent the wide array of interests embodied within the visitor attraction sector and considers at what level strategy should be developed and applied. A case study then follows of the attractions strategy for England in 2000. Finally, a broad overview for the future development of visitor attractions is offered.

The above theme is also advanced in Chapter 18, where Terry Stevens provides an insight into the emerging new geography and typology of visitor attractions. With the demand for traditional attractions down in a number of mature destinations, there is a significant question mark over the viability and survival of many attractions, at least in their current form. Arguably, new forms of attractions, attraction management and marketing strategies are required to secure the longevity of the sector, as indeed are alternative approaches to the funding and financing of future attraction developments. Innovative products are also required to meet the needs of changing patterns of leisure behaviour, with leisure shopping, eating and drinking, and entertainment now impinging heavily on the domain of visitor attractions development and management. There is also likely to be a level of convergence between the management of both individual and collaborating attractions and the wider destination, the interrelatedness of the tourism product becoming much more of a reality in the early years of the new millennium.

16

Rediscovering the imagination: meeting the needs of the 'new' visitor

Richard Voase

Aims

The aims of this chapter are to:

- explain how 'new' visitors are a product of cultural postmodernization
- introduce two kinds of 'new' visitor: 'thoughtful' and 'smart'
- show how 'active' and 'passive' modes of experience require redefinition
- suggest that the alleged 'dumbing down' of culture is a fallacy
- recommend the strategy of ensuring a 'popular' threshold of engagement.

Introduction

This chapter aims to offer insights into the character of the 'new' visitor, into the visitor experience, and into the act of 'consumption' by which the visitor ingests satisfactions. Its content applies principally to visitor attractions of a cultural or heritage nature, but there are also wider implications. There are three key features to the chapter. The first is an examination of discourses in common circulation: discourses about the 'thoughtful' consumer, the 'smart' consumer and the 'dumbing down' of culture. The second is the impact of technological change on the way in which human beings use and consume information: this has been termed 'cultural postmodernization'. The third is an examination of the way satisfactions are generated by an encounter with a visitor attraction. An important dynamic is the relationship between so-called 'active' and 'passive' modes of consumption, and it will be seen that a re-evaluation of our understanding of these terms is desirable. The chapter concludes by suggesting that a 'popular' approach to the promotion of cultural and heritage attractions is a recommended and rational strategy for engaging the 'new' visitor. A case study of the Royal Armouries Museum, Leeds, UK, documents the prima facie effectiveness of such a strategy in a major heritage-based visitor attraction.

'Discourse' and 'ideology'

In order to make this study fully intelligible, it is important to clarify the meanings attached to these two terms. A 'discourse' is a recurring message, or set of messages, which passes back and forth across a range of forms of communication. For example, the alleged 'dumbing down' of culture is a charge which may be advanced by intellectuals who are cultural conservatives; it thus becomes the subject of comment in broadsheet newspapers. It is then discussed around tables in public houses, and also features in academic books such as this one. Thus, the phrase 'dumbing down', and the views attending it, constitute a *discourse*. 'Ideologies', by contrast, are as invisible as discourses are visible. They are embedded in discourses; they are obscure but powerful meanings which underpin a discourse (Purvis and Hunt, 1993). So, for example, the ideology embedded in the 'dumbing-down' discourse is that to be 'dumb' is a mark of undesirability. The reader might take the point of view that the undesirability of 'dumbness' is so obvious that there is no need for discussion. This point of view would be, in fact, clear evidence of an ideology at work (see Althusser, 1992). When such ideologies are contested, the result can be refreshingly entertaining. The film *Forrest Gump* was an affectionate portrayal of a protagonist whose wisdom and humanity more than compensated for his lack of intellectual prowess. Ideologies are rooted in ideas; they are constructs for shaping meanings, rather than templates for realities.

Cultural postmodernization

The most comprehensive study of the theorized cultural shift from a condition of modernity to postmodernity, and its impact upon tourism, is that of Urry (1990). This chapter is not the place to rehearse the full range and complexity of these arguments, but one aspect of the debate is crucial to the present purpose and it is summarized here. The starting point is the miniaturization and spread of IT and its consequences (Lyotard, 1984), which unfolds as follows. The increase in television output by means of satellite transmission and augmentation of terrestrial channels, the cheapening and proliferation of desktop computer technology and, most recently, the arrival of the Internet and the World Wide Web, have progressively led to a saturating of populations in the advanced world with informational messages. This has led to a democratization of knowledge; everyone can become an 'expert' of sorts. A highly informed, highly educated, well-travelled population is less easily 'led' by appeals to traditional loyalties, such as nation, class, trade union or political affiliation. Hence, individuals are more apt to gather around issues which they themselves have chosen, leading to the proliferation of special interest groups around environmental issues, conservation, alternative medicine, and so on (Economist, 1994). As individuals gather around chosen interests rather than around traditional loyalties, traditional methods of classifying people and anticipating their behavioural and consumption habits, by socioeconomic classification, place of residence, level of education and gender, become increasingly challenged. A structural de-differentiation within society has emerged (Lash, 1990).

The proliferation of the transmission of information, and its democratization, has also led to two other consequences. The first involves the blurring of boundaries between cultural forms such as art, music and travel (Jameson, 1984; Laermans, 1992; Urry, 1990). For example, academic history, when popularized through the medium of television, loses its perceived elite status when it shares a medium with soap operas and quiz shows. Similarly, the deployment of three operatic tenors to accompany a soccer World Cup celebration, in Italy in 1990, was arguably instrumental in removing opera, in the perception of the global public, from the opera house to which it had been hitherto confined. The second consequence is that as cultural knowledge proliferates and spreads via the electronic media, it loses, not unexpectedly, some of its depth. For example, to convey the essence of England under the Tudor monarchs within the space of a fifty-minute documentary, and make it engaging television, demands some

257

selection of material. Similarly, a global football crowd may be enchanted by five minutes of the aria *Nessun Dorma*, but may baulk at the prospect of enduring the full duration of the opera from which it was extracted. The demands of the medium become predominant, or as McLuhan memorably observed, 'the medium is the message' (McLuhan and Zingrone, 1997: 151). In the words of Jameson (1984: 60), the consequence is 'the emergence of a new kind of flatness or depthlessness, a new kind of superficiality in the most literal sense'.

The second consequence, crucial to our present understanding, is that this proliferation of knowledge involves not just the dissemination of superficial expertise, but its commercialization and commodification. 'Knowledge is and will be produced in order to be sold, it is and will be consumed in order to be valorised in a new production: in both cases, the goal is exchange' (Lyotard, 1984: 4). So knowledge proliferates and enables the individual to acquire expertise, and increasingly it proliferates on the basis of economic exchange. For example, that which is known as 'heritage' is arguably 'history' in a selected, packaged and consumable form.

The 'new' visitor

At this point the question of the 'new' visitor is addressed. Most practitioners and academics agree that visitors are changing, and that the 'newness' has something to do with increasing levels of sophistication. But like the 'new tourism' (Poon, 1989), the 'new museology' (Vergo, 1989), *The New Sex*[1] and, for that matter, 'New Labour' (Fairclough, 2000), the 'newness' is defined in very general terms. The 'new' visitor is in danger of becoming, if he or she is not one already, a *discourse*. However, there are already two marked discourses concerning consumer types which have been circulating in recent years, and an appraisal of these reveals that cultural postmodernization has arguably produced, simultaneously, two very different species of sophisticated 'new' consumer.

The first of these will be styled the *thoughtful consumer*. A decade ago, consultants and research organizations began suggesting that future consumers would be variously 'added-value seekers' (Henley Centre for Forecasting, 1992) and 'thoughtful consumers' (Martin and Mason, 1993). These 'new' consumers were discursively linked, in terms of their interest in visitor attractions, with 'a shift in emphasis from passive fun to active learning' (Martin and Mason, 1993: 34) and a general interest in active rather than passive leisure pursuits (Euromonitor, 1992). Ideologically, the discourse was the bearer of assumed values of active = thoughtful = learning. Implicit in these linkages is an assumed binary opposition with passivity, which in turn can be linked with the opposite of whatever 'thoughtful' may be – 'dumb', perhaps? The point to be understood is that these linkages, in ideologically set combinations, are erroneous and misleading. Obviously it is possible to be an educated person and enjoy passive pursuits. Equally, it is a mistake to conclude that thoughtful people, on a day out, expect to assume an active burden for digesting the experience on offer at a cultural or heritage attraction. These new consumers, sated with messages about the past which are as depthless as they are democratized, embark on a love affair with history in its consumable form, known to us as 'heritage'. This presents challenges to museums professionals: see Davies (1989) for an illustration of the intensity of the debate at the end of the 1980s.

The second species of sophisticated, 'new' consumer will be termed the *smart consumer*. If the thoughtful consumer responds primarily to the postmoderniza-tion of knowledge in terms of its proliferation and accessibility, the smart consumer responds primarily to its commodified character. The discourse of 'smartness' appears to have begun, like the discourse of 'thoughtfulness', in the early 1990s. Allied victory in the Gulf War was aided by the deployment of 'smart' missiles, which know where they are going. Some automobile manufacturers have produced 'smart' cars, which are unconventionally effective in urban driving and parking situations. Similarly, marketing staff at two major cultural/heritage attractions, in discussions relating to the changing nature of consumers, reported the existence of both the 'thoughtful' consumers, who were ready to engage with the collections, and 'smart' consumers, who were alert to commercial gimmickry and who saw the visit essentially in terms of a transaction, in which economic exchange value was a key feature. These *smart* visitors were, in essence, consumers who had lost their innocence (Voase, 2002). A hypothetical example may illustrate the difference. A 'thoughtful' and a 'smart' consumer both buy a comparable work of art by a contemporary artist. The 'thoughtful' consumer buys it because he or she likes it, and because the picture resonates with values and memories deep in his or her personal psyche. The 'smart' consumer also quite likes the picture, but the primary product benefit is that the work will increase in pecuniary value. The author would also like to point out that he regards these rationales for ownership to be different from the rationale, so meticulously researched by Bourdieu (1984), whereby original works of art are appropriated as a means of demonstrating social distinction.

'Consuming' the visitor attraction

How do visitors 'consume' the objects and interpretive material which they encounter in a visitor attraction? The vital point is that meaning is not intrinsic to externalities, such as the objects and interpretive material encountered in a museum, but is *authored by the visitor in his or her own mind* (Campbell, 1990). Meaning resides not in externalities but is defined in the mind of the reader at the point of reading; an insight afforded by the analytic paradigm known as post-structuralism. Outside an encounter between a reader and a text, there is no meaning. As Derrida (1998: 158) famously observed, *'il n'y a pas de hors-texte'* (there is no outside-text). In Campbell's (1994: 510) words: 'The individual can be seen as an artist of the imagination, someone who takes images from memory or the immediate environment and rearranges or otherwise improves them so as to render them more pleasing.'

This effect was ably demonstrated by research undertaken at Madame Tussaud's, in London, during the 1980s. What was apparent was that the satisfactions which visitors derived from the encounter with a wax figure did not reside in the artistry with which the likeness had been fashioned. Rather, satisfaction resided in the exploration of the memories, feelings and emotions which the visitor associated with the person represented by the wax figure. As a result, Madame Tussaud's was remodelled. Wax figures were removed from their roped-off compounds and placed into settings where visitors could walk around them, touch them and simulate interaction with the person represented by the figure. This relationship could be further simulated by having oneself photo-graphed with the wax figure, photography having been a practice which hitherto, at Madame Tussaud's, had been proscribed (Yorkshire TV, 1986).

The implication is, thus, that visitors will bring with them to the museum, in their minds, a set of memories acquired through previous exposure to the subject matter represented by the collections of the museum and a set of anticipations based on those memories and constructed through daydreaming (Campbell, 1994; Kelly, 1997). These daydreams, we can be certain, will not be anticipations based on purely intellectual memories. For example, in the case of a museum displaying and interpreting weapons of war, the anticipations are more likely to relate to personal memories of relatives involved in armed conflict, the fear experienced while watching documentary footage of war situations or simulations in fictional war films and vicarious concern for victims. Daydreams are not primarily constructs of the intellect; they are constructs of the emotions. As shall be seen, such insights have formed the basis for the promotional strategy of the case study chosen for this chapter, the Royal Armouries Museum in Leeds.

First, however, further comment is needed on the two discursive features mentioned earlier, and which are arguably crucial to an understanding of the landscape of contemporary consumption. The first will be styled 'the dialectic of the active and the passive', the second 'the discourse of the dumb'.

'The dialectic of the active and passive'

It has been shown earlier that agents of the circulation of the discourses surrounding the 'new' consumers are apt to link 'active' modes of consumption with 'thoughfulness' and 'learning', and 'passive' modes with 'fun' and whatever may be implied to be in binary opposition to 'learned'. The suggested term was 'dumb'. It has been argued that these ideological linkages are erroneous and misleading. However, there are deeper problems. The first problem is that it is arguably unsafe to assume that terms such as 'active' and 'passive' are in binary opposition to one another. Rather, they are extremes on a continuum of experience. For example, angling is an essentially passive pastime. It involves sitting by a river or canal for many hours, waiting for a fish to bite. But a retired person who pursues angling as an interest would be discursively regarded as active, and may attract comments such as, 'oh yes, he is very active, he gets himself out once a week to go angling'. Similarly, a group of young friends travelling by train to an arena in a city to hear Robbie Williams issue his injunction to 'Let Me Entertain You' are active in constructing and organizing a day out, even if, as audience members at the concert, they are essentially passive and it is Mr Williams who is doing the entertaining.

The second problem with attempting to label certain pursuits as 'active' and 'passive' is that many pursuits are difficult to categorize in this way. Take, for example, the reading of books. To sit in an armchair for an hour is not most pundits' idea of active consumption, but in a very real sense book reading is 'active' in that it is a mental activity requiring the deployment of intellectual skill. Moreover, the precondition for book reading is the equally active task of informing oneself of what is available, selecting a book, and borrowing or buying it. And it does indeed appear that British people are becoming more active as readers and owners of books. In 1996, two-thirds of adults were in the habit of reading books, compared with a little over one-half in 1976 (ONS, 1998). This increased bookishness is not entirely surprising when one considers the major increases in admissions to tertiary education in the UK – an increase of 75 per cent between 1990 and 1995 (Marshall, 2001).

It is maybe useful to contrast the intellectually active but physically passive pursuit of book reading with that other armchair pursuit, television viewing. This is widely regarded as the apogee of passive consumption. Televised output has, of course, expanded greatly during the last twenty years. For example, over the six-year period from 1985/6 to 1991/2, average weekly broadcast hours on terrestrial channels in the UK increased from 477 to 632 hours. This represents an increase of 30 per cent, and does not take into account the proliferation of satellite and cable channels over the same period (PSI, 1993). It may therefore come as a surprise to learn that, over a similar period, British adults actually started watching less television – from 27.1 hours per week in 1985 to 25.2 hours per week in 1994 (PSI, 1996). Admittedly the overall scale of watching remains considerable, but it is clear that television viewing has not expanded in tandem with the expansion of television output. What can perhaps be safely concluded is that viewers are, by necessity if not by disposition, more *selective* in their viewing. Furthermore, in common with book reading, television viewing now, in contrast with, say, twenty years ago, involves a range of pre-conditional planning tasks: deciding which programmes to record on video for future viewing; deciding which satellite, cable or digital channels are suitable for subscription. While less time is being spent on actual viewing, more time, and mental effort, is being expended on the *act of choice* in viewing. So, consideration of the nature of book reading and television viewing strengthens the notion that the UK population is becoming more active and thoughtful in the broadest sense. Why, then, has a whole discourse emerged surrounding the alleged 'dumbing down' of society?

'The discourse of dumbing down'

First, the nature of this discourse needs to be specified. The gist is that, for example, school examinations are becoming easier, university standards are being lowered by 'trendy' degree courses (Daily Express, 1996; Smithers and Roff, 2000), democratization of culture has led to erosion of standards (Hartley, 1999) and that a concomitant shortening of attention spans has led an assemblage of 'dumbing' effects, including the tabloidization of the broadsheet press (Engel, 1996; Greenslade, 1997). The pervasiveness of sound bite and spectacle in contemporary cultural expression is taken as indicative of a seldom articulated but clear inference that a dumbed-down culture, hand in glove with a dumbed-down education system, is producing dumb consumers. However, it does not take many moments' reflection to realize that these claims are not based on observations of cultural *consumption*; they are based on observations of cultural *production*. It is arguably fallacious to infer that, because cultural producers allegedly supply 'dumb' material, the consumers themselves are 'dumb'.

Investigative journalism has yielded some interesting comments on school examinations. Those of the present day were found to be no easier than those of a few decades ago. However, they were qualitatively different: the present-day candidate was required to be more competent in explanation, rather than in description; the emphasis had shifted from 'what' and 'how' to 'why'. Also, the present-day papers were apt to be carefully phrased in contemporary English in order to be easily understood or, in contemporary jargon, 'accessible' (Elliot-Major, 2000). In other words, the demands on the candidate were no lower than several decades ago and, depending on the value placed on exercising the mind rather than the memory, the present-day papers were arguably more demanding. But at the interface between production and consumption, usefully termed the 'threshold of engagement',[2] the candidate encounters a paper which is friendlier and easier to understand than its equivalent of several decades earlier. Similarly, in the case of the broadsheet press, the popularization of approach should not necessarily imply superficiality. One broadsheet editor argued cogently that the deployment of spectacle (tabloidization) does not necessarily betoken lack of depth (Rusbridger, 2000).

Linking technological change and consumption practices

So, it does not follow from an apparently 'dumb' threshold of engagement, that content is dumb or that consumers are dumb. There remains, however, the question as to why the 'dumbing down' of the threshold occurs, if as has been shown earlier, the 'new' consumers of both kinds are more knowledgeable and sophisticated. Why must the threshold be visually eye-catching (spectacle) or orally ear-catching (sound bite)? For the explanation, we return to the post-modernization of culture and, in particular, the writings of Lyotard. A consequence of the democratization of knowledge, itself a consequence of the miniaturization of machines and the means of transmitting information, argued Lyotard (1984), is that the big, unifying ideas of modernity – we could mention nationhood, organized religion, monolithic political ideologies – no longer carry the influence they once had. Their component parts are still around, in the form of lesser narratives or to use Lyotard's (1984: 37, 60) term, *'petits récits'*. These are arguably identifiable with the proliferating special interest groups, mentioned earlier, which have been so successful in recruiting support in the past twenty years. The emergence of flexible (post-Fordist) production and the substantial replacement of mass markets by segmented markets are arguably other manifestations. In this way, technological change can be seen to be the direct antecedent of the proliferation of information and its consequence the sating of consuming populations with informational words and images. Quite apart from the explosion of media output of all kinds, the volume of paid advertising in the UK doubled between 1975 and 1991: expenditure rose from £2700 million to £5400 million at constant 1985 prices (Waterson, 1992). As these proliferating lesser narratives all clamour for attention, it is unsurprising that, in order to get their messages heard, the threshold of engagement is popularized. As a result, sound bite and spectacle are now an integral part of journalistic, commercial and political discourse, but this is not to say that content is 'dumb', nor should it infer that consumers themselves are 'dumb'.

Case study: the Royal Armouries Museum, Leeds, UK[3]

Armed with these insights, the manager of a visitor attraction can reasonably conclude that content should offer the scope for exploration for the 'thoughtful' consumer; price and value should offer a deal to satisfy the 'smart' consumer and the initial contact with the visitor, via promotional material, should offer an arresting and popular proposition which appeals, not so much to the intellect, but to the emotions. Such a policy, implemented at the Royal Armouries, can be linked with significant improvements in visitor numbers. First, some background. The Royal Armouries, which opened in 1996, is an example of a trend whereby collections held by the UK's national museums have been relocated to provincial outstations. Initial annual visitor numbers exceeded 300 000, but thereafter showed a worrying downward trend (see Table 16.1).

Table 16.1   Royal Armouries Museum: annual visitor numbers

Year	1996 (part)	1997	1998	1999	2000
Number	324 110	345 705	292 658	177 334	158 274

Source: Royal Armouries Museum.

The arrival of new marketing staff in the summer of 2000 facilitated a reappraisal of promotional policies. The collections, consisting of weapons and armour from multiple time periods, vividly interpreted, combined with a building which was dramatic in terms of scale and space, were felt to be positive assets. There was felt to be adequate scope for an in-depth exploratory experience in which the emotions, as well as the intellect, could feature. However, implements of war do not have an immediate and obvious appeal to the general public. Indeed, their connotations are, unsurprisingly, somewhat negative. For that reason, a new promotional policy was conceived. The intention was to portray the visitor experience as an encounter with a range of narratives which appealed to all the senses. In the words of the museum's Marketing Operating Plan for 2001/2, this shift involved the replacement of a 'cerebral appreciation' with an 'emotionally driven call to action'.

The principal proposition of the new brochure was to 'discover your sense of adventure'. This was supported with sub-propositions within the brochure to 'see the splendour', 'touch the reality', 'hear the stories', 'smell the fear' and 'taste the victory'.

This approach was adapted for the purpose of business-to-business marketing in the form of attracting sponsorship. A named individual in the targeted business would receive a succession of postcards (Figure 16.1).

These mailings were followed up by a phone call from the museum and, subject to level of interest, a personal visit and the handing over of a full brochure. The revised promotional policy was accompanied by an increased emphasis on special events as a provider of a popular 'threshold of engagement' for the visitor. Self-evidently, it is difficult to document an empirical link between changes in promotional policy and changes in visitor numbers; however, month-by-month attendances show a consistent improvement from October 2000, in comparison with the previous year. Table 16.2 shows visitor numbers up to the time of writing, September 2001. The monthly visitor numbers for the financial year 2001/2 remained confidential at the time of writing; hence the author is grateful to have been allowed to cite the aggregate figure for April to September 2001. A comparable aggregate figure for 2000 is indicated.

Table 16.2 Royal Armouries Museum: month-by-month visitors

Year	1999	2000	2001
January	9 830	7 038	9 030
February	18 456	14 449	20 656
March	14 434	10 372	15 051
April	17 267	21 157	
May	12 670	13 038	(aggregate total,
June	16 868	11 842	April to
July	19 088	14 792	September 2001
August	28 771	22 435	was 154 425)
September	11 165	9 538	
October	14 022	18 395	Not yet available
November	8 008	9 602	Not yet available
December	6 755	5 614	Not yet available
Total	177 334	158 272	199 162 (to Sept.)

Source: Royal Armouries Museum

Figure 16.1   Royal Armouries Museum promotional postcards

Conclusion

This subject area is the object of continuing research on the part of the author, but it is suggested at this stage that there is prima facie evidence for the following three propositions, of which managers of visitor attractions can usefully take note.

First, cultural postmodernization has led to two kinds of 'new' visitor: the 'thoughtful', and the 'smart'. The former is a product of the proliferation of knowledge under the postmodern condition, the latter a product of the commodification of that same knowledge. Second, discursive references to 'active' and 'passive' leisure are arguably misleading in the new cultural climate. The terms require redefinition, since to be physically inactive does not betoken mental inactivity. Third, the 'dumbing down' of culture is in fact a lowering of the threshold of initial engagement on the part of cultural producers. Consumers themselves, far from being 'dumb', are increasingly complex. The evidence of the Royal Armouries Museum, where promotional policies based on these insights have been implemented, suggest that this approach should be seen as a rational strategy, and can be an ingredient for success.

Notes

1 The title of the first book by the fictional anti-hero, Howard Kirk, in Malcolm Bradbury's celebrated novel *The History Man*.
2 An excellent term for which the author is indebted to Nick Thompson, formerly of the Royal Armouries Museum.
3 This case has been prepared from interviews with and information provided by Royal Armouries staff. The author acknowledges with gratitude the assistance and information provided by Nick Thompson, formerly Head of Sales and Marketing, and Gillian Harnby, Sponsorship Manager, both of the Royal Armouries Museum, Leeds.
4 This compares with an aggregate figure of 92 802 visits for the same months in 2001.

References

Althusser, L. (1992). Ideology and the ideological state apparatus. In *A Critical and Cultural Theory Reader* (A. Easthope and K. McGowan, eds) pp. 50–58, Open University Press.

Bourdieu, P. (1984). *Distinction: A Social Critique of the Judgement of Taste*. Routledge.

Campbell, C. (1990). Character and consumption: an historical action theory approach to the understanding of consumer behaviour. *Culture and History*, **7**, 37–48.

Campbell, C. (1994). Consuming goods and the good of consuming. *Critical Review*, **8**, 503–520.

Daily Express (1996). Farce of useless degrees. *Daily Express*, 21 August.

Davies, M. (1989). A loss of vision. *Leisure Management*, **9**, 40–42.

Derrida, J. (1998). *Of Grammatology*. Johns Hopkins University Press.

Economist (1994). A nation of groupies. *The Economist*, 13–19 August, p. 25.

Elliot-Major, L. (2000). Have exams got easier? Dumb, No. 1: 1066 and all what? Supplement to the *Guardian*, 28 October, pp. 10–14.

Engel, M. (1996). Papering over the cracks. Guardian 2. Supplement to the *Guardian*, 3 October, pp. 2–4.

Euromonitor (1992). *The European Travel and Tourism Marketing Directory*. Euromonitor.

Fairclough, N. (2000). *New Labour, New Language?* Routledge.

Greenslade, R. (1997). The Telegraph, 'it is a-changin'. Media Guardian. Supplement to the *Guardian*, 3 February, p. 5.

Hartley, J. (1999). Someone's dumb. *Guardian*, 5 March, p. 20.

Henley Centre for Forecasting (1992). *Inbound Tourism: A Packaged Future?* Henley Centre for Forecasting.

Jameson, F. (1984). Postmodernism, or the cultural logic of late capitalism. *New Left Review*, **146**, 53–92.

Kelly, J. (1997). Leisure as life: outline of a poststructuralist reconstruction. *Loisir et Société/ Society and Leisure*, **20**, 401–418.

Laermans, R. (1992). The relative rightness of Pierre Bourdieu: some comments on the legitimacy of postmodern art, literature and culture. *Cultural Studies*, **6**, 248–260.

Lash, S. (1990). *Sociology of Postmodernism*. Routledge.

Lyotard, J.-F. (1984). *The Postmodern Condition: A Report on Knowledge*. Manchester University Press.

Marshall, J. (2001). Vision of lifelong learning put at the heart of OECD target. *Times Higher Education Supplement*, 6 April, p. 11.

Martin, B. and Mason, S. (1993). The future for attractions: meeting the needs of the new consumers. *Tourism Management*, **14**, 34–40.

McLuhan, E. and Zingrone, F. (1997). *Essential McLuhan*. Routledge.

ONS (1998). *Living in Britain: Results from the 1996 General Household Survey*. Office for National Statistics and The Stationery Office.

Poon, A. (1989). Competitive strategies for a 'new tourism'. In *Progress in Tourism, Recreation and Hospitality Management: Volume 1* (C. Cooper, ed.) pp. 91–102, Belhaven.

PSI (1993). *Cultural Trends 17*, **5** (1), Policy Studies Institute.

PSI (1996). *Cultural Trends 25*, **7** (1), Policy Studies Institute.

Purvis, T. and Hunt, A. (1993). Discourse, ideology, discourse, ideology, discourse, ideology . . . *British Journal of Sociology*, **44**, 473–499.

Rusbridger, A. (2000). Versions of seriousness, Dumb, No. 2: down the tubes. Supplement to the *Guardian*, 4 November, pp. 14–17.

Smithers, A. and Roff, A. (2000). Are new 'vocational' degrees worthless? Saturday Review, *Guardian*, 19 August, p. 2.

Urry, J. (1990). *The Tourist Gaze: Leisure and Travel in Contemporary Societies*. Sage.

Vergo, P. (1989). *The New Museology*. Reaktion.

Voase, R. (2002). Rediscovering the imagination: investigating active and passive visitor experience in the 21st century, *International Journal of Tourism Research* (in press).

Waterson, M. (1992). *The Marketing Pocketbook*. Advertising Association and NTC Publications.

Yorkshire TV (1986). *The Marketing Mix*. Programme One. Channel 4 Television.

17

A national strategy for visitor attractions

Victor T. C. Middleton

Aims

The aims of this chapter are to:

- outline the broad context within which any strategy for visitor attractions is likely to emerge or be designed within a tourism master plan
- summarize the circumstances that warrant a strategic approach to attractions and discuss who is likely to be responsible for its development
- identify the five critical dimensions of strategic analysis using trend data drawn from UK research
- provide a case study of the attractions strategy for England in 2000, indicating the process and main components, and highlighting the case for research
- offer a broader view of attractions for the twenty-first century beyond the traditional approach to sites that are provided primarily for the purpose of sightseeing.

Introduction

The [visitor attractions] seam is very rich: historic houses, castles and cathedrals, gardens and zoos, museums and theme parks, architectural masterpieces and icons from our industrial heritage, bird sanctuaries and London Eye. Foreword to *Action for Attractions* (ETC, 2000).

Context for a national strategy

For a developing country committing itself to tourism development as a new sector of its economy, a strategy for visitor attractions will invariably be an element of an overall tourism strategy or master plan – strategy will exist from the outset. For a developed country such as England, however, with over 150 years of continuous tourism development, strategies are only likely to emerge when specific structural problems and difficulties are perceived.

England is the largest country within the UK, registering some 85 per cent of recorded visits to known visitor attractions. Many of them have a history of over 100 years. But neither government nor tourist boards saw reason to devise a national strategy for visitor attractions until the late 1990s.

Recognizing the role and value of attractions as a key motivator for visits to leisure destinations, tourist boards in the UK took an interest in the sector from the mid-1970s. Numbers of visits recorded annually at known attractions had first been gathered since the 1960s, but significant research development dates back to 1977, when the first annual self-completion questionnaire survey of attractions was carried out in England (extended to the rest of the UK on a comparable basis in 1989). In a wide and disparate sector of some 6000 known attractions it is impossible to create a credible strategy without adequate management information to base it on and research developments are, therefore, a useful indicator of strategic interest and development

In order to conduct an efficient survey, it was first necessary to devise a standard classification for attractions and operational dimensions that attractions would recognize and respond to. Operational dimensions include the size of attractions measured in numbers of visits per year, percentages of all visits represented by those who pay for admission, those who are overseas visitors, those who are children, and so on. The standard classifications, although they are now dated (see below), provide the basis for defining the visitor attractions sector in any country and they are reflected in Chapter 1 of this book.

The evidence and trends emerging from data collected on a broadly comparable basis for over twenty years between 1977 and 1998 provide the information basis for the development of a strategic approach to visitor attractions in the UK. So 1977 was a far-sighted development that has served the attractions sector well. Once established as an annual series, however, there is enormous pressure on tourist boards not to change definitions because tracing trends over the years is generally considered to be more important than findings on specific topics. In the UK the need for comparability has tended to trap the data on attractions into 1970s' definitions and a focus for action that appears increasingly less relevant to the circumstances of the first decade of the twenty-first century (Middleton, 1999). At the time of writing, following a strategic review process carried out in 1999/2000, the design and implementation of the UK's annual survey of visitor attractions was out to tender and it is not yet clear how the survey will develop.

Under what circumstances is a strategy for attractions needed?

If the demand for attractions is growing, the sources of capital and revenue funding are secure, and the sector is able to sustain itself and fund the necessary processes of renewal and refurbishment, the need for a national strategy is limited, with scope only for limited action. The minimum strategic input is to organize research for the sector, co-ordinated on a national basis, and organize occasional forums for the airing of issues and the dissemination of good practice. This, indeed, was more or less what was done in the UK for the best part of a quarter of a century until 1995. There was not much need or reason for government or its agencies to interfere further.

On the other hand, if demand is falling, sources of capital and revenue funding are under threat and survival becomes an issue, the case for strategic intervention increases. When, as in the UK since 1995, government action through National Lottery funding and through subsidizing national museums to provide free admission radically and rapidly distorts the established patterns of growth, change and competition in the sector, imbalances occur that require strategic intervention. With the benefit of hindsight, the UK attractions research reveals a growing imbalance between a massive growth in the supply of visitor attractions and an effective plateau of demand for most of the 1990s. Although the UK economy expanded strongly from 1993 to 2000, it is now clear that demand, at least for traditional attractions as measured by tourist boards, was growing slowly at best and for some sectors it was declining. The need for strategy stemmed directly from that realization.

Strategic intervention is further justified where visitor attractions are not just part of the commercial provision for tourism that can be allowed to expand and contract with market rhythms, but also represent key and often irreplaceable elements in each community's heritage, culture and physical environment, and contribute to the quality of life of residents. Supply and demand for hotels, local transport operations and retail provision may be left to market forces but *laissez-faire* is not a relevant approach to visitor attractions that are core to each community's sense of history and place. Nor is it likely to encourage the level of multicultural provision and 'access for all' that are part of the UK government's objectives. Such objectives are not commercial and generally convey additional costs to those that seek to deliver them. The government clearly recognizes this for the few national institutions it supports directly, but there are less than twenty of them, and the same case applies in principle to at least 3000 of the 4000 attractions known to operate in England in 2000.

The circumstances that led to the formulation of national strategy in England

From an appreciation of British research evidence, and drawing on experience, it seems fair to conclude that a national strategy for visitor attractions is justified where all or most of the following conditions apply:

1 There is evidence that the capacity of visitor attractions is growing faster than the overall rise in demand over a number of years, with the inevitable result that more and more attractions are competing for the same core market and *average* numbers per year for individual attractions are falling.
2 There is evidence that the visitor market is mature (year-on-year growth is relatively static) and that key sectors of demand for attractions are declining. In the case of England, the domestic staying tourism market, measured in nights, has declined over the years since the mid-1980s. The education (schools) market has declined as transport costs have risen and other pressures have been placed upon the school timetable.
3 There is evidence that major new competitors for leisure demand have emerged and are drawing in out-of-home leisure expenditure that might otherwise have gone to traditional attractions.
4 There are destabilizing effects of sudden massive injections of unantici-pated capital into an already saturated market. In the case of England, the funding by the Heritage Lottery Fund and the Millennium Commission has ploughed hundreds of millions of pounds every year between 1995 and 2000 into major new attractions, mostly to be run by the not-for-profit sector. This investment in capital projects only, not revenue funding, occurred at exactly the time when capacity was already exceeding

demand. Although only open for a year, the Millennium Dome alone absorbed some £750 million, equivalent to a payment approaching £150 for every visit made.

5 It become evident that large, newly-opened projects are putting established attractions at a massive disadvantage (this is especially likely when they are provided 'free' to the user). This applied not only to commercial attractions but also to other attractions that have no option but to charge for admission to pay their wage and other costs. The fact that most new projects will not meet their annual revenue projections in the short- to medium-term adds another twist to the destabilizing spiral.

6 There is significant expenditure on other major urban regeneration projects. In the 1990s, much of this expenditure in the UK was contributed through European economic regeneration funding. Many fragile European regions faced with the loss of their traditional industry have targeted leisure, tourism and retail as core sectors for economic revival. On unfounded expectations of ever-rising leisure and tourism demand, visitor attractions are normally part of that perceived way forward.

7 There is a steady decline of local authority annual revenue funding for traditional attractions such as museums and galleries, as they face other spending priorities and are forced to contain their overall budgets.

8 The industry structure is one in which the great majority of players are very small businesses indeed, with only a handful of larger operators capable both managerially and financially of marketing themselves professionally and organizing their own data collection.

9 There is a lack of management information – the 'management information deficit' – that cannot be tackled by individual small players.

10 The attractions sector is distinguished more by non-commercial operators, such as trusts and other not-for-profit institutions, than by commercial businesses.

Critical dimensions for strategic analysis

Drawing on UK experience, there are five key statistical dimensions of the visitor attractions sector that, taken together, are likely to indicate the need for a national strategic response. These cover demand and supply, and the business operational characteristics of the sector. The UK data is shown in four tables:

- visitor demand and capacity of supply (having regard to new attractions opening)

Table 17.1   Trends in number of visits to attractions in
England, 1978–98

Year	Historic properties	Gardens	Wildlife sites	Museums and galleries
1978	100	100	100	100
1982	85	98	85	91
1990	112	139	127	112
1994	109	162	111	119
1996	116	174	117	121
1998	117	170	129	121

Notes: Indices 1978 = 100; 1978 chosen as base year because it was
the high level of 1970s.
Source: *Sightseeing in the UK* (1998)

- size of attraction
- types of attraction and their ownership characteristics
- the management orientation or business philosophy (free or charged).

Table 17.1 shows the trend as an index of the total number of visits recorded at the main types of attractions in England (1978 = 100) on a broadly comparable indexed basis. Apart from gardens, the data reveal only very minor growth in *total* visits during the 1990s. In reading this table one must also have regard to Table 17.2, which shows that almost half of all attractions available in 1998 (before most of the new Lottery funded attractions had been built) opened in the two decades from 1980. As a result, the *average* number of visits per attraction had been declining.

Table 17.3 is one of the most instructive for strategic analysis. The typical visitor attraction in the UK is a very small business indeed: some run only by volunteers. Note that 76 per cent of all attractions achieve less than 50 000 visits a year. Divided by 365, with allowance for seasonality, a busy day for many attractions is therefore less than 100 visits per day for several months of the year. Only 2 per cent of attractions get more than 500 000 visits a year, and most of those are free at point of entry, and in or near to London. The attractions sector, for the most part, is a cottage industry with a lower revenue turnover on average than the typical urban corner shop.

Table 17.4 shows the share of visits by type of ownership. Note that 13 per cent of all recorded visits were to government-owned attractions (37 per cent of

Table 17.2   Years in which UK attractions opened to public

Year first opening	Historic properties %	Gardens %	Museums and galleries %	Wildlife sites %	All %
1990–98	9	19	16	26	20
1980–89	17	26	28	29	27
Subtotal	26	45	42	53	47
1970–79	15	18	20	19	19
1960–69	8	13	10	11	8
Pre-1969	51	24	28	17	26
Total	100	100	100	100	100
Actual number of attractions known in 1998	1418	347	1724	300	5890

Source: Sightseeing in the UK (1998)

museum visits) and 29 per cent to those owned by local authorities. Table 17.4 also reveals the variety of attractions to be embraced within a strategy. For England this ranges from museums and galleries to gardens, zoos and farms open to visitors and managed as attractions as well as production units. The size variable

Table 17.3   Size of visitor attractions in the UK by annual visits recorded in 1998

	Historic properties %	Gardens %	Museums and galleries %	Wildlife sites %	All %
Less than 5000	37	35	34	14	29
5001 to 20 000	27	34	33	26	28
20 001 to 50 000	17	15	18	25	19
50 001 to 100 000	10	7	8	13	10
100 001 to 500 000	8	8	6	20	12
Over 500 000	1	1	1	2	2
Total	100	100	100	100	100

Source: Sightseeing in the UK (1998)

Table 17.4   Share of visits to attractions by type of ownership and proportion of annual visits that are free at point of entry

	Government owned %	Local authority owned %	Other* %	Free visits %
Historic properties	21	10	69	30
Gardens	22	20	58	34
Museums and galleries	37	33	30	60
Wildlife sites	1	7	92	9
Country parks	6	84	10	98
Farms	0	11	89	24
Leisure parks	0	0	100	49
Steam railway	0	1	99	1
Visitor centres	8	33	59	55
Workplaces	0	0	100	73
Average percentages	13	29	58	55

Note: *Other is a combination of private ownership, institutional ownership and trusts and charities as well as commercial sector. In these categories commercial ownership predominates only in leisure parks, including theme parks.
Source: Sightseeing in the UK (1998)

is critical within type as, for example, museums range from the British Museum in the heart of London, with over 4 million visits a year and a budget of millions provided by the government, to tiny one-room collections run by volunteers that tell the stories of remote rural areas.

The management orientation or business philosophy is essentially an issue of whether an attraction is a commercial operation intended to provide a return on capital invested, as major theme parks such as Alton Towers and Blackpool Pleasure Beach are; a not-for-profit operation that is nevertheless required to generate all or much of its revenue budget from earned income in order to survive, such as Beaulieu in the New Forest or Beamish Open Air Museum in the North East; or a fully-subsidized institution providing its services without charge to the user, such as many local authority museums and (since the end of 2001) all the national museums in London and elsewhere that are funded directly by the Treasury. Under current circumstances even the fully-funded institutions are expected to generate some income from their resources but the management style is not the same as for those for whom earned income is the primary means of survival.

What should be the principal components of a national strategy for visitor attractions?

Experience in the sector over many years suggests the following are the seven key factors that are likely to be considered for action recommendations in any national strategy for attractions:

1 The collection and dissemination of effective research on a comparable national basis. Useful data must be timely, believable and actionable. In practice, national data are likely to have two dimensions over and above what attractions can undertake by way of their own market research. The first is overall visitor demand data; the second is research into the characteristics of the supply and operational data.

2 Application of expertise to the analysis and communication of trends and their implications in terms which smaller attractions in particular will be able to understand and respond to.

3 Advice, and perhaps support, on assessing quality of visits and providing customer assurance, for example, by conducting and subsidizing benchmarking studies whereby individual attractions can determine how they rate against the averages for their category (size and type). For example, benchmarking might be done by category/size for visitor enjoyment and value for money ratings, expenditure per capita on site, proportion of annual revenue spent on marketing, and so on.

4 Collection and dissemination of good practice examples in visitor attraction management and operations.

5 Co-ordination and possibly funding for/provision of training and management development.

6 Influence over funding bodies concerning the criteria they apply to bids from new and existing attractions including advice to government on the way in which taxes in the sector are imposed and collected.

7 Influence and advice to public-sector bodies, especially local authorities, that they may consider in relation to their own decisions on planning and funding activities for attractions in their areas.

Naturally, with developments of information communication technology, a national attraction strategy is most likely to be developed and implemented through websites with either open or protected access. Communication of data, other research and good practice are logical and obvious developments. Although such communication was not available nationally in the UK in 2001, it is certain it will be developed in the near future.

Who should be responsible for a national strategy?

Logically, in devising a strategy, a government or a national tourist board is likely to look to a representative trade body with whom to consult. In England, however, this is no easy task. Given the disparity of the 'rich seam' of attractions, each category tends to have its own trade association and there are at least twenty of these active in England, from the Association of Leading Visitor Attractions (ALVA) and the Association of Independent Museums (AIM), via cathedrals and churches, gardens and museums, to zoos. There is no natural affinity between these groups, which (other than ALVA which is defined by size) tend to comprise the whole gamut of very large and very small, commercial and non-commercial, rural and urban locations and professional and non-professional. All have some right to consultation but it would be bedlam to involve them all in an attempt at dialogue.

Case study: attractions strategy for England[1]

Under the devolution of government for England, Scotland, Wales and Northern Ireland established in the late 1990s, tourism in the UK is deemed to be a devolved responsibility. Each country is responsible for its own strategic approach and, while collaboration is encouraged, there is no provision for co-ordination. Accordingly, the English Tourism Council has developed its strategy for England:

> with the help of a group of leading attractions professionals working together for the good of the sector. It aims to improve understanding of the dynamics of the sector and identifies a number of areas where government and industry can work together to improve the quality and viability of the sector for the longer term. (ETC, 2000: foreword)

The second sentence of the quotation succinctly summarizes what a national strategy can hope to achieve within its stated overall remit of improving quality and viability of the sector. The stages whereby it was developed for England were as follows.

1 An initial expert working party on the future for attractions was convened by the English Tourist Board in 1996/7, recognizing that all was not well. A report was produced that identified all the main issues and drew on available research. Although it was not published, the report alerted the ETB to the shifts in demand and supply, and problems arising, and it was an important input to the work that

followed. It also identified many of the people who could contribute to the debate.

2 The ETB was restructured by government in 1999, charged with a strategic remit to improve quality and sustainability, and renamed the English Tourism Council. The ETC targeted the attractions sector as one of its priority areas for strategic initiative.

3 In line with government views on extensive consultation before action, the ETC established an Attractions Round Table in 1999 of some twenty-one individuals from all sectors of attractions who were invited to meet on several occasions to debate all aspects of a strategy. The individuals also commented on drafts of the strategy.

4 Other organizations were invited to comment on the various drafts and at least fifteen did so in 1999/2000. As a result, the ETC can properly claim that all concerned with national issues, and representatives of most of the different types of attractions, either did contribute or had an opportunity to do so. The issues were further debated in the ETC's National Tourism Forum in April 2000.

5 The finalized strategy, entitled *Action for Attractions*, was published in mid-2000, and widely distributed at a price of £10 for all who did not qualify for a free copy. In common with all such strategies the document tends to be replete with copious *coulds* and *shoulds* and not too many *wills* and statements of *costs* and *human resources to achieve*. Bearing in mind that ETC resources for direct involvement in the strategy are limited by government decisions and financial backing, its main recommendations (shortened for the purposes of this chapter) may be summarized under seven main headings. Readers should consult the original document for full detail:

(a) Recognition of the weaknesses of research in the sector and decision to put out the main survey (*Sightseeing in the UK*) to external tenders. From 1976 to 2000 the survey had been conducted 'in house' or on a consultancy basis by the person involved from the outset. It had no external advisory panel during that time.

(b) Linked to advocacy for attractions to improve their standards and increase visitor satisfaction, specific recognition of deficiencies in training from 'front-of-house' staff to the need for 'continuous professional development [for management] across the whole sector' (ETC, 2000).

(c) Advocacy for benchmarking to improve and share data on the operational performance of attractions, building on work initiated by regional tourist boards and others.

(d) Support for quality assurance schemes developed by regional tourist boards and development of a national visitor attractions charter of good practice.

(e) Recommendation that funding agencies should, as a principle, switch priority from funding new attractions to bids for improving existing attractions.

(f) Recommendation that 'any changes in the tax system should encourage reinvestment'.

(g) Recommendation that government planning guidelines for local authorities dealing with attractions should be reviewed nationally and that better co-ordination of planning for attractions within a regional context should be implemented with the support of regional tourist boards.

The strategy expressed the need for the formation of a standing cross-sectoral attractions advisory body, under the auspices of the ETC, to keep the strategic recommendations under review and advise the ETC and government as appropriate. Such a body was established in 2001.

A broader view of attractions for the twenty-first century

As a member of the Attractions Round Table and Tourism Forum, the author of this chapter sought to widen the traditional tourist board definition of visitor attractions on the grounds that its thinking and conceptualization were actually rooted in the 1960s and 1970s, and locked into an inward-looking annual 'sightseeing' survey that maintains agreed definitions for the sake of comparability but ignores the competition emerging outside those definitions. Long-established thinking dies hard and in 2000 there was no consensus for change. The detailed case for widening the concept was published earlier (Middleton, 1999). The case is that major retail-based out-of-town centres, such as in the Metro Centre in the North East and Bluewater Park in the South East, have brought across the Atlantic an original enclosed shopping mall development process that developed significantly in the 1980s and 1990s from retailing into the construction of day-out destinations designed to absorb leisure time and leisure expenditure within secure, all-weather complexes offering a mix of entertainment, hospitality, events and speciality retailing that cater for all in the population. All the new centres demonstrate the type of impressive and flamboyant architecture and design that are intended to stimulate and appeal to the popular imagination, replicating in many ways the styles that also distinguish major theme parks.

Increasingly operating for eighteen to twenty-four hour days, and all the year round, the biggest of these new leisure destinations draws up to 35 million visits a year. Just two of them are equivalent in size to all the visits in a year, including tourism visits, to Britain's 2500 museums and galleries put together. Competition of this level is absorbing the expanding day-visit leisure time of an affluent population that traditionally went to sightseeing attractions. This appears to be the greatest strategic challenge facing the visitor attractions sector in the first decade of the new century and it is disappointing that the ETC attractions strategy does not deal with it other than in vague terms of 'new competition' for leisure spending.

Conclusion

In developed countries such as the UK, a strategy for visitor attractions must reflect market maturity (demand) for traditional sightseeing options, and aim to achieve balance between demand and supply. For a quarter of a century, capacity simply grew on the assumption, fostered at the time by tourist boards, that demand would follow. Whatever else, that is no longer a tenable assumption.

A key issue for research and strategic thinking is the continuous review of new opportunities for leisure time and expenditure, and of the changing nature of leisure provision – beyond the issues of tourism demand and beyond the boundaries of traditional sightseeing definitions.

Strategies for attractions have to reflect the key issues of size of businesses in the sector and the fact that much provision is of a non-commercial nature. There is a strong case for allocating most support to attractions that contribute most to their local communities, including commercial attractions that meet that criterion.

Given the disparate nature of attractions it is certain that strategic involvement has to be based on enabling, facilitating and leading by research and information provision. It is not possible to impose policies on the sector.

Finally, reflecting the fragmented structure of the sector, strategy has to reflect networking development for small operations, assisting them to achieve some of the economies of scale and management skills enjoyed by their commercial competitors. Developments of information and communications technology over the last decade provide ideal means of supporting networks and their strategic development will be of primary importance in any national strategy.

Note

1 Sources referred to in writing the case study include *Cultural Trends*, Lockwood and Medlik (2001) and Middleton (1998; 2001).

References

Cultural Trends. Series of quarterly reports on trends in cultural attractions. Public Studies Institute.

ETC (2000). *Action for Attractions*. English Tourism Council.

Lockwood, A. and Medlik, S. (2001). *Tourism and Hospitality in the 21st Century*. Butterworth-Heinemann.

Middleton, V. T. C. (1998). *New Visions for Museums in the 21st Century*. Association of Independent Museums.

Middleton, V. T. C. (1999). The new resorts for the 21st century? *Insights*, **10**, A7–A12.

Middleton, V. T. C. (2001). *Marketing in Travel and Tourism*. 3rd edn. Butterworth-Heinemann.

Sightseeing in the UK. Annual series of reports on the traditional visitor attractions sector, published jointly by the tourist boards for England, Scotland, Wales and Northern Ireland.

18

The future of visitor attractions

Terry Stevens

Introduction

Over the past twenty years there has been an unprecedented growth in the number of traditional, stand-alone
visitor attractions, such as museums and heritage
properties, visitor centres, farm parks, aquaria and
theme parks. In many countries, supply has more than
doubled in this period. In recent years, the attractions
industry has faced intense competition from a wide
range of rapidly emerging, innovative leisure products.
Evidence suggests that in many mature tourism destinations, demand for traditional attractions is actually now
in decline. There are real fears for the viability and
survival of many of these attractions. At the same time,
however, some major new players in the industry are
responding strongly with the development of an exciting new genre of attractions. Some of these are being
built in unusual venues, thus creating very different
tourism destinations for the new millennium. Over the
next ten years there will emerge a new geography and
typology of visitor attractions. These developments will
require different forms of management and organizational structures if they are to work. The concept of
multifaceted and multi-occupier sites is likely to provide the key to achieving success in this industry.

The changing role and status of visitor attractions

In the 1970s and 1980s visitor attractions became widely regarded as an essential feature for any successful tourist destination development. Gunn suggests in his book, *Vacationscape* (1988: 37) that 'without developed attractions tourism as we now know it could not exist; there would be little need for transportation, facilities, services and information systems'.

Throughout the 1990s, however, the role and status of the traditional attraction has become less relevant to consumer needs, with the survival of many attractions becoming more precarious. The market is responding with a new generation of visitor attractions with many specifically designed to be 'destinations' in their own right. These 'destination attractions' offer consumers a comprehensive range of services and facilities for entertainment, shopping, eating and drinking, and other aspects of leisure. They are also being developed in unusual locations that require designers to use place-making skills to create this renaissance in the attractions industry. As a result, the term 'visitor attraction' now encompasses a wide range of products making a succinct definition both elusive and increasingly irrelevant.

Around the world the attractions industry does not have an easily accessible or central source of data about trends and markets. Indeed, it is in only a relatively few Western countries that data is collected in a systematic way. For example, in the UK and Ireland, the national tourist boards each maintain an annual record of visitation to the majority of their attractions. These data are submitted voluntarily by individual operators and, as a result, the sample is not always consistent and the information submitted is unable to be validated. This voluntary recording of information and the partial coverage of the population base characterizes the way information is collected on attractions in other countries. It is also the approach adopted by the representative or membership bodies, such as the International Association of Amusement Parks and Attractions (IAAPA).

In the past five years, designers, operators and investors have attempted to reinvent the concept of the visitor attraction in response to the changing patterns of consumer demand. Much of this activity has built upon the pioneering work of Disney with its resort developments in the USA, Japan and France over the past thirty years, but breaks new ground as a number of key strategic trends testify. These trends evidence a post-Disney reshaping and redefining of the attraction industry.

Such trends have already emerged in North America and Western Europe and are predicted to impact worldwide over the next ten years. They include the following trends:

1 The emergence of a new geography of destination attraction from development in association with other sectors of business or tourism, for example, as part of corporate brand development or as an integral feature of a sports complex. These will develop in Western countries, together with Malaysia and Australia.

2 Innovation to create a new generation of all-inclusive, multifaceted destination attractions with year-round operation, appealing to different markets at the same time. These projects are introduced to assist the regeneration of urban areas with the large-scale resort destinations being used to 'kick-start' a tourism economy in locations where relatively cheap land prices allow easy land assemblage to take place. Increasingly these types of developments will be located in countries with emerging economies as in Eastern Europe or South America.

3 The current polarization of retailing activity from the entertainment and enjoyment aspects of day-trips is rapidly eroding and will soon disappear, so that shopping and entertainment will become fully integrated with the attraction.

4 The investment appeal of these developments will lead to fresh sources of funding and finance being introduced to the sector. In return the investors, especially institutional investors, will require a more professional approach to the management of the attractions, essentially reducing the risk potential. This will result in the emergence of a number of specialist destination management companies operating on a worldwide basis leading to the further globalization of the industry.

These developments result from the changing patterns of leisure behaviour leading to the growth of demand for leisure shopping, eating and drinking, and entertainment as essential components of a day-trip. According to recent research, shopping for pleasure has now become one of the most important out-of-home activities in the UK. In the USA, shopping malls are now among the top tourist attractions in ten US states. A special study by the US Department of Commerce and the Taubman company examined shopping and cultural/heritage tourism, and confirmed the interdependence of shopping and visiting attractions among overseas visitors to the USA.

Increasingly, leisure consumers are becoming constrained by complicated lifestyles and are seeking leisure offers that are more in touch with their needs. The markets most likely to visit attractions are the more affluent (as measured in disposable income per capita, ownership of property and household conveniences), better educated, older, more travelled and experienced in quality service and facilities, and more sophisticated in their use of leisure time and

Table 18.1 Projected versus actual
attendance growth among IAAPA
member attractions, 1991/2 (%)

Region	Forecast growth	Actual growth
Europe	4.0	2.0
Canada	1.0	−1.0
USA	4.0	3.9
Pacific Rim	8.0	9.4
All regions	6.0	6.8

Source: IAAPA (1992)

sources. Clearly these characteristics change according to specific types of attractions with theme parks attracting younger markets and families.

Throughout the 1980s the visitor attraction industry was one of the most dynamic sectors in tourism development and investment. New developments in the sector were outpacing closures at a rate of up to five to one in many parts of the world. According to IAAPA's *1991 Investment Survey*, growth had been especially pronounced in the Pacific region in the early 1990s (see Table 18.1).

In Europe, where the attractions industry, especially in the cultural and heritage sectors, has a long tradition, there was, according to Lavery and Stevens (1990), the scope for further development of different types of attraction. This opportunity has been borne out in the findings of recent research in *New Visions for Museums in the 21st Century* (Middleton, 1998), which noted that in the UK alone, 50 per cent of the 6000 attractions have opened since 1980. In Wales, it is estimated that some 300 new attractions have entered the market since 1989, effectively doubling the supply in a decade. Meanwhile in Ireland 50 per cent of all fee-charging attractions have opened since 1990.

Given the apparent slowing down of the US market, especially for large-scale theme park development, US interest and expertise looked to the opportunity to develop the relatively untapped potential in the European and Asian markets. In the early 1990s interest was shown in attraction development by US companies in the Pacific Rim region and in Western Europe.

At the beginning of the 1990s, the attractions industry worldwide was in an optimistic mood. In Europe the prospect of the opening of EuroDisney in 1992 had a positive impact on the investment strategies of existing European parks. Disney's confidence in the European leisure and tourism markets encouraged others to invest in these countries. Awareness of attractions was at an unprecedentedly high level and financial institutions began to consider attractions more seriously as investment opportunities.

This euphoric state was, however, short-lived. The need for Disney to move vigorously in 1994 to cut its overheads at EuroDisney; to restructure, refinance, drop prices, recast its marketing strategies and relaunch as Disneyland Paris after a disappointing initial showing, sent a chill wind through the industry across Europe. Recovery is now complete with 2002 witnessing the opening of Walt Disney Studios as the second theme park in Paris and numbers of visitors stabilizing at 12 million per annum.

In the UK, where attractions had been opening at a rate of more than 100 a year, concerns were beginning to be expressed about oversupply. This, coupled with the well-publicized failures of Royal Britain and Space Adventure, both located in London, together with the inability to bring the Battersea Power Station project to fruition, resulted in the temporary slowing down of annual growth in new attractions by the mid-1990s. The situation was exacerbated by the failure of several major millennium projects, including the Millennium Dome, to achieve their stated targets. A similar trend was also identifiable elsewhere in Northern Europe.

However, there has been a revival of interest in Europe at the end of the 1990s with, for example:

- the announcement in 1999 of a 100 million guilder (2.20371 guilders = 1 euro) investment by the USA-based Six Flags European Division into Walibi Flevo and its rebranding as Six Flags Holland
- continued heavy investment at several long-standing theme parks in Europe
- Universal's 37 per cent stakeholding of Port Aventura. Universal acquired their interest in the Spanish theme park in July 1998. Other shareholders are La Caixa (the Catalan bank), 37 per cent, Anheuser Busch (US brewers), 20 per cent and Acesa, 6 per cent. This redevelopment of Universal Port Aventura extends over the next twelve years and is designed 'to become a whole holiday destination, providing accommodation, shopping and entertainment. This reflects the need to provide guests with a consistent and holistic level of quality throughout their entire stay as is achieved at the Walt Disney World resort and the Universal Studios Escape in Orlando' (Stevens, 2000: 67).

A number of public limited companies also exited from the attractions sector in 1999. This was particularly observed in the UK where, for example, Granada sold its American Adventures theme park in Derbyshire. This was followed by a management buyout of its Camelot Park in Lancashire. As a result, Granada was left with Granada Studio Tours in Manchester, but even this closed in 2000. Elsewhere, the Tussauds Group (Alton Towers, Chessington World of Adventures and Thorpe Park) was sold by its parent company, Pearson, for £352 million to Charterhouse Development Capital.

New markets for visitor attractions

Other investors and developers were, however, taking advantage of this dynamic environment to explore new markets, new types of investments and fresh locations. The subsequent development of these new forms of attraction destinations has had a profoundly debilitating effect on many parts of the traditional attraction industry throughout Europe and North America.

In terms of the new geography of the attractions industry, the first activity occurred in Europe where the focus of attention shifted from Northern Europe to Southern Europe, and especially to mainland Spain and Italy. The Middle East also became a new geographical focus for the search for theme park and water park developments, especially by North American groups and their 'local' (often European) partners. The focus for investment has also shifted away from the theme park per se to the inclusive all-weather, mixed retail, entertainment and leisure developments in out-of-town locations.

Over the past five years, Europe has witnessed an explosion of out-of-town retail and leisure parks that characterized urban planning in the USA in the early 1990s. In Europe, these developments have included the brand name factory outlets, such as those developed by BAA/MacArthur Glen in Wales and in Austria. They also include the regional complexes such as the Bluewater Leisure and Retail Park in Kent – a 1.6 million square feet, £700 million development for 30 million customers – and a similar scale development, the Trafford Centre, in Manchester. Such developments are not, of course, a particularly European phenomenon. In Santiago (Chile) the Ministry of Public Works has delivered a request for proposals for the Metropolitan Ecological, Entertainment and Cultural Complex. This will be a 395-acre zoo, sports and entertainment facility close to the city centre. In Seoul, the COEX Plaza is a 95 000 square metre development by the Korean International Trade Association and incorporates an aquarium, a multiplex and a series of international lifestyle tenants at the heart of the city.

Ironically, however, despite these warning signs, in many parts of Europe there has been an unprecedented surge of investment in new attractions over the past three to five years. This has been due to the availability of European Regional Development Fund (ERDF) monies for attraction development in many parts of the European Union, especially in those regions in need of economic regeneration where tourism has been seen as offering this potential. In the UK the advent of National Lottery funds since 1995 has prompted much speculative and spurious attraction development.

A number of key questions emerge from this analysis. First, is the shift of market interest simply a function of oversupply and market fatigue with the traditional attractions industry, or does it reflect a more significant structural shift in demand with consumers seeking a new generation of attractions? Second, how is the industry responding to these challenges and what format will the successful attractions of the millennium take? In short, does the traditional attraction have a future and how can it survive in the face of these challenges? Deloitte & Touche, in their 1997 *Survey of Continental European Visitor Attractions*, concluded that Western Europe was going to witness the growth of a more sophisticated, technology-led attractions sector, appropriate for a mature market. This would contrast with a culture and heritage-orientated market for Central and Eastern Europe.

Worldwide theme parks and amusement parks enjoyed a good year in 1999 (Table 18.2), but this was a turnaround for the top fifty most visited parks, which had suffered a 6 per cent decline in visitors in 1998. The picture in 1999 is not consistently positive, however, either globally or regionally. In each case there have been winners and losers, while the top ten parks in the USA contributed 46 per cent of total growth. Other smaller parks suffered a continued downturn in business.

In South America the top ten parks saw a 10 per cent decline in attendance, while the sector as a whole was down 4 per cent overall. Europe's top ten parks and the top fifty in North America grew attendances by 6 per cent and 3 per cent respectively. Once again, however, the growth is dominated by a few large-scale operations.

Walt Disney Attractions is ranked first in the top amusement/theme parks worldwide (Table 18.3) and, although it has far fewer parks than that of Premier Parks (thirty-five), it does have the largest cumulative attendance at its nine theme parks.

Attraction visitors, especially the resident day-trip market, are now confronted with a wide range of options and choices, and there is evidence to suggest that,

Table 18.2 Top twenty amusement/theme parks worldwide, 1999

Rank	Park	Country	Attendance (millions)
1	Tokyo Disneyland	Japan	17.45
2	Magic Kingdom	USA	15.20
3	Disneyland	USA	13.45
4	Disneyland Paris	France	12.50
5	Epcot	USA	10.10
6	Disney – MGM Studio	USA	8.70
7	Everland	South Korea	8.64
8	Disney Animal Kingdom	USA	8.60
9	Universal Studios (Orlando)	USA	8.10
10	Blackpool Pleasure Beach	UK	6.90
11	Lotte World	South Korea	6.10
12	Yokohama Sea Paradise	Japan	5.67
13	Universal Studios (Hollywood)	USA	5.10
14	SeaWorld Florida	USA	4.70
15	Huisten Boch	Japan	4.03
16	Nagashima Spa Land	Japan	4.00
17	Busch Gardens Tampa	USA	3.90
18	Six Flags Adventure	USA	3.80
19 =	SeaWorld California	USA	3.60
19 =	Knotts Berry Farm	USA	3.60

Source: Stevens & Associates (2000)

given this broad choice, a visit to an attraction is becoming less important and, more significantly, less relevant to the needs and the demands of the consumer. The local resident and tourist day-trip markets are increasingly searching for innovative attractions that provide a multiple range of 'things to do'. These markets are seeking one-stop leisure solutions. As consumers of attraction products, the tenet 'money rich, time poor' is particularly apposite. The research emerging from a number of different sources confirms, however, that holidaying tourists will continue to prioritize a visit to an indigenous icon, or 'signature', attraction that reflects the local culture or heritage.

In the future attractions must, therefore, be able to meet a wide range of customer requirements that embrace retail, entertainment, education and fun in a safe, comfortable, quality environment. Increasingly, these attributes are to be found in abundance in the new generation of destination attractions being specifically designed for this purpose. They are much more difficult to provide in

Table 18.3   Top ten amusement/theme park chains worldwide, 1999

Rank	Name	No. of parks	Attendance worldwide (millions)
1	Walt Disney Attractions	9	89.20
2	Premier Parks/Six Flags	35	47.50
3	Universal Studios	5	20.90
4	Anheuser Busch	9	19.60
5	Cedar Fair Ltd	8	13.50
6	Paramount Parks	5	12.29
7	Grupo Magico Int.	7	8.96
8	Blackpool Pleasure Beach	3	8.10
9	The Tussauds Group	3	6.30
10	Silver Dollar City	3	4.60

Source: Stevens & Associates (2000)

the more traditional attractions. As a result, at the end of the 1990s, many of the traditional non-signature attractions in Europe were under threat and extremely fragile.

In the USA it was generally thought that the attractions industry in general was immune to these trends. However, this might not now be the case. It has been suggested that the success of new attractions in the Orlando region has been the result of capturing market share from existing operations, adding to the pressures on the attraction sector from other leisure products. There are now regular reports in the specialist press that a combination of unpredictability in the weather, vagaries in international currency exchange rates, continued growth worldwide for overseas travel and an ever-increasing range of leisure options have resulted in a decline in the overall demand by consumers for the traditional visitor attraction. Investors are already taking the prospect of creating modern attractions in these economies very seriously.

There is also a need for high levels of product development in the existing attractions, particularly in terms of the catering, retailing and events offered, in order to stimulate repeat business from local residents. The importance of developing multiple sources of revenue is clearly a key feature of successful attraction management.

So what will future attractions be like and where will the successful attractions be located? Some experts argue that the key to future attraction development will be in creating and controlling intellectual properties and brands. In order for attractions to compete successfully with home shopping and home entertainment, they must develop unique experiences incorporating themed retail and entertainment with powerful brands that cannot be duplicated. To date, the USA has served as a laboratory for the attractions business, with a significant influence from Hollywood. As a result, the USA remains the most innovative environment for developing many forms of new attraction concepts and developments. This has been especially the case in the context of the emergence of what has become known as 'corporate lands'.

The consolidation of major media and entertainment companies and mergers with telecommunications conglomerates will further fuel the potential to integrate different forms of marketing to promote a brand. This diversity of corporate interest will increasingly include the development of a new generation of corporate attractions.

Industrial attractions

Industry tourism, based on visitor attractions at factories, is not a new phenomenon. Factory tours and museums have existed for many decades. Most have offered basic facilities and services for visitors, generally providing opportunities to see products being manufactured and the ability to purchase at an on-site shop, often at discounted rates. It is estimated that in France some 10 million visits are made each year to over 5000 industrial sites. In the USA a recently published directory lists some 300 industry attractions, while the British Tourist Authority has a schedule of some 314 workplaces open to visitors in the UK.

The EU has introduced a series of initiatives in recent years to encourage regions to promote and highlight the tourism potential of their indigenous industrial heritage as part of a strategy for overall economic development. As a result, the South Wales and Ruhr coalfields have encouraged the development of coal mining attractions while in Lecco (Northern Italy) the potential of the silk industry to contribute to tourism development has recently been explored.

It is in the corporate sector, however, that the most dramatic new forms of industry tourism are taking place. A number of high-profile companies have actively developed their attraction product at their main point of production. Successful examples are shown in Table 18.4. The demand for this type of attraction product has grown significantly in recent years.

As a result, some key operators have recently announced major expansion plans for the further development of their factory-based attractions. For example,

Table 18.4   Examples of successful 'industry' visitor attractions

Name of company	Country	Industry	Visitors per annum
Coca-Cola	USA	Beverage	2 000 000
Hershey	USA	Chocolate	2 000 000
Kellogg's	USA	Food	1 000 000
Volkswagen	Germany	Cars	1 000 000
Swarovski	Austria	Crystal	650 000
Cadbury	England	Chocolate	500 000
Waterford Crystal	Ireland	Glass	400 000
Guinness	Ireland	Beer	400 000
Parfumerie Fragonard	France	Perfumes	300 000
BNF Sellafield	England	Nuclear energy	200 000
Glenfiddich	Scotland	Whisky	180 000
Heineken	Netherlands	Brewing	90 000

Source: Stevens & Associates (2000: 75)

Guinness has replaced the Hop Store Visitor Centre with a new £70 million attraction at the Old Brewery in Dublin (Ireland) called 'The Storehouse' and Wedgwood has opened a new £5 million visitor complex at its Barlaston (England) factory in 2000.

The media and entertainment industries have also played an active role in the development of larger-scale visitor attractions and should be regarded as being part of this corporate form of visitor attraction development. The obvious examples are Universal Studios, and MGM with Disney.

In the absence of any single, large-scale corporate attraction in any particular region, there are opportunities for similar but smaller-scale operations to collaborate to develop a tourism strategy themed on the dominant type of local industry. This form of clustering helps create a critical mass of visitors and provides a range of attractions and other services.

There is a number of particularly interesting examples of this form of industry tourism where the 'corporate' approach is balanced by a wider concern to increase the tourism business within a destination. In Scotland, for example, a number of distilleries have formed a strategic alliance to promote various whisky trails. In Stoke-on-Trent in England, companies involved in the pottery industry work collectively to promote the region's ceramic heritage and in 2002 will open a combined visitor centre, Ceramica, as a focus for this activity.

Sports-related attractions

The concept of developing attraction-based destinations as a strategy to enhance a corporate brand is now also being enthusiastically adopted by some of the world's leading sports clubs and sporting venues. The importance of exploiting the value of a brand in sport has matured rapidly over the last twenty years, due primarily to the exposure to global markets provided by satellite broadcasting. In this context, the interests of sportswear manufacturers such as Nike, Reebok and Adidas are inextricably linked to successful clubs, mega-sporting events (such as the Olympic Games and the football and rugby World Cups) and, by association, the venues in which the sports are played.

These manufacturers have a sophisticated understanding of the importance of brand extension through exposure and the creative diversification of their marketing activities. The emergence of Niketown in the early 1990s, first in Portland (1990) and then Chicago (opened in July 1992) represented a new form of retailing environment. The merchandise is given a setting using museum-type exhibits incorporating artefacts and pictures of sportsmen and women wearing the Nike sportswear. As a result, Niketown can be regarded as an attempt to bring the corporate 'attraction' onto the high street and a significant shift towards fully integrating the retailing experience with that of the attraction.

Significantly, the opening in 1996 of Sony Wonder on New York's Madison Avenue represents further corporate recognition that leisure retailing is becoming more inclusive and interchangeable. Coca-Cola's investment in the temporary sports village in Centennial Park during the 1996 Atlanta Olympics was clearly a concept designed to merge interactive sporting experiences with retailing, while forging brand identity. As such, this initiative heralded the beginnings of a fresh cohort of attraction developments based upon sports clubs and venues.

Sports clubs are now recognizing the importance of building their brands, principally as the means of generating the essential revenues to invest in the best players and to create stadia that provide yet further opportunities to diversify their commercial potential and create profits for their shareholders or members.

Manchester United's Old Trafford and Barcelona's Nou Camp stadia have been the venues for the two clubs' successful museums for over fifteen years. Barcelona Football Club's museum, with over 500 000 visitors per annum, is Spain's second most popular museum (after the National Museum in Madrid). Manchester United has recently refurbished its museum, which accommodates over 200 000 visitors a year (excluding visits on match days). Both museums are incorporated into the stadia and enhance the stadium tour, which is offered as part of a wider attraction package.

This format of the sports club, or sport museum, within the stadium is found at a number of internationally known sporting venues. In Europe it is estimated that there are between twenty-five and thirty major sports museums of which perhaps one-third are located in stadia. In the USA there are some ninety sports halls of fame, of which approximately 25 per cent are located at or in stadia. Some examples, including the Daytona and Indianapolis motor-racing circuits in the USA, provide interactive attractions with strong heritage or museum features. At the Newmarket Racecourse in the UK, at the Kentucky Horse Park (home of the Kentucky Derby) and at the Irish Stud near the Curragh in Ireland, attractions have been developed to celebrate the sport of horse racing.

Creating visitor attractions with ancillary visitor services and facilities associated with a sport, a sports club or a stadium is, therefore, a logical extension of their portfolio of commercial activities. This potential has become more important over the past ten years as clubs, sports organizations and cities have invested heavily in the redevelopment of their existing stadia or have created new stadia. The 'cathedrals' of sport have to operate on a daily basis if they are to make a positive contribution to the economy of their host city/region and to the turnover of the owner. The potential for these major landmark buildings to become destination attractions has only recently been recognized.

Other types of sports venues besides soccer are now examining the implications of this form of collaboration and synergy. This is well evidenced with the proposal for Philips Electronics to develop a £250 million International Sports Village in Cardiff (Wales) that will incorporate sports visitor attractions, stadia, artificial snow centre, sports-related retailing and hotels. In short, this project represents a combination of the all-inclusive themed destination and the concept of the branded attraction. As such it may represent the next phase in the development of the stadia as described below.

As the bidding process intensifies among those countries and cities wishing to host the major global sporting events, such as the Olympic Games, the football and rugby World Cups or one of the Formula One Grand Prix races, there will be increasing pressure to find imaginative designs for the sustainable use of the stadia constructed for the events. This will result in greater attention being applied to the seventh and eighth phases of the author's evolutionary model of attraction development (Stevens, 2000: 82). Complexes will be specifically designed to operate as year-round destination attractions.

If the current trends of the merging of corporate interest with sporting events and teams continue to strengthen and the brand leaders in sportswear continue to innovate and lead brand marketing, then it is very likely that the sports venue will become a major part of the geography of visitor attractions in the next twenty years.

The synergy between sport and tourism, especially in the attractions sector, is set to expand dramatically. These new destination attractions will offer a diversified range of services and facilities. This, combined with ever-increasing customer expectations, will necessitate the use of specialist operational companies and a range of different occupiers capable of providing added value with their own brand relationships.

These types of multifaceted, multi-occupier solutions will become standard practice in the attractions sector over the next decade. It is a solution that is relevant to attractions of different types and sizes. The economies of scale explicit in the large-scale operations hold obvious appeal for their party involvement. However, there is scope for smaller attractions to offer creative conditions that will allow specialist interests to flourish within an attraction. For example, at the Powerscourt Estate in Dublin, the historic house and gardens are operated by the owners of the estate, the Slazenger family. In order to diversify the appeal of the property to meet modern market demands in the competitive Irish attractions marketplace, the owners have developed the core of the historic house as a quality craft and specialist retail area with a quality catering offer (coffee shop, restaurant and functions). The success of the venture is due to the involvement of specialist retailers and caterers to manage the provision of these aspects of these products. The combined operation currently attracts over 350 000 per annum and a further 25 per cent increase is projected for 2000.

Conclusion

The next ten years will see remarkable changes in the geography and nature of the visitor attraction industry. The changes currently being experienced in consumer demand will lead to a considerable number of casualties among traditional attractions. Many will become increasingly irrelevant to the interests of the market.

The future is likely to remain relatively positive for those signature attractions that are regarded as 'must-see places' on most tourist itineraries. Equally, those attractions that continue to innovate with their product and become market, or customer, focused are more likely to survive. This will necessitate a real commitment to quality as well as becoming price competitive and developing multiple sources of revenue.

In the meantime, the next ten years will see the emergence of the next generation of destination attractions. Many of these will use the Disney model as the prototype for the new genre of attractions. These will provide all-weather, inclusive resort products but operating on a smaller scale than Disney and sited in unusual locations. Others will be founded upon new types of destinations in urban centres. Sports complexes will also emerge as the venue for much of this new investment.

It can be argued, furthermore, that the emerging economies will soon create resident markets with disposable income and aspirational demands for entertainment and enjoyment in unusual settings. These countries will also offer attractive land and property deals to investors. As a result, there is likely to be a burst of interest in the potential to create these new destination attractions in these countries.

Both of these trends effectively use the concept of the 'destination attraction' to create new tourism destinations in their own right. Under these conditions, Gunn's original testimony to the power of the attraction as the main energizer of tourism in a region appears to remain true even under these new conditions. If, however, the attraction is to remain the 'lodestone' for tourism, the industry must accept this redefinition, be prepared for casualties and adopt new ways of working.

References

Amusement Business (1999a). *Top 20 Amusement/Theme Parks*. December.

Amusement Business (1999b). *Top 10 Amusement/Theme Park Chains Worldwide*. December.

Deloitte & Touche (1997). *A Survey of Continental European Visitor Attractions*. Deloitte & Touche Consulting.

Gunn, C. (1988). *Vacationscape: Designing Tourist Regions*. 2nd edn. Van Nostrand Reinhold.

IAAPA (1992). *Amusement Industry Abstract – Business Managers Survey*, 1. International Association of Amusement Parks and Attractions.

Lavery, P. and Stevens, T. (1990). Attendance trends and future developments at Europe's leisure attractions. *Travel and Tourism Analyst*, **2**, 52–75.

Middleton, V. T. C. (1998). *New Visions for Museums in the 21st Century*. Association of Independent Museums.

Stevens, T. (2000). The future of visitor attractions. *Travel and Tourism Analyst*, **1**, 61–85.

Conclusion

Alan Fyall, Brian Garrod and Anna Leask

The task set for this book was deliberately an ambitious one. Rather than simply to report on how visitor attractions have been managed in the past and are being managed at present, this book has sought to make a series of short forays into the future. The intention has been to spy out the landscape that lies immediately ahead of the visitor attraction sector and to chart some of its major features. The purpose of this concluding section of the book is to draw together the intelligence that has been gained and to present an overview of the management challenges and opportunities the authors of the various chapters collectively believe to lie in the near future for the visitor attraction industry. This, we believe, will provide the reader with further insights into the 'new directions' in which the management of visitor attractions might be well advised to head as the first decade of the new millennium continues to unfold.

The changing market for visitor attractions

Most of the chapters in this book predict testing times ahead for the visitor attraction industry. In the aftermath of the 11 September 2001 terrorist attacks on New York and Washington, DC, it is clear that many 'world-class' visitor attractions will be hard-pressed to achieve their visitor number targets in the coming season, as people prefer to stay at home rather than to venture abroad. Experience shows, however, that such influences tend to be relatively short-lived, with the desire to travel sooner or later overcoming personal safety fears. Nevertheless, visitor attractions are likely to take a hard hit; in some cases this may prove a knockout blow.

This having been said, the larger, more established visitor attractions cannot afford to be complacent as the shock waves of the 11 September 2001 attacks eventually begin to subside. The major markets for visitor attractions are currently replete with challenges for visitor attractions, and these challenges look set to intensify rather than decrease in the medium term. Changing patterns of leisure, an increasingly crowded attraction marketplace and the impacts of new technology are all anticipated to present serious challenges to the visitor attraction sector. New directions in the development, management and marketing of visitor attractions will need to be identified and engaged with if such challenges are to be successfully met.

Stevens, in the final chapter of this book, prophesies a stark future for both larger and smaller visitor attractions. For smaller attractions, the major threat is that changes in consumer demand are increasingly rendering their product offerings irrelevant to the needs of the market. The result may be that many of the weaker lights will inevitably be extinguished from the visitor attraction map over the coming decade. For larger, 'must-see' attractions, meanwhile, Stevens argues that the danger comes in the form of fierce competition from the advance troops of a new army of 'destination-style' attractions. Wanhill, meanwhile, identifies the globalization of the visitor attraction market as a potential threat to many existing visitor attractions. With acquisition driving the globalization process rather than organic growth, such attractions need to beware of being swallowed up by the emerging breed of multinational giants. The imperative for larger attractions will therefore be to become more innovative with their product offerings, develop a much stronger consumer focus, embrace the need to develop quality and be prepared for casualties along the way. Braun and Soskin make a similar point in the context of the 'living laboratory' of Florida's theme parks, where market consolidation has already led to new relationships emerging between visitor attractions and new pricing strategies being adopted as a result. Attraction managers might anticipate further consolidation, leading to further changes in the strategic environment, in the near future.

New management approaches

While Stevens paints perhaps rather a bleak picture of the future of visitor attractions, other chapters in this book are more optimistic about what lies ahead, though none is entirely confident of a bright future for all. The position usually taken is that even smaller, traditional-style attractions can prosper in the changing market for visitor attractions provided that they either smarten up their management approach, perhaps even adopting new management approaches when existing approaches are deemed no longer helpful or appropriate.

Where the chapters taking this more positive view differ, perhaps predictably, is on the question of which elements of the management process require reform. Watson and McCracken, for example, highlight a need for visitor attractions to adopt a more human resource management focused approach to their management. After all, if visitor attractions are essentially people-centred activities, improved human resource management is likely to provide a coherent response to the challenges faced by the sector both now and in the near future. Garrod, meanwhile, adopts a sustainability approach, arguing that heritage-based visitor attractions in particular should be more concerned with the task of walking the fine line between enhancing the accessibility of the site for current generations and protecting the authenticity of the site in the interests of posterity. Xie and Wall also take up the torch of authenticity, although in the very different context of visitor attractions based on ethnicity. Central to their argument is that while authenticity may be a multidimensional and slippery concept, it is nevertheless one that those responsible for managing visitor attractions must come to terms with or else risk failure. Both Boyd and Fyall, meanwhile, stress the importance of marketing in the successful management of the future visitor attraction, yet even then their emphases are rather different. While Boyd argues for a widening of the marketing approach to include people, programming and partnership, Fyall highlights the central importance of developing collaborative partnerships in the marketing and promotion efforts of visitor attractions.

If there is agreement among the various authors of the chapters of this book, however, it is that 'new directions' in managing visitor attractions must be identified as a matter of urgency. It is clear that existing paradigms do not provide an adequate basis for the future prosperity of the visitor attraction sector as we know it.

Continuing challenges

Various chapters of this book also identify a number of perpetual challenges for the visitor attraction sector, one being the influence of seasonality. Robbins, for example, identifies seasonality as a constraining factor in the development of transport-based attractions, even when they are also oriented to serving the mobility needs of their local community. Goulding, meanwhile, argues that seasonality is a broad and complex phenomenon that goes beyond the immediacy of the marketplace. He goes on to argue that while there is much that attractions can do to address the seasonality of their operations, many will have to accept that developing a year-round operating season is an unrealistic target. Such attractions should therefore concentrate their efforts on adapting to the seasonal 'downtime' in more innovative ways.

The role of technology is highlighted in a number of the chapters in this book, and it is clear that information and communications technology is set to play an increasingly central role in various management functions, including marketing, promotion, interpretation and education, and visitor management. While this much is agreed, there would appear to remain very real differences on the matter of whether this might be a good or a bad thing. In Chapter 3, for example, Wanhill points out that the most recent radical innovation coming from the 'imagineers' of the giant US theme parks is to combine the physical and virtual world using state-of-the-art technologies. However, the costs associated with such innovations have tended to be immense, so that only parks that are located within their own resort destinations have been able to bear them. This further increases the competitive advantage of global chains over their smaller independent rivals. Wanhill goes on to note the many worries that have been expressed about the popularization of the attraction 'imagescape' through the use of technology, such that the medium becomes emphasized at the expense of the message. In Chapter 16, meanwhile, Voase presents the rather different view that rather than 'dumbing down' the cultural visitor attraction experience, the use of new technology has enabled the proliferation of knowledge in society more generally. This in turn has changed the nature of the visitor experience: rather than undermine or dilute it, managers of visitor attractions have been able to lower the threshold of engagement of the experiences they offer. As a result, two new breeds of visitor can now be identified: the 'thoughtful' visitor, who is the product of the proliferation of knowledge in the technology-dense postmodern society, and the 'smart' visitor, who is the product of the commodification of that same knowledge.

Many of the chapters in this book note the growing recognition of the sustainability imperative among managers of visitor attractions. Garrod argues that sustainability is central to the mission of heritage-based visitor attractions, and therefore that managing visitor impacts on the attraction site should be seen as fundamental to the role of the visitor attraction manager. If today's visitors compromise the very things that they are coming to see, then clearly it will not be possible for future generations to witness these treasures in all their splendour. In some cases, all that may be left is a virtual representation of the artefact in question. Hall and Piggin make a parallel argument in the context of the management of World Heritage sites, where inappropriate visitor activity and behaviour may endanger the brand image of World Heritage status, which depends on the vicarious consumption of supporters who may never visit the site in person. Robbins, meanwhile, highlights the potential for transport-based attractions to provide more sustainable alternatives for those travelling to, from and within tourism destinations.

Prideaux identifies a number of continuing challenges for attractions located in peripheral areas, including overcoming lack of accessibility on the part of visitors, coping with competition and gaining local community support. Certainly it would appear that as the degree of peripherality increases, so the issue of scale becomes more important and the risk of failure increases. He goes on to argue that if the countryside is not to be littered with the wreckage of failed visitor attractions, developed using public funds in the name of supporting local communities, funding bodies will need to examine the long-term viability of such attractions much more carefully. Meanwhile there is much that peripheral visitor attractions can do to secure their viability in spite of their location, including encouraging visitors to overcome the effort and inconvenience involved in travelling to out-of-the-way places by providing them with high-quality visitor services and experiences not found in the core.

Finally, it is clear that visitor attractions will continue to be challenged by ever more rapidly changing visitor motivations as we move into the new millennium. Nowhere is this better illustrated that in the case of religion-based attractions which, as Shackley notes in Chapter 10, have generally been experiencing growing visitor numbers in spite of the increasing secularization of society. One can only speculate as to why this might be the case: perhaps today's visitor is seeking to spend leisure time in holy places as a substitute for personal prayer and worship; perhaps visiting religious sites represents a new form of pilgrimage. What is clear, however, is that visitor motivations across the visitor attraction sector as a whole are changing rapidly, yet for the most part they remain seriously under-researched and, as a result, poorly understood.

New drivers of attraction development

A number of the chapters in this book identify the considerable tensions that underlie the management of visitor attractions. This is made clear in Chapter 1, where Leask argues that the multiple stakeholder interests involved in a given visitor attraction, be they related to education, revenue generation or conservation, inevitably lead to management conflicts as visitor attraction managers are pulled between these often competing demands. The past decade has seen the visitor attraction sector widen as visitor attractions continue to broaden and deepen their stakeholder relationships, taking visitors and the local community into their web of stakeholder interests. It might therefore be expected that such management conflicts will intensify in the future. Meanwhile, Shackley argues that such conflicts are particularly evident among religion-based attractions, where managers are expected to juggle the opposing interests of worshippers, visitors, the local community and conservation. It is clear that one of the new drivers of change in the visitor attraction sector in the coming decade will be the increasingly intense interplay in an ever-widening stakeholder base.

In Chapter 5, meanwhile, Henderson argues that visitor attraction development is rarely driven by economic forces alone. Visitor attractions are also employed by national governments and their agencies in exploring, discovering and expressing various dimensions of their national and cultural identities. Political and social factors are hence at least as important drivers of visitor attraction development as economic forces. This would certainly seem to be true in the two case studies Henderson develops. In the first, that of Hong Kong, the development of visitor attractions has been central in reaffirming the distinctive local culture following the return of the former British colony to China. In the second, that of Singapore, visitor attractions have been used as a means of assisting the social integration of culturally disparate local communities. While it might be argued that exporting the Disney theme to France and Japan represents the working of a rather similar agenda, it is interesting that Disneyland Paris has recently found it expedient to draw back on some of the more overtly American cultural features of its product.

Finally, many of the chapters in this book argue that collaboration will be increasingly important in the future. Indeed, in Chapter 15 Fyall argues that collaboration represents a lifeline for smaller, independent visitor attractions that are threatened by the changes in market conditions referred to earlier in this conclusion. He goes on to argue that the success or otherwise of collaboration lies in how well individual visitor attractions prove willing and able to work with one another. It is clear that in order to achieve this, individual visitor attractions need to adopt a less proprietary and more holistic approach to management and marketing, viewing competitors not as a market threat but as a source of potential future strength and collaborative survival. This theme is also taken up by Boyd, who argues that developing partnerships will be a key factor in determining the success or otherwise of strategies to promote the sustainability of the visitor attraction sector. Middleton, meanwhile, argues that networking will be essential to the development of a strategy for the development of the visitor attraction sector in England. Given the fragmented nature of the sector, any such strategy will need to be supported by collaboration among individual operators, enabling them to achieve economies of scale and to develop the management skills enjoyed by their commercial competitors. Information and communications technology arguably represents an ideal means of supporting such networking.

Endnote

It is clear that managers of visitor attractions must respond to survive and thrive in the changing market. With the need to generate additional revenue streams, meet profit forecasts and market the attraction product to an ever more fragmented, more demanding and more fickle visitor base, the task facing many operators of visitor attractions is immense. Of particular concern is that so many attractions are important intrinsic elements of our physical, cultural, scenic and environmental heritage, and cannot easily compete in the arena of commercial rivalry. Hence, the ease with which some operators of visitor attractions in danger are likely to be able to, or consider it right to, accommodate many of the new management approaches discussed throughout this book is debatable. After all, the significance of so many attractions lies in their very existence, not their ability to meet the needs of the short-term whims of the market and ability to break even with operating costs covered by admissions and commercial revenue. It is thus so ironic that as societies in the developing world become more affluent and more able to afford to sustain these 'community' assets, which so many attractions represent, so the myopic preoccupation with commercial autonomy is threatening their continuity.

There can be no doubt as to the seriousness of the challenges facing visitor attractions and the force of the new drivers shaping attraction development. In this respect, this book offers many valuable lessons for the visitor attraction sector to consider, adopt and, hopefully, implement successfully. The challenge is, however, formidable, as the threat to the continuing existence of non-commercially viable visitor attractions that are not otherwise subsidized is clear. Economic and employment criteria ought not to be the sole measures by which attractions are judged as to whether they survive or fail. The attributes of many attractions are important to national, regional and local cultural and social values. All such attractions are important to global heritage. While there is an undoubted case for selectivity and rationalization among attractions, it is of great importance that in any case of threatened viability or closure, the intrinsic aspects are thoroughly appraised, recorded and assessed. Criteria must be found to evaluate and recognize the overall 'worth' of attractions to the community as genuine cultural assets. Society at large must find ways of balancing the books of those attractions which incorporate such assets, but whose survival is otherwise threatened by the fierce, and predominantly short-term, economic criteria upon which 'success' is increasingly judged in the developed world. This book raises many important questions and offers several valuable 'new directions' for the management of visitor attractions. Yet, success and survival are for many, far from assured.

Ken Robinson CBE
Chairman, English Tourism Council Visitor Attractions Forum

Index